D1761003

From Feminist Theology to Indecent Theology

Readings on Poverty, Sexual Identity and God

Marcella Althaus-Reid

YORK ST. JOHN
COLLEGE LIBRARY

WITHDRAWN

17 MAY 2025

scm press

York St. John College

3 8025 00462168 9

All rights reserved. No part of this publication may be
reproduced, stored in a retrieval system, or transmitted,
in any form or by any means, electronic, mechanical,
photocopying or otherwise, without the
prior permission of the publisher,
SCM Press.

© Marcella Althaus-Reid 2004

British Library Cataloguing in Publication data

A catalogue record for this book is available
from the British Library

0 334 02983 X

First published in 2004 by SCM Press
9-17 St Albans Place, London N1 0NX

www.scm-canterburypress.co.uk

SCM Press is a division of
SCM-Canterbury Press Ltd

Printed and bound in Great Britain by
Biddles Ltd, www.biddles.co.uk

Contents

Acknowledgements

It has been said already: theology is a journey. It is a tentative journey though, in which our understanding of the relationship which is at the core of our faith (God, ourselves, others) changes and changes us in the process. This book brings together, for the first time, 12 years of that journey which made Indecent Theology, that is, a feminist Latin American theology which is political, postcolonial and Queer.

To acknowledge the people who have shared this journey with me is a daunting task. There are so many. I would like to acknowledge and thank some of those who have contributed to and challenged my thought and praxis over the years: Steven Mackie, Ofelia Ortega, Daphne Hampson, Dan O'Connor, Elizabeth Stuart, Alison Webster, Lisa Isherwood, Maria Pilar Aquino, Jaci Maraschin, Alistair Kee, Beatriz Melano, Tim Gorringe, Peter Selby, Anne Hepburn, the people of the 'Theology at the Edge' project from Edinburgh, Eilidh Whiteford, Alastair McIntosh and José Miguez Bonino. Also, the Friends from the Dundee Meeting House (Quakers) for so many years of loving support. Not to forget my students and colleagues at New College, Edinburgh.

I would particularly like to thank my dear friends and colleagues, Professor R. S. (Sugi) and Dr Sharada Sugirtharajah for the enrichment that our shared intellectual discussions on postcolonialism have brought to me. Through their friendship I have been able to live and do a kind of theology which for me has always been 'home'.

I would like to thank Anna Hardman who was the Senior Editor of SCM Press when this project was born, who received the idea of this book with enthusiasm, and to Barbara Laing, current Senior Editor, for her support in finalizing this project.

Y Nueva York sigue vacía.
Para P.

Introduction

From Feminist Theology to Indecent Theology:

On Going Beyond

To 'go beyond.' Or decode the Christic symbol beyond any traditional morality. . . . The spirit? Not, this time, the product of the love between Father and son, but the universe already made flesh or capable of becoming flesh, and remaining in excess to the existing world.

Irigaray, 2002, p. 58

'What has sexuality to do with a Feminist Liberation Theology?' I was speaking some years ago at one of the annual conferences organized by the Britain and Ireland School of Feminist Theology, when a distinguished feminist liberation theologian raised that question. I had presented a paper concerning the necessity of starting to produce a kind of 'outing' theology,[1] a Liberation Theology which would be committed to honesty, done with courage and would deal with issues of sexuality and poverty. But my colleague could not understand the inclusion of sexuality in a paper about women and poverty and she persisted with her question of why a Liberation Feminist Theology needs to use the word 'sex'. Many other participants joined in the discussion, but the theologian addressed me personally. 'Marcella, I have known you for your commitment to a theology done from the perspective of the poor – especially poor women – but why are you now talking about sexuality? Have you left aside your identity as a liberationist?' My colleague was right in that I was originally trained as a liberation theologian, although Paulo Freire would have said that 'training' is not the right verb to use here. Freire used to speak about 'acquiring style' rather than getting training. Acquiring style implies flexibility and the capacity to reconsider strategies of teaching and learning according to the context. But the point is that I am a Latin American theologian who studied Liberation Theology as a 'walk' (*caminata*) or as a 'style' and not only as a piece of history. Doing

---

[1] The paper was published under the title 'Outing Theology: Thinking Christianity out of the Church Closet', *Feminist Theology,* no. 27, May 2001, pp. 57–67.

Liberation Theology involves more than reviewing the historical accounts of Medellín and Puebla. It is a style, a way of doing Theology which requires the liberationist to continue walking along that path. This theological journey involves taking risks. The first generation of liberation theologians experienced real risks and danger as they unmasked different forms of oppression. So it was that Enrique Dussel, one of the most important theologians of the movement, had to take his family into exile from Argentina when a bomb was planted in his home.[2] The Brazilian educator Paulo Freire told me how he had to fly immediately from Brazil one day when his life was threatened by the dictatorial regime. When, in El Salvador, the military came for Jon Sobrino he happened to be out of the country. They murdered six of his Jesuit colleagues and two women workers in the Oscar Romero Pastoral Institute, dumping the body of one of the priests in the office of Sobrino as their calling card. This is what it means to say that to do Liberation Theology was to take risks. In its formative years it was not acceptable to church or state. Liberation theologians were subject to persecution, to silencing, to dismissal, to ridicule in the academy and in the media.

But times change and subversive theology becomes incorporated: church leaders claim that they themselves have always been liberation theologians. They guarantee to the state that there is no danger here. Liberation Theology can now be taught safely to undergraduates. It is acceptable in the academy, entertaining to the wider public and a valuable commodity for publishers. Having reached calm waters, why would I as a feminist liberation theologian risk rocking the boat by introducing such a scandalous theme as sexuality, especially when it is not the theology of sanctified sexuality? This is a different risk, the risk of losing the good will of the religious authorities and the approval of the academic community. Worse than that, is there not the risk thereby of betraying the cause of the poor in my own continent?

Betrayals

The fact is that few accusations could be more hurtful to any intellectual such as myself, born and bred in Latin America, than betraying the cause of the poor. But women doing theology are always accused

---

[2] Enrique Dussel wrote in the Foreword of his influential book *Filosofía de la Liberación* (Mexico: Edicol, 1976), p. 10 : 'This short book appears without any bibliography because the books of my own library are very far away in my homeland of Argentina. This book is written in the suffering of my exile' (my translation).

of betrayal. We have been courageous enough to become unfaithful to patriarchal ideologies in theology, just as liberationists exposed the class interests of those wielding power in the church. To these examples can be added the list of theologians who have courageously shown their profound disrespect to the white, postcolonial theologies of oppression. There has emerged a wide and wonderful spectrum of Feminist Liberation Theologies,[3] including the sisters from Asia, the *mujeristas* from Hispano America, the womanists, the Aborigine theologians, the African theologians. New examples of contextual theologies appear continually.

Of all the contextual theologies unveiling different ideological issues in theology, Feminist Theologies are the ones which have produced the most severe criticisms of Christianity. The critiques of theology stemming from feminism have destabilized the deep foundational patriarchy at the base of theology. Feminist theologians have been in this sense the great betrayers of the ideological patriarchal God. Gender and sexuality do not subvert Christianity in the ways that other theologies do, that is by simply problematizing the politics of religious representation and allowing a more genuine theology to resurface. No, Feminist Theologies represent an authentic Christian conversion, a turning away from the structures of patriarchal sin and a reading of the Scriptures which throws the texts into crisis. And there is no turning back. Conversion, it goes without saying, is about ethical betrayals. It means turning our backs on a whole ideological symbolic order that is sinful. Conversion takes us into the holiness of betrayals, the unveiling of ideologies of death. Feminist Theologies started with a gendered form of suspicion towards ideological themes in theology and in its methods. They left nothing untouched, beginning with the reading (and the text formation) of the Scriptures, and proceeding to suspicion about the way traditions and church history have been developed around androcentric worldviews, arriving finally at suspicion about the way that Christianity has understood God. Systematic Theology could never be the same again. If Liberation Theology took many years to become established – and it still meets with resistance in some academic and church circles – what can be said concerning Feminist Theology? The struggle here has been and still is even more fierce, because the discourse of gender threatens the core of patriarchally constructed religious representations and their production of sacred meaning. We

---

[3] In this book I shall be referring to Latin American Theology and to Latin American Feminist Theology, hence the terms are in singular form. Yet, it is not satisfactory to refer to Feminist Theology or Liberation Theology in the singular because this style of doing contextual theology is now to be found worldwide.

must be proud to be called betrayers, if our unfaithfulness to patriarchal ideology opens up the possibility of discovering God anew. Here is the parallel with Liberation Theology: the subversive has become acceptable. Gender studies have been incorporated into Christian theology. Gender suspicion has become an important and respectable element in many hermeneutical circles. Are we once again risking rocking the boat? Are we not just going too far if we add also what we can call 'radical sexuality' to our questioning?

To go back to our original question: what has sexuality to do with Feminist Liberation Theology? The answer is simple: everything. For every theology is always a sexual theology and it is necessary to uncover not just the gender codes but the sexual (ideological) assumptions of Christian theology, ecclesiology and the methods of theological inquiry which have pervaded our understanding of Christianity. Sexual ideologies are foundational in economic and political structures of oppression, just as they remain foundational in our understanding of ourselves and ourselves in relation to God. As Lisa Isherwood has said, 'When women no longer understand themselves as consumable goods for the delight of men it will have an effect on the way they consume . . . [This] will have both economic and ecological benefits' (Isherwood, 2000, p. 161). And to this I should want to add that, from this perspective, only a political Feminist Theology has the capability of de-articulating the present gender ordering of the market system and liberating not only humanity but also God from the narrow sexual ideological confines in which God has been located.

Have I then betrayed the cause of the poor? Have I betrayed Liberation Feminist Theology by unveiling the deceitful ways in which heterosexual ideologies systematically pervade and domesticate that great rupture in the knowledge/experience of God as presented by Liberation Theology? Yes, I have. As I have said previously, the poor and Christians (even in the Latin American Christian communities) are sexual beings. Yet, sexuality and poverty are the great taboos of theology. How can we be true to the origins of Liberation Theology? By rehearsing the theology of an idealized past and entertaining ourselves by repeating anecdotes from Vatican II or episcopal conferences? My path has been to develop a sexually explicit Liberation Theology which I have called 'Indecent Theology', as a continuation of Liberation Theology in all its transgressivity and agency. It is a path from the margins of sexual and economic exclusion towards an understanding of a larger Jesus, a greater God and an infinitely wider Christianity that will not need to be, in the words of Irigaray, the 'product of the love between Father and son' (Irigaray, 2002, p. 58), but among other, more Queer but no less tender lovers.

This book

From Feminist Theology to Indecent Theology is then, in a sense, a reply to that question concerning theology, sexuality and poverty which my colleague formulated some time ago. I have since then heard it repeated from time to time, though interestingly by European, but not by Latin American, women. The question is still one about trans-gressive sexuality and political theologies. It is about God and the gendering orders of geopolitics.

This book is about a journey and a complex one at that, but one on which I have not been alone. I have been accompanied by many partners in an interdisciplinary dialogue, from Feminist Liberation Theologies and postcolonial readings, to postmodernism and Queer theory. The book is divided into three parts. In Part One, 'Troubling Theology: Liberation Theology Meets Sexuality', I show that the encounter between Liberation Theology and sexuality is not an unnatural one. On the contrary, it is surprising that such an encounter has not been produced earlier. The three chapters included in this first part show some of these first encounters of the (sexual) 'third type' in the context of Liberation Theology. Chapter 1, 'Walking with Women Serpents', is a reflection on the incarnation of Jesus. It adopts the perspective of the encounter of a messiah born in times of not only political and religious upheavals in Israel, but also a messiah whose sheer presence in the world seems a direct confrontation with patriar-chal powers. Using a style of doing theology traditional among Latin American feminist theologians, 'Walking with Women Serpents' uncovers some of the confrontations that have been hidden in our reading of the gospel narratives concerning the birth of Jesus and the killing of the innocents. Behind the scenes concerning the birth of Jesus there is a story of power and domestic violence, of the killing of children and women and the horrors of power exercised against women which comes from a highly ideological heterosexual frame-work.

Chapter 2, 'When God is a Rich White Woman who Does Not Walk', addresses the false construction of a general identity of Latin American women, based on class but also on cultural and racial issues present in the continent. Using a materialist perspective, I reflect on a Mariology of Liberation to focus on the difficulties of too easily iden-tifying Marian worship with liberation in Latin America. Moreover, a postcolonial reflection shows us that the sexual ideology behind Mariology might well be responsible for more than just gender structures in the continent. Economic and political structures may also depend on *Marianismo*, or the ideology sustaining 'femininity' and *machismo* among the poor.

Chapter 3, 'Do Not Stop the Flow of My Blood', further explores the role of denunciation and the unveiling of sexual ideologies which should come from Liberation Theologies. It is in that way, and informed this time by Paulo Freire's dialectical method outlined in his *Pedagogy of the Oppressed* (1993), that I address the tension in Jesus' ministry concerning women's consciousness. There are several issues here. The first is that the consciousness of Jesus was subject to historical limitations. This could be the starting point for a more mature Christology among Latin American women who need to challenge the patriarchalism which was embedded in the discriminatory social and religious traditions of his day and also in bureaucratic canons and legislation. This raises the question of how to construct a liberative Christology which has the courage to face Jesus' historical shortcomings. For example, how to reconcile the picture of a Jesus who while charitable and compassionate towards individual women, does not concern himself with the reform of harsh laws. The answer is to produce a dialectical Christology which takes seriously the historical role that women have played in the making of the Messiah, both in his own community where he grew up as a child and in our present circumstances.

The common theme running through these three essays is the attempt to do a Liberation Theology from the perspective of poor women, addressing with honesty the questions which come from poverty and sexuality. These questions include the following. How did patriarchalism (as an ideology sustaining imperial power) react to the presence of the Messiah? It may be that the first confrontation of Jesus was with domestic violence. Or, how can Mariology claim to liberate women whose foremothers fought against *Conquista*? They suffered rape and death at the hands of the Marian conquistadores, the same hands which bore the banners of their white, European lady. Or again, how can poor women continue to develop a christological project in which Christ grows historically along with with women's consciousness?

Part Two of this book, 'Indecenting Theology: Undressing Sexual Ideology in Theology', continues by applying to Liberation Theology a hermeneutical suspicion constructed from Marxist analysis and sexual theory. Chapter 4, '¿*Bien Sonados*?', is a critique of the way that Liberation Theology manifests only a secondary concern for women's issues. This can be seen when a theological interest in women is added as an appendix to a general theology of the poor, or when space for women's theological reflection is restricted to Mariology, especially a Mariology which suits the interests of the church. This chapter is the text of a paper that I presented at a conference at Newman College, Birmingham, at which Jon Sobrino also spoke. We were the only two speakers from Latin America, yet Jon Sobrino not only refused to enter into any dialogue with my reflections, but even in his own presentation he ignored every issue of gender. It is not easy for a Latin American woman theologian to find companions in the struggle even among those who have otherwise done so much for the cause of God's Kingdom in the continent. It is my hope that those who led the way will not be content to stand still. My farewell words to Sobrino were 'We need to keep walking . . .'.

Chapter 5, 'On Wearing Skirts without Underwear', shows already the seeds of a theological rebellion in the making. This is not the first paper where I used the term 'Indecent Theology',[4] referring to a way of doing theology outside the parameters of decency/indecency. These parameters have dominated Latin American society, especially through the mechanisms by which sexuality and Christianity have been closely linked in regulating the lives of women. In this chapter, the christological theme which started to be reflected in the previous chapters of Part One becomes overtly and critically involved with heterosexual ideology. The attempt here is to think how Christology can be done outside the limitations of heterosexuality while still retaining the economic and political perspective of Latin American women. What would happen if we challenged the women who usually appear in Liberation Theology, the ones from whom christological reflections come? It is well known that liberationists have made a plea to have an option for the poor, but, especially, the rebellious poor.[5] This concern is carried forward and deepened in Chapter 6, 'A Woman's Right to Not Being Straight'. Here theology itself and not just Christology is questioned, this time from a human rights perspective, from another dialectical pair related to 'decency/indecency', namely 'normal' (heterosexual) women and 'para/normal' (non-heterosexual) women. This chapter reflects on how a theology which is a theology of liberation, which claims to be a theology done at the margins, for the margins, can locate itself within the ideologically centred heterosexual paradigm. This is what I have called 'indecenting', that is, a way of doing theology which deconstructs its implicit heterosexual assumptions, while giving a voice to the voiceless women of Liberation Theology.

Part Three, 'Postcolonialism, Feminism and Liberation', considers the encounter of postcolonial suspicion with Liberation Theology, basically through the irruption of the discourse of poor women in

---

[4] The first time that I used the term 'Indecent Theology' was in a paper presented to the College of Le Sante Union, Southampton, for a Summer School at the invitation of Professor Mary Grey in 1996. The women present engaged immediately with my idea of linking theology, poverty and radical sexuality. My praxis as a feminist theologian of liberation became clearly 'indecent' from that day.

[5] For this point, see for instance the *Central American Kairos* document (New York: Circus, 1988).

theology. The chapters in this part are 'Does the Church need Theology or Vice Versa? A Materialist Analysis Concerning the Current Theological Industry and Its Church Market', 'Doing the Theology of Memory: Counting Crosses and Resurrections' and 'Gustavo Gutiérrez Goes to Disneyland: Theme Park Theologies and the Diaspora of the Discourse of the Popular Theologian in Liberation Theology'. These chapters are concerned with a political postcolonial analysis of theology. They explore the way in which systems of theological legitimization continue the deregulation of the theological productions of the Other, making theology into a marketable product and trivializing the authenticity of subversive voices in Christianity. However, from the voices of women in El Salvador, a popular yet nuanced theological analysis comes to challenge us to reconsider the presence of God among women, not only peasant but also guerrilla women. Unfortunately, the mechanisms of colonization in theology still exist and function. 'Gustavo Gutiérrez Goes to Disneyland' explores a theme that I developed later in Indecent Theology, that is, the process by which Liberation Theology became almost a site of tourist attraction through the marketing processes of North Atlantic Theology. In that sense, Liberation Theology was disempowered while readers in Europe and the United States were able to acquire by a process of theological expropriation a new, more meaningful identity. The North Atlantic reader became a prophet. The decline of the church in the West and the disillusion that many Christians felt with the church as an institution was healed by the construction of the figure of the prophet-theologian which was built around themes of Latin American nativism.

Part Four of the book, 'Indecent, Radical, Queer: The Future of Feminist Theology of Liberation?', takes the discussion of Queer theology and Liberation Theology to a deeper level. '*Rejunte*: A Theology from Excluded Love' brings together issues of economic exclusion and love, reflecting on the family from a Queer, transversal perspective rooted in poverty, alienation and the spirituality which people develop in times of globalization. Exclusion is not only an economic category: it is also an affective one. Christianity is destabilized by processes of exclusion because theology is by tradition normative. This means that the best and most compassionate efforts in theology should not try to adapt and reformulate institutions such as the family, when the economic agreements surrounding the family no longer exist. New economic and affective ways develop and therefore new ways of loving people and understanding God are unveiled. What can Christian theology learn from that?

Chapter 11, 'A Profane Book of Saints: *San La Muerte*', continues the theological reflection on *Rejunte* Theology. There is a 'Queerness' in popular theologies from the margins, such as in the worship of *San La*

Muerte (St Death) where spiritual challenges and a stranger, Queer God of the poor emerges. It is interesting to reflect on how these popular theologies arise from the experience of the *cotidiano* (every-day life) of the excluded and how their Queerness consists in chal-lenging the vision held by Liberation Theology of the 'everyday life' of the poor. A Queer popular theology is an unruly one. It may bring some chaos and disorder to the affective ideology of Christian theo-logy, but its contribution is immense. In a way, the God of the excluded can only be revealed in the community of the excluded and *San La Muerte* is an example of a divine worship organized around different ways of thinking economically and sexually, and yet, abundant in solidarity and generosity.

Chapter 12, 'Scenes from Queer Cruci/Fictions: *Matan a una Marica* (They Killed a Faggot)', is a Queer and liberationist manifesto for the reading of the Queer God in Jesus. What is at stake here is how to think in a different way and to write a Christology that might allow us to engage with a Queer God. A Queer God: a stranger at the gate; a God that has been excluded by sexual and economic normativities but also by sexual epistemological conventions. This chapter is therefore an attempt to render in crisis the heterosexual epistemology behind the christological reading of the gospel and to read his crucifixion from the cruci/fiction of the innocent death of a transvestite in Buenos Aires. A Queer Christology must also be a grounded Christology, reading the life of the poor and marginalized from the economic and sexual hegemonic orders of our world.

This collection is by no means exhaustive of the concurrence of themes and analyses that a multidisciplinary theology such as Indecent Theology intends to be. However, it shows that there is no 'fashion' stance in choosing a dialogue with Queer theory, just as there has been no fashion stance in using a Marxist understanding of ideology as a method to explain relations of production, not just in church and society, but also in theological processes. From Feminist Theology to Indecent Theology is not a progressive development. Rather it is a transversal (Queer) one in that we can see how a high sexual suspicion concerning epistemology starts a process that both unsettles and discovers. In this discovery new understandings continue to interrogate the praxis of the church as action and reflection from 'the margins of the margins' where a true marginal God refuses to leave and be co-opted by the centre.

Part One

Troubling Theology:
Liberation Theology Meets Sexuality

Introduction

Beyond the well-known 'option for the poor', what characterized Liberation Theology was the alliance between a powerful ideological suspicion concerning how class formation had influenced faith and Christian teaching, and a genuine praxis of transformation of the unjust structures of society. That 'ideological suspicion' was a characteristic which was not original, fortunately, in the history of Christian theology, but for the first time it was solidly and coherently applied. It is true that voices of protest had already denounced the unholy alliances between church and state and the conviviality of ecclesiastical and secular power, from the writings of the Fathers of the church to the many radical writers of Reformation times. However, Liberation Theology went a step further by systematically and structurally using the concept of ideological formation in order to unveil class economic interests embedded in theology. Such interests, argued the liberationists, influenced ecclesiology (the organization of the churches), dogmatics (the corpus of the orthodox doctrines) and Christian ethics. From the way parishes were organized, preventing poor people from being full participants of their Christian communities, to the individualistic understanding of sin, the presence of ideological interests needed to be confronted.

However, using ideology *à la* Marx, as a method to unveil the non-neutrality of theology when it comes to power relationships, was only the beginning of a long process. It was the occasion for black and indigenous Latin American people to address the same ideological questioning, now applied to issues of race and gender. This led to reflection on theology and poverty in the multiple combinations of discourses on gender, class and race. For Latin American women, it meant what came to be called the unveiling of the 'triple oppression'. In practice it produced a search for a liberation from theology, which needed to come not only from a gender suspicion but from one based on gender and poverty, analysing the difference that being an indigenous or black woman in Latin America makes in the life of the poor.

The challenge then was multiple: a different methodology (or a different emphasis) was required. First, there had to be theological recognition of the women's *caminata*,[1] taking account of the fact that there were women also doing this walking. Second, what was at the stake was the idea of theology as a creative path of acting and reflecting about the presence of God in our lives. Women highlighted the fact that theology should be a kind of enterprise of opening up new roads, taking the old paths when needed but at other times deviating from traditional roads in order to explore new fields. Since Liberation Theology was from the outset a biblical theology, these new roads were biblical ones. The women's *caminata* required a different engagement with the Bible, new questions concerning the patriarchal structures of sin needed to be unveiled in the Scriptures. One of these questions which I thought particularly important related to Jesus the Messiah and sin, not just individual sin but the structures of sin. Latin America has a history of violent, criminal, systematic and structural opposition to courageous, prophetic voices. High-profile examples include the assassinations of Archbishop Oscar Romero of El Salvador and Bishop Juan Gerardi of Guatemala. This invites the theological question of the ministry of Jesus as critical of the structures of gendered sin. It is not enough to say that on an individualist level Jesus confronted patriarchalism (unevenly) among friends and acquaintances. The liberationist perspective demands a structural level of analysis here.

It occurred to me that the killing of the innocents in the Gospels, read from this perspective, might show how domestic violence relates to the coming of the Messiah. According to Josephus, Herod was a wife-beater who finally succeded in killing his wife. His mother-in-law managed to escape from his brutality by pretending to be dead in a coffin.[2] I therefore suspected that domestic violence, the oppression of the Israelites (politically, economically and culturally) and the killing of children were profoundly linked as forces in opposition to the birth of Christ. In that case, as is argued in Chapter 1, we are confronted with an enmity or opposition that is intrinsic between Christ and patriarchy, or between God and patriarchy. This is to say, the Messiah's birth was opposed by the same forces of patriarchy represented both by a military empire occupying Israel and the figure of Herod as a domestic abuser.

The *caminata* proposed here is one of structural denunciation. It disengages itself from the readings of the Bible that at that time

---

[1] *Caminata* is the Spanish word for 'walk'. It is traditionally used in Latin American Liberation Theology to indicate a style of 'doing' theology in a community process or 'walk'.

[2] Cf. The *Works* of Flavius Josephus, Book XV, iii, 2 and 4.

attempted to deal with women's liberation from oppression by focusing on the narratives concerning the Virgin Mary. The Messiah's birth
was resisted by patriarchal ideologies of power, and this has little to
do with the narrative of Jesus being born in a story characterized by
submission and acceptance. Mariology in Latin America has suffered
from its beginnings from the predominance of male theologians. They
may well have had good intentions. They may have inadvertently
opened the way for Latin American women to start to do a Mariology
of Liberation. But the outcome was a truly innocuous Feminist
Liberation Theology. They emptied the discourse of gender, poverty
and class and prevented consideration of more radical, revolutionary
possibilities. Paul Ricoeur has been influential on Liberation
Theology and it is at this point that we can make use of his concept of
demystification in relation to the Virgin Mary. After all, Mariology
has been at the root of 500 years of the oppression of women under
Christianity in Latin America. We must honestly face the fact that
although in Latin America Mary is sometimes hailed as a powerful
liberator of women and the poor, we have yet to see any evidence of
it. The reality is that the Virgin Mary has become a white, rich God
who, being depicted in many statues, cannot walk and was never
imagined as having to walk. As such, Mary is the symbol of the
anti-*caminata*. The claims for her as a force for liberation all stem from
contemporary biblical exegesis. But the actual symbolism of Mary in
Latin America today is quite the reverse. The fact that it is still necessary to denounce the real effect of Mariology today is a reflection on
the fact that Liberation Theology has never cared to develop a
Christian ethic of sexuality. It has used a progressive Marxist analysis
to understand ideological formation processes related to class issues.
However, when it comes to matters of sexual ethics it has maintained
an unreconstructed pre-conciliar position. This is nowhere more
evident than in Mariology where it betrays any liberationist standpoints with a heavy patriarchal understanding of life and society.
Therefore, while some liberationists were considering the wisdom of
traditional economic systems found in the indigenous nations, it did
not occur to them to look equally at constructions of sexuality and
gender codes prior to the arrival of Christianity in the continent, codes
which still survive and are influential, although marginalized. These
issues are taken up in Chapter 2, 'When God is a Rich White Woman
who Does Not Walk', a call for greater attention to be paid to the
actual mechanisms of how sexuality and Mariology work, and the
consequences, methodologically and theologically. It is also an early
presentation of the argument that sexuality is foundational in the
system of class structures in Latin America.

At this point it became evident that the *caminata* proposed here
was dialogical. It is curious how Paulo Freire has been taken more

seriously by many ordinary women in the continent than by academics. While theologians of liberation were writing on issues related to conscientization, dialogical education and processes of transformation, women in Basic Communities just got on with the job. Chapter 3, 'Do Not Stop the Flow of my Blood', is about taking seriously the challenge of dialogical processes in theology, as is already done in community work. The desire to use dialogic methods in Christology comes from the desire to have a coherent, liberative praxis in our thinking/doing of theology. Contrary to what the Boff brothers suggest in their *Introducing Liberation Theology* (1987, p. 13), there should not be a 'class division' of labour in a Liberation Theology. A hierarchy of knowledge, that is, 'professional theologians' versus 'people's theology', cannot exist if liberationists are coherent with their hermeneutical circle of suspicion.

If women were to develop a Liberation Christology in a hermeneutics of gender and sexual suspicion they would need to use a different methodological stance from the patriarchal ones. An attempt to reread Christ, then, across the web of ideological constructions should be dialogic. Women and all the oppressed and marginalized people of our world need dialogue. *Los pobrecitos de Dios* (the poor ones of God) need a dialogue among equals: they do not need a Christ-Emperor to instruct them. Instead of that, we need the Christ of the Gospels, who entered into dialogue and discussed things with friends and neighbours, using precisely that method rediscovered by Freire of 'problem posing' issues and answering questions with questions. A Feminist Liberation Theology cannot proceed so far, only to stop and adapt feminist issues into the framework of patriarchal ideology, just as there can be no compromise between capitalist spiritualities (such as consumerism) and class analysis in Liberation Theology. However, the problem is how to develop an alternative Christology which steps out of the gender ideological framework, while allowing Christ to be Christ. Chapter 3 attempts to do that by using a dialogical methodology in theology. It considers the role of the community, and women in the community, in the formation of Christ, what I call 'the social construction of the Messiah'. It sees Jesus in his process of growing up as a person and as a messiah, confronting people's expectations but also discovering himself in them. An authentic dialogical process implies that people in communities are able to challenge each other and to learn from each other. And it also means that a dialogical Christ is more than Jesus because it lovingly acknowledges a community that nurtured Christ, taught Christ, challenged Christ and was a participant in dialogue with him. And Jesus, in his process of becoming the community Messiah, may at times have fallen short of expectations. For instance, in the episode of the woman suffering from a haemorrhage, Jesus did not acknowledge the structures of sin surrounding the religious laws of pollution and the conceptualization of menstruation as part of a patriarchal ideology that denigrates women's bodies.

To stretch the hermeneutical circle of suspicion to these limits has been not only necessary but a part of doing the *caminata* with creativity and courage. Perhaps one of the first lessons for us as Latin American feminist theologians has been that we do not need to justify God. In the presence of hunger, political persecution and centuries-long injustices, we do need to justify God's apparent silence. Instead of that, we try to do a theology which is both honest and courageous, because the art of posing the right questions is still as important as obtaining the right answers.

1

Walking with Women Serpents:
Women's Ministry and Economic Oppression

The first thing that we are going to do is to bring geopolitics into theology. The second thing, is to declare (even if it is only for ourselves) our bias or prejudices, the ones we take with us when we do theology. Neutrality only helps to maintain the status quo, and therefore declares a position. My first bias, or presupposition for interpretation, is that we have conflicting spaces incorporated in our theological discourses, as for instance the spaces of the first world and the third world.

Any attempt to produce a liberating theology needs to consider how knowledge is invented, and why and how certain ideas become authoritative paradigms, while others do not. Every epistemological construction we use has been developed with a purpose, and coming back to geopolitics we will say that knowledge comes from certain spaces of legitimization. For instance, there are political spaces which, due to their economic and military supremacy, impose ideas that tend to disempower other spaces. We will call these other spaces 'peripheral', because they are located around the centres of power (which are the centres of knowledge and of interpretation). This periphery can be looked at as the space of the 'Other', or the different or not normal. For instance, during the *Conquista* of America, America was the Other for the Europeans; during processes of colonization, the colony functions as the periphery to the centre of economic power of the dominant country.

The space located in the periphery of theology that we are going to consider today is women, and women from Latin America. Latin American women are the third world of the third world, and a theology with a bias towards the poor can only find its most radical option when it focuses on poor women.

We are going to use a *mujerista*[1] perspective. *Mujerista* is a word

---

[1] *Mujerista* Theology has been developed by Ada María Isasi Díaz with the Hispanas women in the USA. It takes seriously the cultural and political environment of their community. See Isasi Díaz, *En la Lucha/In the Struggle: A Hispanic Women's Liberation Theology* (Minneapolis: Augsburg Fortress Publishers, 1993).

related to *mujer,* which is the Spanish for woman. It is a theological dialogue between Theology of Liberation, Feminist Theology and Theology of Culture. In this way we make sure that we bring to the discussion all the spaces of women in Latin America: their economic oppression, their invisibility in church and society, and their cultural space. The *mujerista* concern is not, however, restricted to a discourse of equality between men and women, but is one of liberation.

I am concerned with the interpretation of texts. My concept of text is very wide. I would like you to consider that a text is not only a written discourse, but that the arts, architecture and social structures of our society work as texts which can be interpreted. The churches and their traditions are like texts in themselves, which must be read together with the Scripture, to enable us to understand more of their identity.

Another important text to interpret is the historical one, especially from the perspective of marginalized people, but then we must consider an alternative concept of history. To work with historical data to try to search for the identity of the text (for example, historical reference of things being said, facts, etc.) will always challenge us to confront what Haydn White said: 'Facts do not speak for themselves. The historian does.' The historical discourse is an interpretation, and sometimes even an interpretation of previous interpretations, of past events.

The second presupposition to take into account is that if God is God, not of the dead but of the living (Matthew 22.33), our reading of the Scripture should have characteristics of life in it, such as birth, creation, recreation, movement and novelty. Most of the time, the traditional interpretation made by the church has fixed the meaning of books, stopped the interaction between text and reader in the name of dogmas, and therefore has kept the experiences of the life of believers outside the interpretation of the living Word of God. The churches have many times been nearer to ideological production than to allowing a community to work on its own process of understanding.

To analyse this phenomenon, we need to go back to geopolitics. There are basically two kinds of readings: the one which interprets to legitimize structures of power, and the one which questions the interpretation and the power itself. Following the French philosopher Paul Ricoeur, we will call the reading which questions 'a reading of rupture'. This is produced by the positive role of the imagination of a community, in an ongoing process of interpretation of their own faith and everyday reality. The text that we interpret also interprets us: this is a process of self-understanding. This concept is very important, because if we read the text of the church without a critical interpretation, we accept a definition of our being-in-the-world, without confronting this with our life experience. Any uncritical reading, which I will call naive, is a contradiction of the interpellative nature of the Word of God, which I believe permanently opens a project of being in the world, according to our historical circumstances.

If there is something that is central to the New Testament it is Jesus' insistence on this 'communitarian reading of rupture'. 'How do you read?' is the permanent question that Jesus brings to the people, constantly challenging traditional interpretations that are dead, that is, immobile, and that do not allow the production of meaning between the Scriptures and the readers. The rupture suggested by Jesus is a rupture produced by faith, not by an individual but by a whole community, in a dialogue which includes emotions and data from daily life experience – mostly from marginalized people. This is perhaps the difference we perceive when we read the Gospels, and when we read the Letters of Paul. In the Gospels, everything Jesus said provoked either opposition or acceptance; that is, his word was discussed by people, with examples taken from their own life. The Messiah has a dialogical role: meaning comes from dialogue with the community. In the Letters, we confront a monologue; there are no people, no second version of things that happened. The feeling of authority is overwhelming.

How do we read in Scotland, where I live, and in Latin America? If we want the sort of reading which interprets the Bible and allows us to be interpreted by such a reading? Our answer is: It is a reading *with* our poor (not *for* them), and it must feel like walking alongside the poor on the same road, sharing the same life experiences, observing, judging, acting and celebrating together. I will call it 'walking with women serpents'.

Walking with Women Serpents

Walking with women serpents is a method to read our texts, from women's perspective, which includes the political and the cultural, and privileges a marginalized group of poor Latin American women. We are used to a universal reading of the Scriptures (for example, 'for all humanity'), without suspecting that such an ample perspective excludes a lot of people from marginal groups. The universal reading is really European, male and white. To read from a different perspective does not sound 'legitimate'. But this is the point: it is not a legitimate reading that we want, since legitimization is the instrument of support of patriarchal ideologies, inside and outside the churches. Our interpretation wants to rescue elements of illegitimacy and subversion.

We propose first, *to walk with;* second, with women serpents.

To walk with is at least to have a path in common, but different companions on our route. They are different in the sense that they are not 'images of ourselves'; they are women from another culture, have another vision of the world, and a different reality. It is our experience meeting with the experiences of others. We can then say that *to walk with* is an expression of solidarity, a sharing of experience of the 'everyday nature of *Otherness*'.

Our companions are women serpents. This requires some explanation. From the different cultures we have in Latin America, I am highlighting one, the Náhuatl culture, which was part of the Mexican empire before the invasion of America. These lands were lands of women serpents. What does this mean? It means that the symbols of the serpent and that of femininity were inextricably united in a dialogue with the sacred. Serpents were a symbol of the sacrality of women. The dualistic pantheon of the Mexicas (for whom God was neither male nor female but 'dual') was inhabited by god/desses represented as serpents: for instance, the goddess Cihuacóatl, whose name means 'the Woman Serpent'.

Women had priestly roles in the temple. The sacrality of Mexica women was never questioned, and it was related to their daily life and economic activity. The serpents were a symbol of wisdom, and union with God. It is a pity that when the conquistadores brought the Christian religion to these lands, the serpent that for centuries was a symbol of women's wisdom and power became, until today, a negative symbol related to guilt and disempowerment for women. The conquistadores brought to our lands a discourse of legitimization of power and, as such, a univocal interpretation of Christianity and the Scriptures. Univocal, fixed meanings are also characteristic of dictatorships. It is as homage to Latin American women, and my race, that we will walk today with them, reading about women's ministry and economic oppression.

We are going then to walk with women who are alive, and with women who are long dead. Women serpents were massacred 500 years ago, with the invasion of Latin America, but because nobody ever gave them a voice in our theology, I have decided to let them speak and criticize us. The women survivors, humiliated and subjugated until today, still carry with them many of the characteristics of their ancestors, adapted to new circumstances of colonization. The women warriors died in the battle of Tlatelolco, defending their cities, their families and religion, but the survivors are today busily engaged in many battles: political, economic, against subjugation of race and gender, and, some of us, in theological battles.

To walk with women serpents is to let Otherness take the lead for a while, to teach us something new, and, in this case, to share with us the experience of the two big losses suffered at the hands of the European conquistadores: the knowledge of the sacrality of women, and economic independence.

Choosing our tools of interpretation

To read our texts of church, society and Bible as women serpents, we will use first of all a tool that I call 'the mirror of Mama Huaco'. Mama Huaco, first Coya woman and mother of the Incas, has been represented as a woman with a mirror in her hand. The mirror reflects the face of a Coya woman. This is the mirror of Otherness, reflecting the triple Otherness of gender, race and economic exploitation in Latin America.

The second tool has already been mentioned. It is the role of subversion. These tools will make our theology vulnerable, and in a way, as the Asian theologian Kosuke Koyama has said, it will take our reading out of the sphere of our mother tongue and its familiar concepts. This vulnerability will prove at the end to be a source of renewed strength. Latin America was invaded and the faith, language and culture of the indigenous people were banned. Women suffered more than men from the slavery system to which they found themselves subjected, but, especially, they suffered from the division of sacred/profane, which became central to Christianity in our lands. The sacrality of daily life was destroyed, and replaced by a public sacrality, represented by the church supported by the economic power of the colonizers. Temple spirituality was opposed to everyday sacrality.

These women, these Mayas, Incas, Coyas, these Zapotecas, how do we read with them the message of Christ? Walking with their bodies covered with rags, and with their children on their backs, barefoot, illiterate, malnourished: what did we do to them? How did they come to be identified by the rags they use as skirts, the women whose symbol was 'the skirt of serpents' and 'the clothes made of stars'? How have we interpreted the Scriptures for the last 500 years, for these women to be reduced to this appalling condition?

Once the everyday sacrality was dismissed, Latin American women lost their relationship with God and their economic independence. Their skirts, symbol of their femininity and priesthood, were also a symbol of their contribution to the national economy, through the work of their hands. Nowadays their rags are a sign of their complete alienation.

These women are like refugees in their own lands, as women serpents in a quasi-ontological exile. Christian hermeneutics is responsible for that, because it has interpreted their race and gender in terms of inferiority, and has excluded them from any cultural or religious dialogue. Traditional hermeneutics has made of them passive recipients of history, and it has silenced them.

The *Conquista* is an ontological key for Latin America. Latin America is like its women: a symbol of Otherness which the *Conquista* set off on a process of destruction or assimilation. The ego of Europe acted as the centre of interpretation; everything needed to become as it was in Europe, in a process of permanent assimilation or sub-mission. It was the submission of the different, of Otherness, into sameness, the legitimate order of the western world. We can compare Latin American women to a text which has been read from a unique perspective: male, white and from a foreign culture which interpreted Christianity in its own peculiar – convenient – way, to legitimize their power. To speak about women's ministry implies to recognize first of all the geopolitics of Otherness applied against people due to their gender, race and economic dependency, because to speak about women's ministry must challenge us to ask which legitimization of power lies behind women's exclusion from the churches.

From the many discourses we find in the Scriptures, I find one type particularly interesting – the discourses about births. These are narra-tives on the birth of patriarchal culture, people and institutions. All of them are presented with genealogies, a device of legitimization at the time of the writing of the Scriptures. Most of these narratives of births have many elements of rupture in them, and, for some reason, of the rupture of the feminine in them. The stories of women giving birth are elaborated by men, and are a product of their fantasies about women's feelings, needs and biology. However, there are subversive elements in them, because they introduce a novelty in the stories, and the novelty is the participation of women in active roles. For instance the narrative of the birth of Jesus Christ, and the woman who gave him life, Mary. Because I am interested in elements of renewal and life in the text, I find that in this case, the birth of Jesus, we have the coming of the sacred to the world, and the symbolic account of a new interaction of humanity with God.

This encounter between people and the sacred happens in com-munity, and as a traditional discourse of rupture it has elements of strong opposition and social disturbance in it. The narrative of the birth of Jesus is short. With few exceptions, all the stories of women in the Bible are short. Why is this? This is the first element we are going to subvert: the narrated time, and we will do it using the tool of the 'mirror of Mama Huaco'.

This is a human invention, but Latin American women do not participate in the same elaboration of time as Europeans. For instance, in the Andean region, time is not reduced to an abstract sense, detached from creation. This 'world-time' (*mundo tiempo*) has an element that we want to rescue, which is its lack of division between private and public time. The sphere of the domestic and the sphere of the public are somehow interlinked, therefore reducing considerably the division between sacred time and profane time. All this is the time of the wholeness of creation, where the divine and the economic are intimately related. The time of creation, or Pacha Mama (Mother Creation), is the feminine order where communities live without divisions between home-time and church-time.

In the Mary narrative, for instance, the narrated time is short, while the event time is not, because the story has been written from a division of sacred/profane time, which is also a division between domestic and public affairs. But in this narrative, we have a biological time (of nine months from conception till birth), political time (which is the time spent by the King with the ambassadors from the Orient, plus the time of planning to kill the children, and the process of giving orders to the soldiers, and executing them). There is the time of exile (the escape from Judaea, and the settling down in Egypt), and most important of all, the cosmic time, of the dwelling of the Word of God among people.

With the use of the mirror of Mama Huaco, we become aware that, because the texts concerning Mary becoming pregnant, escaping to Egypt and returning are short, we have then to infer that the time of the story belongs to what we identify with short, domestic, women's time. The time of our everydayness which does not take many pages in historical accounts.

Our elaboration of sacred time in relation to women suffers then from the fallacy of reducing Mary the mother of Jesus, a woman, to a domestic, private time, while her participation in public time is almost non-existent. Now, this has an ontological consequence for women in the church, because it means that when we read the story, we elaborate our being in the world, excluded from the perspective of participation in cosmic time, the time of the Word. This shows the dimension of women's exclusion from the field of the public, which is also the field of the cosmic, according to patriarchal interpretation. But if we resist the division sacred/profane and public/domestic, we cannot divide the public-important, the field of titles and recognized functions, the field of the institutions and churches, from the domestic-non-important, invisible life of home. Then Mary and every woman can participate in all times: the biological and the political; the field of intelligence and emotions; the field of leadership and priestly roles, the area where the hands which bake bread are consecrated, and are the ones chosen to distribute it.

Our method of reading the birth narrative of Jesus from this perspective can only start when and if women serpents meet Mary on their road: that is, the encounter of everyday Latin American women with the woman who became de-womanized as a patriarchal symbol of the relation of femininity with the sacred. Does Mary empower women to minister in Latin America? When the churches in Latin America refer to Mary, they always want to emphasize the humility and simplicity of Mary, the peasant girl, with so much in common with our own 'girls' or *chicas* (poor women are always addressed as 'girls' in Latin America, irrespective of their age or marital status). The stress is always on the reply of Mary to the Man-Angel, 'I am the handmaid of the Lord, let what you have said be done to me' (to my body). The time of Mary's reply to the divine messenger is a domestic time, and although it is a short statement of consent, it has become unbearably long in the churches' interpretation, to the point that this reply can still be heard today. These words have been used and abused by churches to tell women their public place in church and society: to reply to any word from whoever is considered a divine messenger, 'let what you have said be done'. From the opposition to women's ministry to the opposition of votes for women, these words from Mary have been used by many churches.

When some years ago I read that the Episcopal Council of my country, Argentina, replied to the petitions of the mothers of the disappeared, who wanted the church to demand from the government the whereabouts of kidnapped relatives, with the words, 'Go and pray to the Virgin Mary', I knew that Mary in Latin America had become a symbol in prison, a symbolic 'prisoner of war'. When I saw that dictators in my continent fiercely opposed the most fundamental rights for women, in the name of the traditional values of the Christian church, and invoked the Virgin Mary in every single discourse they gave, then I also knew that Mary and God could only be liberated in a dialogue with poor women.

What sort of things can be reflected in the mirror of Mama Huaco, when women serpents meet Mary on their road?

• The sacrality of womanhood;

• definitions of wisdom and power;

• issues of *Conquista,* struggle and exile;

• women's suffering as an important hermeneutical clue.

Let us take the last clue, women's suffering. This encounter on the road of liberation produces a process of reading the Bible including Otherness, which is so much needed. Latin America is not Israel; Israel was the conquistadores who came to our lands and told us we were Canaan – pagans, idolaters – and they took our lands and women by divine design, to convert us or to kill us. Women serpents are Canaanites in this sense: they represent the other which is not understood, which is subjected to slavery and abuse, to be domesticated into the order which calls itself reality, or civilization, or the Christian western order.

Why should Latin American women be concerned then with women's ministry, or with ministry in general? What is ministry?

Who has elaborated this concept? Which legitimization of power lies behind it? Can we keep it or not? We must wait some time before considering women's ministry, because first of all we need to produce a less naive reading of the church 's structures.

Any Latin American woman knows that her real priorities are related to the right to a dignified life, where every person can have access to clean water, food, education and health care, but, even more than this, a society where women can exercise a ministry of basic solidarity in the struggle for life. However, these priorities are also intimately related to the economics of women's everyday sacrality. More to the point, any discussion on the distribution of power in Latin America, from our walking with women serpents' perspective, needs to start by understanding female spirituality as central to the relationship of power and production.

Latin American women are concerned with structures of economic and religious power, and their discourses of discrimination and oppression. Economic oppression is violent, poverty is violent. The mutilation of the God who is female into maleness is violent, and the exclusion of women from religious ministry, to which Latin American women are so accustomed in their original traditions, is very, very violent. It violates their sacrality, their sacred time-world conception, and alienates them from a spirituality linked to productive forces, as for instance, their agricultural economy.

If we go back to our idea of using a different mirror to reflect our life, we will be surprised to find that Andean women have an enlightening perspective on Christianity and towards ministry. In their religious universe, there are some characteristics that it is important to mention here:

1. the lack of distinction between the religious and the productive space, that is, between the temple and the cornfield;
2. the lack of a split with everyday life in their elaboration of the sacred;
3. the sexuality of their spirituality: *Pachamama* (sometimes identified with the Virgin Mary) is women's power in their agricultural economy and community life. The *Apus* (male spirits of the hills) have sexual characteristics too, they fall in love, reproduce etc. When people claim to have seen apparitions of the *Apus*, or *Pachamama*, they talk about them as people who eat and work, laugh and celebrate life.
4. worship is related to everyday things: community gatherings of the agricultural year, the offering of *chicha* and a sacramental meal, where women have the key priestess's place. The time-world is female, and this vision of the world is also translated into their society's structures, and, of course, the structure of their religious organization.

Theology of Liberation says that the birth of Christ is the coming of the God-who-is-community or the God-who-is-society. The God whose flesh was made of woman's blood. The idea of a messiah coming to the world has not always been traditionally associated with a man. There was a time when Israel believed in a collective messianism: the community of Israel, as messianic. There is also perhaps a female prototype of a messiah in the Hebrew Scriptures, in the Deuterocanonics of Judith. What we want to say is that the fact that Jesus was a man is not relevant for us, because his messianic role, which was very original, was the creation of a dialogue between Jesus and women, who challenged him with their questions and interpretations. This is our point: although the gospel writers were male and thus their interpretation of accounts is also limited to a male perspective, and in spite of the fact that Jesus was a man, his messianic role was construed by a community of women. 'Who do you say I am?' Jesus *became* a messiah walking with poor women, in a dialogical process of popular conscientization.

This messianic construction started with the woman who received him in her womb and showed him compassionate love (in the Old Testament, the compassion of God is the 'love from the womb'). Mary taught Jesus to speak, and she breastfed him. Even before that, the dialogical construction of the Messiah started with a community of women who received the news of a future birth in the village; especially in the collective work of preparing clothes and sharing their humble food with the future mother. Any Latin American woman interprets Jesus' birth as prepared by a community of hard-working women, as birth still is among the poor women of my culture.

The narrative of Jesus' birth is a violent text because it is a text of the irruption of God during the *conquista* of Israel by the Roman Empire. For Mary, as an economically dependent child-bride, to accept her pregnancy, still single, while society could condemn her, was a situation of confrontation. In Latin America, it still is. For Joseph, to defy the religious law concerning fiancées breaking sexual regulations, was a courageous act and even a reinterpretation of religious laws. It was confrontative too, because it was a clear choice in opposition to the religious establishment of the time. And what can be said about the violence threatened against foreign ambassadors by the government, the fact that a pregnant woman, ready to give birth, could not find a room, the killing of the children in Bethlehem, the escape to Egypt and the years of a family living in exile?

The story represents the violence to which life is submitted in an occupied territory. In this case, God is submitted to institutional violence, and structures of violence particularly addressed against a whole feminine symbolic universe. From the mirror of Mama Huaco, we can see that the feminine of God has been attacked. We will see more about this in a moment.

Herod was a cruel ruler. In Latin America, we call his like *vende patrias* (literally 'sellers of their own country'), a terrible insult. The forces who do not respect the woman, do not respect the children either. And Herod decided that children under two years old should be killed in Bethlehem, because the Messiah was living among them.

How selective are the paramilitary in cases of killing children in the streets of Brazil? Do they check how old they are? How easy is it to decide if it is a girl or a boy while their mothers scream and run in an effort to protect their children? How many mothers have died in Latin America while campaigning for the safe return of their disappeared families? How many women died with their children during Herod's massacre? All of these are important hermeneutical questions when addressed by poor women walking with us on the same road of interpretation.

This blood of women and children was sacrificial blood. There is a thesis from the French anthropologist René Girard that every civilization is built upon a 'founding sacrifice', which in our case Girard relates to Jesus' crucifixion. From our perspective, if there is a sacrificial founding event, it must be this killing of women and children, because their blood was the symbol of the struggle which surrounded the coming of the Messiah. Herod was a patriarch, and also the symbol of patriarchy itself, being related to economic, political, racial and gender oppression. His discourse was univocal, fixed; Jesus was coming with a different interpretation on basic issues such as society, God, the meaning of life and the politics of marginalization.

The point to consider now is that Jesus became a messiah in community, in an ongoing dialogical process with poor women and men. Due to the characteristics of such a process, which is open and participatory, I want to reclaim the freedom for Latin American women to enter this process too, recreating a new dialogue with Jesus, from their present reality. This project of Jesus was opposed in methodology and purposes with Herod's own project. Herod characterizes the opposition to Jesus in the birth narratives, and developed his role in relation to patriarchal patterns of *conquista*, and lack of respect for women. He battered women, with the same feeling of possession over another person's life that he had when ordering the killing of the children in Bethlehem.

We have construed the mirror of Mama Huaco, seeing how the Andean societies are organized according to the politics of the time-world or *Pachamama*. The whole Andean community participates in structures, organized around cycles of births and harvest, with a high concentration of the productivity being in women's hands. The feminine is manifested in this community through its institutions. These institutions have been attacked by a patriarchal project of colonization, whose interpretation of Christianity has proved to be opposed to the ethos of the Andean regions. For instance, the Peruvian theologian, Aurora Lapiedra, has shown how the indigenous population reject the lack of femininity in the churches. The Andean spirituality is related to family and sharing, and the importance of women's role is vital to their development. It is very difficult for these people to see, for instance, that nuns cannot give the bread of communion, while for centuries the Andean women have been presiding at ceremonial banquets and ministering to the community, as part of their special religious role.

From this perspective, we can consider that the messianic project to which Herod and the established church was opposed was a feminine one. By feminine we mean the project of the Other of humanity, coming from the God whose femininity has been mutilated. Patriarchism is the aberration of the worship to the man-God. But our God is not a man-God. Genesis says that we were created in God's image, male and female, and it is interesting to notice that Genesis 1.27 uses two Hebrew words for male and female, which are strongly sexual. These words are also used in the Bible for animals. This element of sexuality in God is very much attuned to the Andean spirituality that we have looked at.

The mutilation of the image of God, using only male language and metaphor to describe God in God's relationship with the creation, is the main reason tor women's exclusion from ministry, simply because Christianity has been appropriated as a male religion. Women's ministry is such a deep issue that it goes beyond an eventual acceptance of women into priestly roles; it works as a challenge to structures of power, inside and outside the church. It has been said that when the poor read the Bible in Latin America, it is like looking at a mirror that reflects the project of the God of liberation, but when theologians do the same, they just find old facts from the past. The reading of the Bible by the poor, and by poor women, is recovering a project of the Kingdom that had been lost, and, at the same time, giving birth to a new church for a new society.

The two projects of Jesus and Herod are reflected in the church which, through its conscientization process and dialogical style, has taken a radical option for the poor and started a movement of renewal of its structures, for instance, in the Basic Christian Communities. This is the church where women leaders are vital to the project of God, and where women's ministry is a fact. Of course this women's ministry is still exercised in exile; in the exile of women serpents from their own culture and female spirituality, and in the exile of the church of the poor. The life of Mary, Jesus and Joseph in Egypt is the life of a

Christian Basic Community, or the church in exile. Another church, fully structured, needed to remain in Israel. Some of its people were traditionalists, some liberals and some were political militants, but it was incomplete without Jesus' own project. At the end, this church – remaining in occupied territory – felt threatened by the new project presented by Jesus.

If the model of the Christian church is a model of a church in permanent exile, as a protest against systems of injustice that dehumanize God's creation, women's ministry is part of the whole conception of the church from the beginning. This model of church is presented in the life of the Christian Basic Communities, where women's ministry is accepted and encouraged by the poor, recognized by a few ministers who work with them but rejected by the established church. The established church is very far away from the slums where the Holy Spirit seems to be pouring out gifts of solidarity and a new understanding of the Gospels among the marginalized.

Women's ministry in Latin America is opposed by a church that has been many times 'pro-Herod', supporting dictatorial regimes that have offered to keep the traditions of the fatherland. These traditions are practices that have kept women and men oppressed during centuries: traditions of hierarchical visions of the world, of masters and slaves, of first and third worlds; traditions of indigenous women servants, kept in illiteracy, as beasts of burden, beaten by their employers, women without surnames or age, without civil rights, *chicas* (girls). From these women God has raised a church. With these women, Latin American believers have started to do theology. Under these women's ministry, the church in exile which is the church of the poor in Latin America, has survived and flourished. Walking with women serpents can teach us that the full femininity of God is a mystery manifested in the presence of women ministers among the poor. The sign of which was manifested in the living presence of the Word of God coming to a poor woman's womb, and shortly after the birth, escaping from dehumanizing structures of violence which were controlled by a man who beat his own wife, and finally killed her.

Gustavo Gutiérrez, the Peruvian theologian, has said that Latin America must recover the full symbolism of the 'beaten Christ of the indigenous people', the one who suffered together with them the iniquities committed against them by the conquistadores. Perhaps we must recover, too, the memory of the women beaten by Herod, and the 'beaten Mary of Latin America' symbolized by centuries of oppression and violation of the most fundamental human rights of women.

Egypt, once the land of bondage, became the country of exile for the Word of God, when God was politically persecuted. Once the symbol of oppression, it then became the land of survival. Somehow Christian women in Latin America have been going to 'Egypt' for a long time, to the Egypt of the church in exile, the Christian Basic Communities.

They have found there that they can participate in a new definition of the church, and women and men's ministry, in an everyday spirituality which requires the presence of the female face of God, and the femininity of the project of the Kingdom being restored. The coming of the God-who-is-society needs to become the God-who-is-feminine.

We are still there, worshipping and doing theology. What is not clear is whether we are going to go back from Egypt, so the Word of God in the Scriptures can one day be interpreted as saying, 'From Egypt I have called my daughter', or if it is part of God's purpose with God's church for us to remain there and build a new church. In any case, the existing church which supports the project of patriarchism, and refused to confront the division of classes in Latin America, will not be happy to recognize its own divisions and contradictions. The issue of women's ministry will always confront us with the reality of economic oppression, and the ontological exile of women serpents from the religious and social structures of Latin America.

2

When God is a Rich White Woman who Does Not Walk:

The Hermeneutical Circle of Mariology and the Construction of Femininity in Latin America

A group of poor Latin American women were doing theology, discussing the role of the Virgin Mary in their lives. Asking themselves if they identified with the Virgin Mary in their sufferings, one of them, looking at the Virgin's statue, said, 'No, because she has expensive clothes and jewels, she is white and she does not walk.'[1] This statement, which comes from a community of women reflecting about their faith, has implied hermeneutical questions concerning the role of Mariology in the construction of femininity in Latin America. Such questions relate to an analysis of our sexuality in its many components, such as experience, gender role and identity, desire, biology, reproduction, racial and economic factors and femininity as the construction of femaleness by society. This analysis, in our context, should be based on the important worship of *La Vírgen* in Latin America. As these women from Argentina have said, she is white, rich and passive, and although they do not identify with her, she plays a very important role in their lives. Since nature and culture are not two separate things, femininity and sexuality have been built together conceptually around the worship of *La Vírgen* in Latin America.

The criticism of the role of Mariology is the key to understanding how the interdependent relation between *machismo* and *hembrismo* works in church and society in Latin America.[2] *Machismo* can be defined as the permeating patriarchal ideology which has characterized Latin American history since the *Conquista* in the fifteenth cen-

---

[1] From a popular Bible study group gathered in a parish in Buenos Aires, Argentina, 1987.

[2] About the role of *machismo* in Latin America, and the mutual dependence of *machismo* and *hembrismo* in relationship to the worship of the *Vírgen María*, see, for instance, E. P. Steven's article, 'Marianismo: The Other Face of Machismo in Latin America' in A. Minas (ed.), *Gender Basics: Feminist Perspectives on Women and Men* (Belmont, California: Wadsworth Publishing, 1993).

tury. It rules and regulates the behaviour of men, from allowing them to touch women in the streets or public transport, to the complex legal system which condemns women to a life of poverty and brutality. But *machismo* could not exist without women playing a specific part in society, and such is the model called *hembrismo*. *Hembrismo* has its roots in the complex web of the socio-political and the religious life of a continent where church and state have been long-standing allies for domination.

Hembrismo defines a Latin American woman's place, which is her home, or the sphere of the private and domestic. Her bedroom is traditionally the place of the family's saints and the altars of the *Vírgen María*, with candles burning day and night as women pray for specific needs. Outside of these boundaries is the male territory of paid jobs, politics, church, friends and lovers; *machista* culture does not condemn men's promiscuity but celebrates it. The particular type of Christianity which came to the continent with the *Conquista* has set these ideals, especially through the use of the image of the *Vírgen María*. In Latin America the whole social structure of patriarchalism rests upon the pillars of Mariology, which is a powerful tool for perpetuating what Paulo Freire calls 'the naive consciousness' of women in Latin America. Such naive consciousness is the product of the internalization of oppression, and through a process of domestication perpetuates the Latin American stereotypes of womanhood. The main characteristics of this type of consciousness are resignation, passivity and a lack of critical capacity to analyse the situation of oppression.[3]

Mariology sacralizes and dictates how to be a woman in Latin America, and works as the cornerstone of the feminization of poverty in the continent. Although liberation theologians (male and female) seem, until recently, to have been more concerned with a justification of the worship of *La Vírgen* than listening to a genuine criticism of the ideology that supports Mariology, women are starting to speak out.[4] The consequences of such criticism can sometimes lead to a sort of religious ostracism among the theological community of Latin America, and from a segment of the women's population who think that they benefit from the status that Mariology confers to its

---

[3] This analysis comes from the work of the Brazilian educator Paulo Freire, in his book *Pedagogía del Oprimido* (Montevideo: Siglo XXI, 1970).

[4] Women always found a way of speaking loudly against the oppressive Christianity imposed in Latin America. An example of this is the 'Shameless Verses' sung by Indian women of Cochabamba to Jesus Christ, in which they say, among other things: 'You don't put up with me unwed, you condemn me to bear kids, dress and feed them while alive, bury them proper when they are dead. Will you send to me a mate who would give me blows and kicks? Why must every budding rose suffer the same wilted fate?' See E. Galeano, *Memory of Fire III: Century of the Wind* (London: Quartet Books, 1989), p. 143.

followers. However, feminist theologians of liberation, unmasking the patriarchal readings of God the Father, also need to consider his powerful counterpart, God *La Vírgen* of Latin America. Perhaps only then will Liberation Theology be able to confront the relation between sexuality and Christianity in our continent, and start to listen to the voices of women and men who dare to say they are different.

It is well known that Latin America is more a Marian than a Christian continent. To the gallery of white virgins many *Vírgenes indias* (black virgins), like the Vírgen de Guadalupe or the Vírgen del Valle, have been added. The question to ask here is, 'Are they really black?' In this case, the colour of their skin or the ebony hair that falls on their shoulders does not define them as belonging to the black or indigenous race. There is more to race than colour: there is history, tradition, culture and socio-economic definitions of life and expectations which need to be considered when we define a race. *La Vírgen*, with her oligarchic position in society given by the fact that she has a powerful son from a powerful father, and due to the respect that men in society pay to her, is not a woman of the *pueblo*. In any case she is a representative of God, translating the remote desires of God to the poor, and to women the ideology that structures an unjust social order. As the poor women have said, her statues bring to illiterate people the image of a rich, white woman among poor indigenous people.

The fact is that poor women in Latin America do not rely on the Bible for their spirituality (since the church has denied the Bible to our people for 500 years) but they have their own 'Christian texts', made of the legends of the lives of saints, oral traditions of deliverance in moments of poverty or sickness, and the rich iconography of the *Vírgen*. To reread sacred Christian texts means, in this case, to reinterpret, for instance, the particular style of dressing a statue of the *Vírgen* by women of a certain neighbourhood. For some of us, it also means to study the hermeneutical circle of Mariology in Latin America from its roots of blood and violence, in order to open the way for a study of Christianity and sexuality in our continent.

The hermeneutical circle of Mariology

In order to see how women's femininity is built upon the worship of *La Vírgen*, as constructed from a medieval European definition of womanhood, it is necessary to understand the hermeneutical circle of Mariology in Latin America. Some hermeneutical clues for the methodology of Mariology in Latin America, inexplicably neglected in Liberation Theology, come from the history of the *Conquista* in the fifteenth century, when the Christian religion was forced upon the original nations of the continent. The purpose of our analysis is to reconstruct the hermeneutical circle of Mariology from the perspective of those women of the original nations who fought against the banner of the Virgin Mary, and died in the biggest genocide of history. Hermeneutically speaking, we encounter here the same difficulties that we face when reading the Bible, that is, how to interpret the silence of women and their absence from the stories of the *Conquista*. For this reason I have decided to use the references to women's bodies in the texts as hermeneutical clues for understanding the hermeneutical circle of Mariology in Latin America.

I will use for our study some old texts of the *Conquista* written by indigenous survivors, and as far as possible will let these stories of women's bodies speak for themselves.[5] As a result of this, I expect to produce a criticism of the genesis of Mariology in Latin America from the perspective of the women who died under the forces which brought such worship to the continent. Our reconstruction of the hermeneutical circle of Mariology will consider, first of all, the 'voices' of women expressed by feminine elements that come from the texts of the *Conquista*: women's visions, the dynamics of women's clothes before and after the invasion and some clues given by remarks about body language. These elements will be compared with the clothes and body language of the representation of the *Vírgen*, in an attempt to recreate a lost dialogue.

The visions and prophetic voices of the women of the original nations before the *Conquista* are retrospective metaphors of the beginning of the collapse of the original nations' universe. However, their value consists not in their historicity, but in the fact that they constitute a powerful exegesis of the Latin American religious and socio-economic history. Through visions, descriptions of clothes and women's bodies, these women long dead and forgotten are going to unmask for us the face of Mariology in Latin America.

Step one: the visions

The first step of the hermeneutical circle of Liberation Theology always refers to what is technically called 'the guessing stage'. This refers to the presuppositions and context of a specific community, in this case, a community in Mexico before the *Conquista*. The ancient

---

[5] The main texts I used for this study are the *Códice Chimalpopoca: Anales de Cuauhtitlan y Leyenda de los Soles* (trans. from Náhuatl by P. F. Vázquez; Mexico City: UNAM, 1945); the story of the *Conquista* from an indigenous point of view, M. León-Portilla, *Visión de los Vencidos: Relaciones Indígenas de la Conquista* (Mexico City: UNAM, 1980), and Fr B. de Sahagún, *Historia General de las Cosas Nuevas de España* (Mexico City: Pedro Robredo, 1938).

texts say that there were a series of *prodigios* (signs) or visions that announced the forthcoming tragedy to the people. There were several visions at the time, but I will concentrate on one of them, because of its significance in relation to women.

The Vision of the WOMAN.[6] The Mexicas had a dual divinity, who lived in the 'Land of the Duality'. Sometimes the divinity was represented as a male God, and other times as a female God. The distribution of male or female representations for the same God followed cultural reasons, although the boundaries of femininity were less defined than they are now for ourselves. For example, the main female divinity of the Mexica pantheon was the *Cihuacóatl* (the WOMAN or the woman serpent) and she had priestesses and priests in her temple, both of them called *Cihuacóatl* or 'WOMAN'. The statues of the WOMAN that survived the destruction of the conquistadores belong, no doubt, to a lost aesthetics. It is difficult for us to perceive the love, strength and compassion that those women obtained from a female deity whose representation is a fierce and sinister serpent, with a surprisingly non-human quality. I feel that today we would relate more effectively to a picture of a modern computer, and adore it, than to the representation of the WOMAN. It belongs to a lost aesthetics that accentuates our distance from women of the original nations. Their femininity was made of a power which today terrifies us, and a compassion which is not submissive. This is the first clue to understanding the women who fought against the imposed Mariology, the key to try to re-create the lost sexuality of the Latin American women.

The WOMAN was an agrarian deity, patroness of the people's economy (there were public demonstrations of Aztec peasants at her temple, asking for fair shares in the harvest), a warrior, and a mother for the mothers dying during childbirth. She was a god of passion and compassion. The story that concerns us says that, ten years before the *Conquista*, people woke up in the middle of the night hearing the cries

---

6 The name *Cihuacóatl,* that I translate here as WOMAN, is composed of two parts: *Cihuatl* (woman) and *Çoatl* (serpent), but *Çoatl* also means 'twin', and, in an abstract sense, 'duality'. This is very relevant because the Nahuas believed in a pantheon of a dual God, 'The Lady of the Duality' and 'The Lord of the Duality', who lived in the Place of Duality. Therefore, *Cihuacóatl* means 'Woman of the Duality', that is, the female-represented God of Duality. For that reason, I prefer to use the word WOMAN to refer to her, instead of 'Goddess', which does not carry the same implications of duality. Apart from that, *Çoatl* is a rare form of *Cihuatl*, 'woman'. Her sex is then doubly emphasized. Cf. A. M. Garibay, *Veinte Himnos Sacros de los Nahuas* (México: UNAM, 1958); also F. Karttunen, *Analytical Dictionary of Náhuatl* (Austin: University of Texas, 1983).

of the WOMAN, although nobody was able to see her. In her anguish, the WOMAN said several times the words, 'My dear children (*hijitos mios*), we must leave this place. Where am I going to take you (to protect you)?' and also, 'My dear children, where am I going to hide you?' The voice of the WOMAN is the only human voice registered in the stories of the visions, and it is interesting to notice that the words are related to an exodus of people with God among them.[7]

Many people heard the WOMAN, and interpreted that a terrible danger was going to come to the nation. A danger from which the WOMAN, even with her terrifying power, could not protect them. She was not an all-powerful God; she was the representation of the divine among women of the original nations, the intelligent warrior who knows when she is going to be defeated, and offers to lead the escape. The WOMAN was the projection of a community and, as such, her power or frailty expresses the boundaries of hope and desire among them. I have considered in a previous theological reflection how the Jesus Christ of the Gospels was, as a messiah, the product of a dialogical communitarian process in which men and women participated, both with their inner oppression, and acquired new conscientization. The same can be said about the WOMAN. However, the community projection which made her is still continuing to take shape in the stories of women fighting for liberation in Latin America. For instance, some forms of the legend of the WOMAN crying in the night have survived until now in Latin America. In some countries she is called 'The Weeping Woman' (*La Llorona*), and in others 'The Widow' (*La Viuda*). Her presence announces death or disaster for the unfortunate who hear her.

From a communal perspective, I have personally witnessed 'the presence of the WOMAN' among us, when women of Argentina, searching for their disappeared children in the middle of the 'dirty war', confronted the power of the military dictatorship with the same strength with which other women, 500 years ago, fought to defend their lives and families. The Mothers of Plaza de Mayo also challenged a model of femininity; they were 'women on their own', without visible men, poor women yet independent, challenging a political and religious system. The newspapers of the time called them 'the crazy ones' of Plaza de Mayo. They were Catholic women devoted to the *Vírgen*, who through their political struggle discovered a new way of being women, and with it challenged the establishment. Sra Hebe Bonafini, one of the founders, was advised by the bishops of Argentina to stop demanding the return of her disappeared children, and instead 'to go home and pray to the *Vírgen María*'. Such is the power of domestication of the imposed Mariology that Sra Bonafini

---

[7] Cf. Léon-Portilla (1980), pp. 2–11; also *Códice Chimalpopoca*, pp. 50ff.

was among the women who needed to reject the worship of *La Vírgen* in which they were brought up, in order to demand justice.[8]

As *hembrismo* is the counterpart of *machismo*, the WOMAN as a feminine invention is the sexual counterpart of *La Vírgen;* she is the metaphor that subverts women's traditional sexuality as construed from Mariology. The point is that behind the *machista* myth that says 'all native women are whores' (and was continued by the dictatorships of the 1970s, who considered that 'all educated women are whores'[9] lies the denial of a sexuality which is different; the sexuality of 'the Other'. An early entry in one of the conquistadores' diaries tells us the following story.

The conquistador took an indigenous woman to his ship and tried to rape her. Apparently, the woman was strong and he did not succeed, but it seems that she finally agreed to a sexual relationship with him, although on her own terms. She did not want the 'missionary position' but took a very active role. The conquistador was shocked by her attitude, and wrote in his diary, 'These indian women are all whores.'[10] The observation of the Argentinian women, 'The *Vírgen* does not walk', refers also to the sexual passivity that is required from women in the continent.

Machista societies have a particular way of destroying the purity of human relationships. Many stories tell about the sensual attraction that the conquistadores felt towards indigenous men such as the Caribes. The Caribes belonged to one of the most beautiful races, traditionally very slender and athletic. Their society approved of homosexuality, and because of that, many of the Caribes' men engaged in loving, trusting relationships with European soldiers, only to find themselves betrayed by their lovers, who ended up denouncing them as sinners, and killing them in barbaric ceremonies where the Caribes were eaten alive by dogs, while the soldiers watched. Many drawings of the time illustrate such scenes.[11]

---

[8] See, for instance, the testimonies of the Mothers of Plaza de Mayo concerning their search for their children and the role of the church in Argentina in J. Fisher, *Mothers of the Disappeared* (London: Zed Books, 1983), pp. 5ff., 111.

[9] The Argentinian media carried a public campaign to discredit educated women, especially sociologists, psychologists and philosophers. A familiar saying of that time was that 'Women psychologists (or philosophers, etc.) are all whores and communists'. The universities were closed, students were persecuted and women were encouraged to return to the traditional roles fixed for them by the church.

[10] Cf. E. Galeano, in *Memory of Fire I: Genesis* (London: Quartet Books, 1985), p. 49.

[11] Cf. León-Portilla (1980), p. 160. There is a picture, called 'Hoja del Aperramiento', showing Mariana elegantly dressed and with a rosary in her hand, standing behind Cortes, as Indians are eaten alive by dogs.

What can we learn from this first hermeneutical step in search of the origins of Mariology in Latin America? First of all, we have the intuition of a different construction of sexuality expressed by their god the WOMAN. This sinister-looking and compassionate serpent is a god who admits her failure (could a male-constructed deity admit a shortage of power?), and is the only voice heard during the premonitions. She tells women that they cannot hide any more, and that they need to take action; the crying expresses her pain but is also the language of a tragic vision which works 'as a text' among people from an oral culture. The intuition of a different construction of sexuality pre-Mariology is also enforced by the differences between *La Vírgen* and the WOMAN. Both of them are patriarchal constructions, yet the WOMAN is of a different kind. Behind the legends about the sexual behaviour of the natives lies the political need to suppress an erotic knowledge which threatened the system in which sex/gender differentiation is a core attribute. From this perspective, the separation between decent, white, rich *Vírgen*-like women and poor, native 'whore women' in Latin America is not a coincidence but part of the social organization which is supported by class divisions.

Step two: women's bodies as clues for the interpretation of Mariology: 'the skirts made of stars and serpents'

The descriptions of women's clothes that we find in texts of the *Conquista* describe not only costumes but also economic and sexual power. The traditional attire of the women of the original nations was a product of their own hands, and as such was a piece of art and the visible product of their participation in the economy of the Empire. I found in one text a metaphor of God's power associated with women's skirts. The WOMAN's skirts were said to be made of 'stars and serpents', of light and power (the sinister power of the WOMAN – sinister because the positive and empowering symbol of serpents for women is lost for our western culture post Genesis 3).[12] The skirts were the symbol of God and of sexuality, and it is interesting to find that the destruction of the original nations is full of stories related to women's skirts.

One story says that when the city of Tenochtitlan was surrounded and defeated by the conquistadores, the survivors, mostly women, escaped to Tatlelolco to continue their battle against the foreign invaders.[13] The women from Tatlelolco fought with arrows; they wore their war emblems and tucked up their skirts to their waists in order to chase their enemies with freedom of movement. The chronicle says

---

[12] Cf. *Códice Chimalpopoca*, p. 7.
[13] Cf. León-Portilla (1980), pp. 112ff.

that these women fought half-naked in the marketplace during five days and nights, defending their lives, families and religion, but unfortunately they were defeated by catapults. In Zanatla, at the door of the temple of the WOMAN, there were hundreds of skulls of women from Tatlelolco killed in battle. It is important to remember that those brave women fought against soldiers bearing the *Vírgen María's* banners, as some drawings of the Conquista represent the battles; a handful of nude women defending a city against the over-dressed European soldiers, and the banners with a fashionably dressed white Mary. It was as if God had come to Latin America as a rich, white, carefully covered woman, to defeat women who tucked up their skirts to fight for freedom and country. The conquistadores interpreted actions like the battle of Tatlelolco with a disapproval of the native women's lack of sexual codes of behaviour. They thought they were fighting against whores, and used Mariology to force them to conform to the sexual patterns of Europe in the fifteenth century. Such a pattern, until today, consists in submission in wealth (for rich women), and submission in poverty (for poor women).

'*The conquistadores tore up the women's skirts.*' Another text tells us how women survivors were gang raped by the conquistadores who tore apart their skirts. Some women apparently managed to escape, and according to this story, they sought refuge in other neighbourhoods and at the riversides. At night, the exodus of people leaving Tatlelolco began. The women gathered some rags and covered their wounds in the dark. In this way, with skirts made of rags, the daughters of the WOMAN escaped; 'the One with the skirt made of serpents; the One with the skirts made of stars'. The story says that the only voices in the night were of women calling their children. Voices of women in the night of 1-Serpent, in the year 3-House, 'My dear children, where am I going to hide you?' Not in their skirts because they were rags now. Only the skirts of the *Vírgen María* shone, in full medieval fashion, on the banners of the conquistadores. For the women who survived swearing fidelity to the Christian faith, it was possible to hide their original worship of the WOMAN in the skirts of *La Vírgen*. This is a metaphor for the origins of the Christian syncretism of popular religiosity in Latin America.

Other stories say that the native women were accused of hiding gold in their skirts. The conquistadores subjected women to humiliat-ing body searches, looking for gold under their skirts. Many drawings made at the time depict scenes like that. There is a paragraph in a text explaining how women painted their arms and faces with mud, to avoid being sexually attractive to the soldiers, who preferred women with clear skins. 'Women with clear skin, chickens and corn' was a permanent demand from the conquistadores. Many women were also marked with hot irons on their cheeks, as a sign of being concubines belonging to their masters. Reading these stories, my attention is called to the comments of the writers concerning the women who were forced to live with soldiers. They say that there were grand-mothers and mothers, separated from their families for ever, in a world which had turned 'upside down': their lives were altered to extremes that are difficult for us to recognize, and although these women lived in a patriarchal society before the *Conquista*, their world had a different ordering of society and religion.

Concerning the mud with which they covered their faces to escape rape, years ago, visiting the north of Argentina, I had the opportunity to speak with a group of young indigenous women. While we were sitting talking in the marketplace, some white men approached us asking for directions. The women, seeing them coming, immediately covered their faces with their shawls in fear that they would be attractive to the men, and would risk being abused, as they explained to me later. When I made the comment that I did not use a shawl, and considered it unnecessary for my own protection, they told me laughing that this was because I was not an indigenous woman.

How can we explain Mariology in Latin America, with its emphasis on motherhood and a culture of 'purity', having produced five centuries of disrespect for poor mothers and abuse of women? The reason is that the Christianity and Mariology which came to our continent were instruments of a colonial project, and as such have a double discourse. Women are differentiated according to race and social class; indigenous women are the non-persons of Latin America. José Míguez Bonino, the Argentinian theologian of liberation, has contributed to the unmasking of the oppressive faces of Jesus in Latin America, in search of the genuine Jesus of liberation.[14] People in the Base Christian Communities have learned that the god of the conquistadores is not the real Christian God, the Jesus who is now represented as an indigenous man, living and suffering among the poor. Yet, work concerning a serious criticism of Mariology has not started, perhaps because Mariology fulfils such a crucial role in the patriarchal order of our society, much more than Christology.

The oppressor of her sisters

Up to this point we have rescued the visions of women before the *Conquista* from a few texts written by people of the original nations. Then we extrapolated from various texts the stories related to

[14] Cf. J. Míguez Bonino (ed.), *Faces of Jesus: Latin American Christologies* (Maryknoll, NY: Orbis Books, 1984).

women's clothes. We discovered that women's skirts were a metaphor of God's power, and we read how their lives, faith and economy
were destroyed through metaphors of the tearing up of the skirts.
Other stories tell us of bodies being marked with hot irons and
covered with mud. In this moment we are able to participate somehow in the genesis of Mariology, sitting in our imagination among the
defeated, raped, rag-dressed women. Using the same hermeneutical
clue of clothes, we will now interpret the image of *María*, and how it
was presented to women of the original nations.

Studying the drawings and pictures of the times of the *Conquista*,
we always find a woman standing near one of the conquistadores,
Hernán Cortés, between him and the defeated natives to whom she is
pointing with her fingers.[15] She is also a native woman, but her finery,
her beautiful long skirts and a rosary in her hands tell us otherwise.
The woman represented in such a way was called Mariana. She was
given a name derived from the Virgin Mary when baptized by the
priest of the conquistadores (perhaps she was the first *María* of Latin
America), and was the lover of Cortés. Her main role was that of
translator – the Spanish conquistadores did not speak Náhuatl and
the natives did not understand Spanish. It is probable that she did not
understand very much Spanish herself, but she understood the
language of oppression: she knew that her masters wanted gold and
riches, and that they were prepared to kill and destroy for them. She
knew then what to say to her fellow countrymen and women. They
needed to obey, give their work as slaves and their riches to the
foreigners, and also to obey their God. At this early stage, according to
the documents that we have, 'God the Father' was represented by
Hernán Cortés (called by her, 'God the Captain'). The natives did not
understand the language, culture or catechism of the conquistadores
and Christianity was represented by living icons. The *Vírgen María*
was represented by Mariana, the translator of 'God the Captain'.

Mariana has become a symbol for traitors in Latin America. People
speak of 'the curse of Malinche (or Mariana)' for those who, forgetting
their own identity, serve foreign interests which oppress our own
people. She is the holy translator of God's desires to Latin American
women: be submissive, be passive and accept abuse and degradation.
The role of Mariana was to crush people's spirits, demanding them to
give themselves to the 'White God' or 'God the Captain'. This is the
very origin of the Latin American Mariology which has been so
important for the male and female role perceptions in society. Mary
was a medieval Spanish representation of a woman expensively
dressed with no more work to do than to hold a child in her arms and
a crown on her head, and, by a curious coincidence, to crush a serpent

---

[15] Cf. León-Portilla (1980), p. 162.

with her feet. Even now she is the symbol of the well-off Latin American woman, going to mass with a shawl on her head and a rosary in her hand, and exuding asexuality even after giving birth to a son (some women in Latin America do not feel that they are really mothers if they only have daughters). She is alone, because men are independent, yet she is well provided for. This is the idea of the traditional Latin American wife, living among children and female relatives, while the husband is away doing his business. Sexually speaking her power is in the reproduction of sons, while native women clean her house and have bastard children with her husband, with or without her knowledge. *La Vírgen* represents a god that Liberation Theology has tried to unmask, a god of oppression. *María/Maríana* is from 'the beginning her own sisters' oppressor' and the counterpart of God the Captain. She also works as a metaphor of women's disunity and lack of solidarity towards each other; if united, they could find the strength that is needed to fight against the several faces of oppression that women suffer in Latin America.

The enthroning of the *Vírgen María* came after the destruction of women's lives, and the banning of their original faith. It presented a different project of womanhood necessary to construct the patriarchal pattern of the colonization of Latin America. This is the *Vírgen* that year after year military dictators in Latin America have worshipped with devotion, adorning her statues with swords and war medals. *Machismo*, woman-hating and Mariology came hand in hand in Latin America. The black virgins that remain black (many have had their faces covered with silver to produce the illusion of whiteness) are, no doubt, objects of popular devotion. Some of them are, somehow, the product of syncretic devotions with female original deities and the *Vírgen María*, like the Virgin of Guadalupe whose temple has been erected upon the ruins of the temple of the WOMAN. However, one can argue that if such worship is liberative, it is not due to the *Vírgen María* but to the presence of the memory of the WOMAN's worship among indigenous people. There is also the perpetuation of a patriarchal construction of femininity which is done through the internalization of oppression in women. Mariology in its origins is, as we have seen, an unequal dialogue between women masters and women slaves. While in Europe it can be said that Mary is a woman 'who is not a woman' (because she is the product of men's imagination), in Latin America we must say that 'she is a God and a woman who oppresses women'.

The face of Mariology in Latin America is the worship of *María/ Maríana*. A *Vírgen* addressed for several countries as 'General of Armies'; her banners were carried during the battles for independence from Spain, but there were other battles in which she was also the patroness of the armies, such as the clearings of the indigenous people of Patagonia in the eighteenth century. The multitude of apparitions of the *Vírgen* in Latin America have never been related to challenging the patriarchal structures of the continent (colonial, sexist, classist and racist structures), but rather to condemn women's new roles in society (for instance, women's vote), and to reinforce women's sexual submission in the continent. The same bishops who asked Hebe Bonafini to pray to the *Vírgen María* witnessed pregnant women suspected of being communists being gang raped by soldiers, and offered the following comment: 'This is a war.'[16] Women prisoners during the dictatorships in Latin America were more cruelly treated than men; women's traditional magazines reinforced the idea of politically aware women as prostitutes, who had departed from the traditional model of the church shown by the *Vírgen María*. A woman who lost her husband and her four daughters (the youngest only 13 years old) during the repression in Argentina told people that a bishop reproached her: 'You should have been a better mother, and told your daughters to follow the example of *María*.'[17]

Can *María* be liberated?

The reconstruction of the hermeneutical circle of Mariology from the perspective of its origins in Latin America is important if we want to understand Christianity and its role in shaping the lives of women in the continent. With the voices of dead women in metaphors of God, clothes, visions and gestures, it is difficult to forget that Latin Americans fought against the *Vírgen*'s banners but were crushed by an ideology called Mariology. Could the *Vírgen María* one day be free of Mariology, and join the cause of women's struggle in Latin America? Will she ever walk and serve us as an interpretative clue for recovering our ancestral erotic knowledge? *María* would then need to speak for herself, and join the voices of poor women in the third world. In Latin America this is an indigenous woman's voice, and requires a pluricultural, multifaith dialogue which has been denied until now. This ecumenical dialogue also needs to accept that sexuality and spirituality, so closely linked among Latin American women, needs to be liberated from the western religious and colonial patterns of the *Conquista*. Only then will Latin American women (and men) be able to discover their real identity, covered by an oppressive religious discourse as mud covered the faces of the women from Tatlelolco.

---

[16] For the words 'This is a war', see Galeano, *Century of the Wind*, p. 234.

[17] The story of the woman accused of being a bad mother comes from a private conversation with a Mother of Plaza de Mayo after an ecumenical worship service in Buenos Aires, 1986.

For Latin American women, to free themselves from God the Captain is not enough; they need to break free from God the white rich woman represented in *La Vírgen,* who is in reality *María/Maríana.* The utopia of the Kingdom for which many Christian people in Latin America live and die, struggling against an unjust system and structures of sin, demands from us a critical revision of our anthropology and theology. The work of women in Christian and other communities shows a sacred discontent with the patriarchal churches. I believe that a critical reappraisal of Mariology is an urgent task, and needs to be done working from the interpretations made by poor women in Latin America over the centuries. Such interpretations come from a slave–owner dialectic, and are reflected in popular sayings such as, 'If you do not fulfil your promises to the *Vírgen* (usually money or presents for the local church) she will take revenge on your children', or 'A *Vírgen* becomes jealous when someone starts to adore another *Vírgen.'* There are thousands of different images with different names of the *Vírgen.* These sayings show us that for some people the worship of *La Vírgen* is a practice of a polytheistic nature, but more than that, it shows that disunity is presented to poor women by God *La Vírgen* herself, who fights for supremacy with other *Vírgenes.*

The work of a liberative Mariological circle of interpretation is complex. It is not a question of merely painting the colour of the face of a statue to make her look dark, or making her dresses more humble. It is about *hembrismo* and questioning our religious constructions of femininity in Latin America; it is about unmasking God the white upper-class woman who has made of us passive supporters of a patriarchal system, best manifested in the military cultures, living examples of the 'cross and the sword'. The focus of our theology should then be our experience as women brought up in the *hembrismo* culture, and from there we should work to find out if there is a *María* among us, in the face of our sisters, a *María* who is a street vendor, a child in the slums, a battered woman and a *chica* cleaning the home of the rich lady. Perhaps only then will God the white upper-class woman become God among us women in Latin America. The beautiful metaphor of the power of God among our foremothers, 'the skirt of serpents and stars', tells us that there is a deep link between doing theology and our sexual identity as women. The God who told them to 'tuck up their skirts' and fight is perhaps telling us now to tuck up our skirts at the moment of doing our theological reflection. Skirts that tell us about our sexuality, and the way patriarchal constructions support our oppressive economy. At least this is what our foremothers of the original nations are telling us, when we look with them behind the mask of Mariology, searching for the roots of our sexual, economic and racial oppression in Latin America, in search of a woman who is not white and rich, and is longing to walk.

3

Do Not Stop the Flow of My Blood:

A Critical Christology of Hope among
Latin American Women

To do Christology from a feminist, Latin American and liberationist perspective always implies beginning with a hermeneutical circle, and the moment of entry to this circle must be a phenomenology of feminine desire. Femininity in this context can be defined in Julia Kristeva's words, 'that which is marginalised in the patriarchal symbolic order' (Moi, 1990, p. 166), and by desire we understand 'a question of significant interrelationship, desire is always the desire of the other'(Mitchell, 1974, p. 396). The manner in which feminine desire is embodied in discourses of sexuality and of institutionalized power in our society (Ramazanoglu, 1993, pp. 239ff.) shows that it is now appropriated and controlled by the patriarchal discourse, the kind of discourse which is the basis of the relations of power and of our basic conception of the same. Therefore a liberationist and feminist hermeneutic always needs to begin with a shared experience among women from which feminine desire can emerge as a 'text' constructed by such community of women, yielding a phenomenological analysis of a hitherto submerged Other, and ultimately a utopian vision that carries us beyond the present symbolic order from which women are excluded.

The kind of community of women from whose experience as text we enter the hermeneutical circle can be described by use of a concept developed by Italian feminists, the concept of symbolic collocation. By symbolic collocation we refer to an understanding of the community of women across cultures and times, not living separately but rather united by a dialogue and permanent rereading of our lives and our identity (Bono and Kemp, 1991).

By such symbolic collocation we rescue ideas and cultural forms from the movement of feminist conscientization understood not in a chronological sequence, but bound to moments, past and present, in the struggle of the community of women in different places and cultures. Among Latin American Christian women this symbolic collocation has brought us to elaborate a critical Christology of hope which needs to incorporate the dialogues, biblical discussions, frustrations and struggles of the women who live in distinct communities and different countries of the continent. Violence, misery and the oppression of *machismo* in the midst of a past of oppression are the key common elements which unite us. Recognizing that not all hope has the possibility of developing a utopia, for in this case the utopia would mean a Christ stripped of his masculinity, we will aim to construct a theology of difference, a human and divine discourse which is *essentially* feminine; hence our present hermeneutic will be characterized by the interpretative keys of a critique of hope: a critical Christology of hope.

The feminine body as a hermeneutical space

To do a contextual Christology, in this case of Latin American women, we must identify the feminine body as a privileged place of desire and its appropriation and control by the systems of power. The body of the poor Latin American woman, malnourished, exposed to continuous pregnancies, violence and hunger, speaks to us of the community which Christ came to save and for which he died, tortured and thirsty. To begin from the bodies of poor women is to recognize in Christology a sexed discourse, a discourse already made from the body of a young man like Jesus and of his experiences of pain and pleasure, of love and dissatisfaction and also of his ignorance of the feminine beyond the cultural constructions of gender of his time and society. The body of Jesus is the body of a man crossed by a divine madness and a sense of mission, where the language of the people and the language of the oppressing Empire and its culture are mixed and produce a meaning of existence from a perspective of collective liberation (Croatto, 1973, p. 108). But it is also the body of a sexed messiah who interpreted the world from a phallocentric perspective, who did not experience the objectified lives of the women of his era. Beyond the few metaphors of Jesus concerning the Motherhood of God,[1] Jesus as God incarnate never gave birth, suckled a child, nor suffered the pains of menstruation.

---

[1] For instance Matthew 13.33 and Luke 13.20–21 (the reign of heaven compared with a woman making bread); Matthew 23.37–39 and Luke 13.34–35 (Jesus speaks about his concern for Jerusalem using the metaphor of the hen and her brood); and Luke 15.8–10 (God is compared with a woman looking for a lost coin).

Key elements for a critical Christology of hope

Starting from a profoundly liberating discourse such as the interpretation of the salvific act for humanity, and within a clear option for the poor Latinas,[2] the following three elements are those that we consider as key for the identification of a critical Christology of hope.

1. The bodies of women must be the first interpretative clue in understanding Christ and the theological discourse of the New Testament.
2. A Christology must be open and in process.
3. Salvation must be understood as a communitarian process.

We will now specify further these elements and how they relate to each other.

1. Women's bodies in dialogue with Christ.

> *Mulher é bicho esquisito . . . todo mês sangra.*[3]

(Cardoso Pereyra, 1994, p. 86)

A group of Brazilian women gathered together to do a theological reflection concerning their identity as women. The women presented a basket of sanitary towels with foreign brand names, written in English which they needed to translate, such as 'Liberty', 'Carefree', 'Miss', 'She'. They also considered how they were taught about menstruation and the names given to it, that is, the euphemisms which show by their very nature that the core of femininity could not be mentioned. Moreover it is bad manners, rudeness or a lack of femininity to mention the word menstruation. In Latin America the names currently used are 'the illness' or 'the visit' (in the sense of an annoying and unwelcome visitor). A Feminist Theology of Liberation among Latinas is basically a theology of the oppressed and as such we must rescue the generative words of the vocabulary universe (*universo vocabular*) of women (Freire, 1970, p. 133) and begin with them the dialogical process of conscientization. The dialogue, in this case is between menstruation as a generative theme of the feminine universe and Christology.

---

[2] Latinas is a convenient Spanish substitute for the rather longwinded English phrase 'Latin American women' which we will be using regularly in this chapter. The noun has a matching adjective which we use in phrases such as 'Latina women'.

[3] 'A woman is an exquisite creature . . . she bleeds every month' (my translation).

2. *An open Christology*

This dialogue between Christ and real women, that is to say women who, in this symbolic collocation to which we have referred previously, confront the past and in the present nearly always begin with the question, 'Who do you say I am?' The question which Jesus directed to Peter in the text of Mark 8.29, however, is the reverse of this; and now it is the poor women who ask Jesus, 'Who do you think we are?'[4] This is a question which is asked both by Christian and non-Christian women who live in a society which is profoundly structured by the symbolic universe of Christianity. In this sense, we talk about women who need to do a Christology 'without Christ' or read the Bible 'outside of the Bible',[5] for this question may seem to make them stand over against the Christ represented in the Bible, as it certainly sets them over against the combined images of this Christ in the structures of power of their society, ideologically informed by a dogmatic, idealist and mechanistic Christian discourse imposed between oppressed and oppressors (Freire, 1994).

However, in asking this question of feminine identity in relation to Christ, these poor women place themselves within a dialogical theology which we have defined as open and in process. Open, because this symbolic collocation permanently permits the introduction of new historical situations and new questionings which come with them; and in process, because it incorporates the continuous process of conscientization between marginalized groups and the oppressed, such as the Latinas. This dialogue between Christ and our lives is then realized within a movement of solidarity which has hopes but which at the same time is critical of limit situations outside of which we have no experience of reflection and action (praxis). We do not know definitely if the critical Christology of hope which we propose is feasible or not or if in achieving efficacy it would cease to be Christology.

3. *Salvation in community*

This praxis is a communitarian praxis where salvation is an integral concept which includes the economic polity and respects the natural dialogical process of the communities. We should note how the Latinas always use biblical texts as referents of the dialogue. However the shift which has been produced in recent years among Latina

---

[4] I have witnessed this process of question reversal personally in my work in popular conscientization projects both in Latin America and Scotland.

[5] See, for instance, my paper, 'Reading the Bible outside the Bible', in which I reflect on an experience of conscientization among poor women in Scotland (papers of the conference 'Called to One Hope', WCC, 1995).

women doing popular theology goes well beyond the traditional dialogue between two situations (the present of the community and the text where Jesus speaks), because it challenges the static and idealistic conception of Christ. Christ becomes a communitarian messiah, made in the midst of a historical process and in dialogue with the people, some of whom are the women.

This conception has as a principal characteristic, the act of Jesus presenting himself as 'messiah in process', becoming Christ in a process of popular conscientization where the roles are reversed, and it is the poor people and the suffering women who teach him, with their questions, their rejections and their proposals, what it means to be God in the midst of the poor. At the same time, in this theological interchange, Jesus also goes teaching the poor people but he does it using the agenda of the people; specifically with the hunger and the oppression of Israel during the Roman occupation. However, for the women who today ask Jesus, 'Who do you think we are?', as yet there is no reply because Jesus was not completely conscientized, except that as God/man he was subjected to cultural and epochal elements which he did not succeed totally in transcending. In reality this is not a new concept, since the Uruguayan theologian Juan Luis Segundo expounded it in the 1970s, in his elaboration of the dialogue between 'faith and ideology' (Segundo, 1982). Segundo therefore says that Jesus had had 'the right faith' but since he had not known how to carry out his objectives in the end his ideology was erroneous.[6] The key then is also to place Jesus in this epochal collocation and permit him to continue with this dialogical process between God and humanity, which is essential for the interpretation of a non-authoritarian and freedom-loving God and a faith which allows different possibilities, which is not closed and definitive.

Freeing the dialogue

> Hope reigned. Spirits forbidden to so much as speak shouted and sang. Minds prohibited from thinking discoursed, and burst the bonds that had held them.
>
> (Freire, 1994, p. 177)

I refer here to the work I have done in recent years with a group of women, rereading the Bible and creating a christological dialogue

---

[6] For Segundo the term 'faith' means goal, objective and in a way it refers to the utopia of the Kingdom. 'Ideology' means the way, the strategy to make such a utopia a reality. This is the same concept used by Paul Ricoeur in his discourse on 'Positive Utopia' in R. Kearney (ed.), *Dialogues with Contemporary Thinkers* (Manchester: Manchester University Press, 1984), p. 30.

from our femininity. I do not refer here to a work that has been realized in only one place and at a particular moment but to a sequence of work realized among different women and in distinct places. Again I utilize here a concept of symbolic collocation to establish continuity of theological thought among poor women belonging to different cultures.[7] In all these dialogues we always started in a spontaneous way from the core issue of our femininity which is menstruation. To establish the dialogue, Christ was 'localized' (in a spatial sense) in the text of the woman with the flow of blood (Mark 5.25–34). The dialogues were developed loosely following a framework provided by the hermeneutical circle of Ricoeur, using as a method of interpretation critical elements of the reader-response school and reception theory, especially of Hans Robert Jauss and Wolfgang Iser.

The hermeneutical process

The Ricoeurian dialectic is based on three key points:

1. It is not possible to know without taking our presuppositions into account.
2. The ensuing dialectic is anti-idealist (anti-absolutist).
3. There is a structure of intentional consciousness in the world of the text and especially in the operation of the dialectical relation between the explanation of a text and the process of understanding it. This intentionality is given by the social conditions of the time and the choice of the author to write a particular text (Valdés, 1987). Jauss uses Gadamer's concept of 'Fusion of Horizons' (Gadamer, 1975), which states that past experiences, embodied in the text, and the present experiences of the reader form a common horizon; Jauss maintains moreover that apart from the study of the production of the text it is necessary to understand how this was originally received (Jauss, 1982). Iser for his part rescues among other things the indeterminacy of the text, allowing the reader to fill in the blanks of the text with their own interpretation (Iser, 1971).

The text in Mark 5 used by the women does not give by title the name of its protagonist but she is identified by that which the text gives us to understand is an excessive menstrual flow. The story starts in this way from a phenomenology of feminine desire, constructed through categories of control of feminine sexuality; in this case, control of the

---

[7] I refer specifically to women of my reflection group in Buenos Aires, the informal group of women doing theology who belonged to the 'Theology and Development' course at the University of Edinburgh (1993/4; 1994/95), and the women of the group 'Theology at the Edge', Edinburgh.

amount of menstrual flow considered as 'normal'. In reality menstru-ation is a cultural construction. Women of different races and cultures begin to menstruate at different ages, which is related to food (the consumption of a diet rich in protein produces early menstruation), but also to factors of a psychological nature, for example, what is expected from them (Shuttle and Redgrove, 1986, p. 26). Recent reports on anorexia in young women also indicate that in Europe there is a tendency among women to menstruate later in relation to previous generations. The statistics which have normalized the age of the first menstruation together with the duration of the cycle gener-ally come from those countries called developed and much of these have been formulated taking into account only one group of women, 'women in cities and enormous American cities at that' (Shuttle and Redgrove, 1986, p. 37).

There is no historical basis for regarding the case of the woman menstruating in the episode in Mark simply as a case of illness. Obviously no woman could survive 12 years or even 12 months with a continuous and excessive loss of blood. However, an irregular and abundant flow could have created mental health problems, if only because she found herself severely restricted in normal social life because of a religious legislation against women's bodies, which the laws concerning menstruation were. The story can also be read as that of a woman who being at the age for the menopause continued her normal cycle.

The women who at a particular moment participated in this christological dialogue with me were informed by the taboos against women menstruating and so, in the first instance, they reproduced the 'liberating' reading they had learned, about the courage of the woman and the generosity of Jesus in stemming her flow of blood. However, menstruation is intimately related with the unique identity of every woman, and in reality the challenge with which Jesus is confronted here is the challenge of a fragmented community and of a human existence reduced to immobility, the lack of human touch, and the imperative of hiding oneself during the menstrual cycle, which can be translated, first, into sexual codes of purity and, second, into a way of structuring relationships of production in our society. In the second moment of our hermeneutical process, then, the groups of women started their questioning.

'She was not a radical'

One woman made this comment, 'She was not a radical.' The woman in the story was not feeling strong enough to mobilize other women into a radical change of structures of oppression. Possibly what she needed was not a blessing from anybody but a conscientization dialogue; however, this is exactly what Jesus could not provide because he himself was not conscientized. Jesus did not show a radical or liberative attitude because his conceptual horizon was limited by his time. A popular messiah with deeper insights into the structures of discrimination and oppression could have established a dialogue with the woman and with the community surrounding them concerning the theme of menstruation and women's oppression. Whereas the only salvific gesture recorded in the Gospels is the suppression of the menstrual flow; he does not challenge oppressive law but stops the consequences of the law by eliminating that considered impure (the flow of blood).

The gesture of allowing himself to be touched by a woman objectified as impure, without producing a violent response, was a radical act for the time, but if we look beyond that, Jesus is still symbolically accepting that in the menstrual blood is the occasion requiring laws of oppression and discrimination. Moreover, given that these were the laws of men which controlled and judicially regulated the fluids of women's bodies, it is also symbolic that it is a man (Jesus) who controls these by stopping them. If one ceases to be a woman, physically speaking, then obviously the problem of women's oppression is eliminated, but as a salvific gesture this act of Jesus may still be oppressive and colonial. It calls for the integration and the suppression of that which is different from men. As a result the community of Latina women continue talking about 'the illness', just as the community of men and women of the era of the Gospels did not become conscientized about what it would mean to be a new humanity.

On the other hand, there are other flows that Jesus did not want to stop, but rather encouraged their development. The flow of generosity, solidarity with the needy, and a religion from the heart and not the Law. However, because he had not challenged the basic political and religious patriarchal structure of his time, much less of our times, the New Testament cannot be understood except as part of an incomplete process of conscientization. Generosity, pardon, reconciliation, justice and peace still have masculine substrata in the message of Christ: those of his experience of life as a man. The act of stopping the flow of blood in Mark is charitable, but at the same time destructive. Several women who participated in our dialogue agreed that it was not the flow of our blood which needed to stop because in it we have the source of our humanity and power.

Christ-Community

In a way similar to that in which the flow of blood of Nicaragua was stopped and the country returned to be subjected to the forces of exploitation and misery, or the flow of blood of the 30,000 dis-

appeared of Argentina was hidden during the so-called 'Dirty War' of
the 1970s, we are still in the case of menstruation conceptualizing and
justifying ideologically a definitive prohibition of the right to be. This
right to be authentic, which our women and our peoples have, is
challenged still in a common crisis, provided by the religious and
civil codification of the patriarchal powers (Irigaray, 1993, p. 53).
The resolving authoritarian discourse, which excludes dialogue, has
made of Christ an individual messiah, not a communitarian one, with
a message fixed in history.

The reading of the word and of the world has taught us that fixed
meaning is a fallacy. It is the subject that conveys the meaning,
through her existential involvement and her critical distance from the
text and reality. The appropriation of meaning implies also a new
understanding of a mode of being in the world (Ricoeur, 1976, p. 93).
Can we therefore return to an authoritarian, individualistic and fixed
christological reading? Or must we consider a model of Christ-
Community? Although incipient, there is a model of dialogical
messianism in the New Testament. Jesus' words and deeds were
frequently questioned or celebrated by the community, but rarely
ignored. There are many instances where Jesus replies to a question
with another question and starts a dialogue, as in Luke 18.18; 12.13
and 10.25 among others. The christological proposal that we are
making goes beyond the idea of an individual messiah and allows
that the production of meaning of the salvific discourse can introduce
different categories.

Jesus can still be made a dialogical messiah by a community of
women; the limitations of Jesus today coincide in great part with the
limitations of women's conscientization. The New Testament women
challenge Jesus with their sufferings, but not with a critical analysis of
them; in this they were different from the apostles, who were able to
introduce critical elements of the political oppression suffered by
Israel under the Roman Empire. Our proposal is to consider which
characteristics a communitarian Christology should have from a
women's point of view and from that of theology of liberation.

A Christology that encourages all flowing

A dialogical and communitarian messiah is in process. In this process
we must add the woman from the text of Mark, the one that I have
shared with women in these last years, and also add ourselves in an
attempt to achieve a fusion of a common collective horizon. What we
need to consider now are the elements which hold the key to a
Christology of critical hope among Latina women, and which we can
extrapolate from life and from the christological dialogues in our

community. Among the classical elements which give Christologies a claim of universality the emphasis is usually given to three themes, namely, to the birth, death and resurrection of Christ. We must ask ourselves if these elements are valid for our proposal or if there are more important elements which arise from women for this critical Christology which we need. Following the same dialogical model, we would wish to rescue the generative themes (Freire, 1993, p. 78), that is, those which define the theological reflection of women, *their* issues, their conflicts with Jesus as well their identification with Christ.

In the story of the woman in Mark we find three main themes that lead us to a critical Christology of hope. The first is related to the fact that she is a woman, that she constitutes part of the feminine genealogy of the dialogical construction of the Messiah. Second, that there is a prophetic dimension in her, a necessary dimension for the progress of the project of Christ-Community. She prophesies with the denunciation of the judicial religious structures that oppress her because of the flow of her blood, the core of her femininity. Third, she is part of the people who, with Christ, elaborate the collective utopia of the Reign of God; she adds a project that is important for half of humanity – the liberation of women from the structures of patriarchal sin manifested in the control of women's bodies. From this starting point we shall analyse these elements in the following way:

1. The birth of Jesus: the generator theme as necessary for constructing a feminine genealogy.

2. The life of Jesus: the incorporation of the community of women as messianic and as part of the project of Christ's community which transcends the individualist concept of Christ as a man.

3. The death and resurrection of Jesus: the construction of a collective utopia for women, critical, hopeful but nonetheless obtainable.

The construction of a feminine genealogy

In the mythology of the birth of Christ we do not have a feminine genealogy. Jesus, according to the Gospels, was not born as the result of a sexual relation between a man and a woman, but rather a woman provided her body as a 'biological laboratory' to reproduce a human being engendered by God. The masculinity of God is the important metaphor here. God assumes the masculine role biologically so a woman could conceive. But the fact that Mary has been construed to be a virgin, that is, without sexual experience before or after the birth of Jesus, means that she is only a rhetorical figure, a disembodied symbol. Jesus is not presented as born from a real woman, that is, a

woman who menstruates and conceives during her fertile cycle, in a
sexual relationship, and eventually gives birth to a son.

There are four women presented in the genealogy of Jesus in
Matthew 1.5 (Rachab, Ruth, Tamar and Bath-sheba) apart from Mary.
Rachab has been identified with Rahab the prostitute (Joshua 2.1, 3;
6.17, 23, 25), Ruth was the Moabite woman who fought for her survival with her mother-in-law, and Bath-sheba the married woman
who bore a son to King David (2 Samuel 11.2ff.). There are obvious
subversive elements in this genealogy, in the sense of sexual trans-
gressions and also in the fact that those women exercised some sort of
political power. However, we are still dealing with a genealogy of
fathers down to Joseph, where Mary is only mentioned in order to
establish that God is the real father of Jesus. The rest of the mothers
are not mentioned, the maternal genealogy is marginalized from
the history of Jesus although symbolically it reappears among the
community of women who nurture his messianic vocation. We have
here two elements to consider: the reconstruction of a feminine
genealogy of Jesus till his birth and the genealogy made up of the
women of his community during his lifetime.

The construction of a feminine genealogy before the birth of Christ,
the foremothers of Christ, is important and has been realized liturgi-
cally in the last few years (*Mandrágora*, 1994, p. 83). The Christian
liturgy is one of the symbolic moments of the announcement of
change and praxis in our communities. The development of a critical
Christology of hope needs practical actions; if not, we are not talking
about the construction of a dialogical messiah, nor of Christ as part of
a process of popular conscientization. A mechanistic and idealistic
conception of the meaning of conscientization is kept at the level of
critical ideas produced, but does not change situations. The word is
read (and interpreted and transformed), but the world is not read to
be transformed (Freire, 1994, p. 107). The liturgical gesture to com-
memorate the foremothers of Jesus is part of a praxis to change
reality, as a gesture of annunciation. In this way we remember that the
blood and flesh of these women, their genes, made the man Jesus, who
had a physical likeness and predisposition to illnesses and gifts and
talents inherited from his grandmothers and great-grandmothers.

This gesture needs to be accompanied by ecclesial structural
changes, especially in the relationships of power based on the exclusion of the wisdom and humanity of the women who were part of
the feminine genealogy of Christ. Still this is not sufficient because we
need to construct a genealogy of single women and women who were
not mothers, together with the others, basically women from the community who instructed the child and the man with their prophetic
voices and their dialogues. Which characteristics should this genealogy have? Fundamentally, it should be based on the concept of sym-

bolic collocation to which we have already referred and include women contemporary to Jesus, those after his time, our contemporaries, and the women who will succeed us one day. We also need to think about our responsibility towards them. Derrida, speaking of a politics of memory, has said that to talk about the ghosts of the future is to talk about inheritance and generations; that there are 'certain others who are not present' of whom we must talk 'in the name of Justice' (Derrida, 1994, p. xix).

Constructing a feminine genealogy of Christ

At the base of this genealogical construction that we are proposing there is a binary construction that we must challenge; it is structured upon the figures of Jesus and Mary. The French philosopher Hélène Cixous analyses patriarchal binary thought as the underlying opposition man/woman which can be found at the base of all the religious and civil myths of our society (Quoted in Moi, 1990, p. 104). She organizes patriarchal binary thought in lists of oppositions, for example:

activity/passivity
sun/moon
father/mother
head/emotion
nature/history

This juxtaposition feminine/masculine is found in the constructions of Mary and Christ. Mary is a masculine construction, the authentic feminine elements of which have been taken away (Hampson, 1993, p. 73). To deconstruct Mariology as an idealization of what it means to be a woman of God is always the first step we must take and in Latin America there have been attempts to do this, such as the work of the Brazilian theologians Gebara and Bingemer among others (Gebara and Bingemer, 1989). But we are still moving in the binary scheme organized by Cixous. The way to escape from this is to construct a genealogy of different women, or at least authentic women and not those that our Christian history has presented to us as models.

We are talking about a different genealogy, using the concept of difference of Cixous (inspired by Derrida). Briefly, this concept explains that meaning is produced in a structural relation (Moi, 1990, pp. 105ff.). The concept of the masculine has no sense without the play of opposition of the feminine, and vice versa. Meaning can never be actualized, but reconstructed, through this process that forces us to refer constantly to the Other.

This Christ-Community is precisely an attempt to give meaning to Christ in a process where the community of women keeps completing it permanently, in the past, present and future. The genealogy of women, such as the woman from Mark (who staked a claim from her body, censured for its monthly production of blood), the women massacred during the invasion of the Americas during the sixteenth century, and the mothers of the disappeared in Argentina claiming the blood of their dead, give meaning to Christ. Without them we cannot understand Christ. It is not Mary but this prophetic community of women which is in opposition to Jesus as the Others, and in this opposition we find the meaning of Christ.

For that reason the construction of this unchronological genealogy requires ongoing and mutual conscientization of women's communities and Christ. Poor women must acquire consciousness that in their struggles they are still 'making' Christ, in the same way that the struggles and frustrations of women in the time of the New Testament challenged him. They left their prophetic message of denunciation against the system which oppressed them that it might continue in dialogue with us.

The prophetic dimension

The Brazilian theologian Nancy Cardoso has written concerning the communitarian prophecy of the Hebrew Testament (Cardoso, 1993, p. 7). Cardoso considers, from a perspective based on Freire, how in Christianity we have tended to construct an individualistic prophetism following the patterns of 'banking' education of which Freire speaks, the characteristics of which are the authoritarian model of teaching (the student as *tabula rasa*) and the undiscussed role of the educator who teaches without dialogue with the educatees (the teacher as agent of the establishment 'banks' received wisdom with the student and the establishment awaits results to its interest) (Freire, 1970, pp. 73ff.). Cardoso considers how this 'banking' model has been incorporated into our understanding of the prophets and the schools of prophets. At the same time, she challenges it with the communitarian model rescued from the stories of Elijah and Elisha. Cardoso identifies the poor, basically women and children, as those who prophesy with the denunciation of their suffering, not through words but through their own bodies.

This is the same point that we have rescued in the figure of the woman with the flow of blood in Mark. She denounces several things. First of all the alienation of a menstruating woman, separated from the world, not allowed to touch or to be touched (and therefore denied love and a full sexual life). Second, the existing legislation concerning women's bodies, with judicial regulations about a woman's biology and hormonal processes, which results in making an object of a human being. Foucault, in his discourse on 'docile bodies' (quoted in Ramazanoglu (ed.), 1993, p. 249) speaks about the discipline of bodies. In a feminist discourse we can speak about how these bodies, disciplined and docile, are gendered bodies, and the bodies of women. The woman with the flow of blood denounces the docility of her body to the religious and civil legislation of her time, which requires that her flow should cease, that she should stop menstruating irregularly, or that menopause should arrive because it is overdue in accord with the poor understanding of female biology that existed.

Third, the woman, in allowing Jesus to stop her flow, denounces the Christian message that does not challenge the patriarchal structures (represented in the story by the oppressive legislation and the disdain of the disciples) but lessens their oppression if the flow of protest and feminine denunciation is stopped. The woman replies to the paternal attitude of Jesus with happiness because nobody in this story is conscienticized concerning the roots of the conflict. Therefore Christ-Community, as a prophetic community, needs to incorporate the present denunciation existing in the alienation of the suffering people, especially women, and to accept this as a true prophecy expecting its fulfilment in justice.

This denunciation, accompanied by the announcement of a new feminist epistemology, is an essential part of a Christology of critical hope. This is a critical, destabilizing style of prophecy and a deeply subversive Christology. It takes us beyond a 'banking' Christology and makes us assume our responsibility as a Christian community to be part of a process of christological development. This brings us to our final point, the resurrection of Christ and the feminine utopia.

The construction of a collective utopia among poor women

According to Ricoeur, the function of myth is to integrate a community. Traditions also fulfil the role of being 'a diachronic process of reinterpretation' (Kearney, 1984, p. 25). The problem arises with the non-liberative elements of myths and traditions, and with the ideology which has stratified and assumed the role of atemporal authority which cannot be challenged, because it obeys the interests of the elite in power. In this case we consider that the patriarchal structures have subsumed feminine traditions and myths which could have been integrated in the community beyond the divisive binary thought signalled by Cixous.

If we consider the christological tradition as part of a hermeneutical process, then we can assume that this genealogy of women prophets which we have outlined can and shall fill a creative and active role in a Christology of critical hope. The exemplary role of the Bible (Kearney, 1984, pp. 29ff.) has created a prescriptive Christology, of a closed order. On one hand this Christology has served us to order the past, and to give an identity to the Christian community, but on the other hand it has fixed the horizon of the future and closed the doors many times to new collective utopias.

The role of closing or opening the past and cultural creation, however, belongs not to an individual (Christ, for example, in the traditional 'banking' Christology), but to a community. It is the community, and in this case the community of women in the symbolic collocation previously described, which through the medium of its active participation in the processes of history can assume a creative role which gives it identity and challenges the symbolic structures of oppression which exist in the 'banking Christology'. This is important, because there is a profound relationship between narrative and action, between praxis and symbolic order.

The presence of this prophetic genealogy in our communitarian Christology produces a process of re-symbolization and the integration of elements of the mythic cultural universe of Latina women: elements of their pre-Christian religiosity, for example, especially those more attuned to a female expression of spirituality, such as the worship of the *Pachamama* (literally, 'Mother Earth'[8]) in Peru, or the Afro-spiritist religiosity of the *Candomble* and *Umbanda* worship in Brazil. Respect towards women, especially towards older women, is greater in this popular worship than in the existing Christianity in Latin America. There have been also several groups of women such as the 'Independent Christian Women' organized by Isabel Ascencio in El Salvador, who were looking for elements of a synthesis among Salvadorean women for a new Christianity and a new feminine spirituality which can be transformed in effective social action.[9]

The construction of a utopia of the Reign of God needs this process of christological re-symbolization which, apart from introducing the community of women to the discourse over Christ, also adds elements which challenge a western elaboration of Christianity. We can also add here the dialogue between gospel and cultures, especially the cultures and religions violently suppressed by the invasion of the Americas 500 years ago. The poor Latina women have a mythical nucleus made up of elements of their own popular religiosity combined with Christianity. The christological dialogue has already

---

[8] *Pachamama* is the Goddess Earth of the Inca Empire. *Pacha* means 'earth, world', and it represents an abstract concept implying not only the animated world but also the cosmic time (Guardia Mayorga, 1967).

[9] See Chapter 8.

started, although not recognized by the churches. However, there are many liberating elements there which can serve for the construction of a positive and efficacious utopia leading to the realization of an integral salvation from the patriarchal structures of civil and religious oppression. Any other construction of the utopia of the Reign of God is idealistic and mechanistic, because it does not consider the circumstances of life of our women and does not understand the notion of process and transformation of meaning in history.

The collectively constructed utopia of the community of women is equivalent to the resurrection of Christ. This time it is not an individual who rises but rather the genealogy of women prophets announcing strategies of action and deep change, which will be useful for the whole community. By liberating women and finding their identity, the whole community of men and women will transform itself at spiritual, political and economic levels.

'Who do you say I am?'

The basis of this feminist and Latina christological proposal is given by the question that women are now asking Christ. This is a question that seeks to initiate a dialogue and not to find a normative reply. This is a transforming question and as such is a challenge to Christology, to the structures of the church and to the division of the forces of production in our society, because all these structures are based in the same patriarchal conception. The flow of our blood as women represents our life and passion for humanity. A communitarian Christology and the Christ-Community that we propose can contribute to a new aesthetic of rupture with an authoritarian discourse which contradicts the prophetic model assumed by many churches in Latin America. The subversion of the political and social discourses of our society cannot be realized without challenging a 'banking' interpretation of Christ and without letting flow a Christology representing everyone (men and women) in all times and circumstances.

Part Two

Indecenting Theology:
Undressing Sexual Ideology in Theology

Introduction

It has been said that by using dialogical methodologies in order to unveil ideological processes in theology, liberationists have produced a new style of questioning. That is also to say, the art of asking the right questions in theology has become even more important than a theology trying to produce the right answers all the time. Is this true? The answer is yes and no. It is true that the right questioning is a key for any effective theological praxis, but it is misleading to think that liberationists do not produce or care about giving right answers. In fact, it can be said that in Liberation Theology the hermeneutical circle or methodology is in itself an answer to theological questions. Liberation Theology was originally a modern theology and although it evolved mainly through the influence of postcolonial theory, it is still a nostalgic theology. The nostalgia is for the utopian Kingdom or, to put it another way, for the consummation of the Christian agency in processes of social transformations. There is also a nostalgia composed of mixed memories from the times when the church in Latin America exercised more power in secular society. Apart from that, another modernist trait in Liberation Theology was its belief in human reason. Was not the attempt to use ideological analysis in order to disentangle theology from spurious class interest itself a desire to rationalize theology? And rationalization produces a certain aesthetic: like the buildings of Le Corbusier; the liberationists were serious, pragmatic writers.

It was almost natural that a Feminist Theology from Latin America would start sooner or later to depart substantially from this model. It started with the style of writing and continued with the questioning of the nostalgia for the utopic Kingdom and the church as an agent for social change. Women, as a traditionally marginalized sector of the church, have little if anything to look back on with nostalgia when it comes to Christian theology. In any case, the utopia needed to be revisited. Theology is a praxis of action and reflection but it is also a genre. That theological genre – that is, the way that theology is written, its style of argumentation and the boundaries it creates for its readers – is what in the end carries subversive elements in our praxis. Theology may or may not reflect society, but it forms it. This is why I began by saying that our methodology is somehow our theological answer. The shift that was produced by Feminist Liberation Theologies towards a more daring, radical and honest theology is a kind of rupture of a new style of writing. Liberationists used to have Marx's *Capital* at hand, but also the works of Ricoeur and Levinas, Gramsci, Mariategui and Fanon. It was time to add other significative thinkers to the list, for instance, Irigaray, Cixous and Butler. The so-called 'French Feminist Philosophers', Irigaray, Cixous, Kristeva, Clément and Wittig, made a considerable impact on the question of how a woman should write. This is what is called the question on *Ecriture feminine*. The style of writing theology is not neutral. Feminist Liberation Theology could not produce an alternative theological praxis without challenging the patriarchal way of thinking and writing which is characterized by exclusion, hierarchical thought and dualism. In the end, it is the strength of patriarchalism as an ideology which subverts the materialism of Liberation Theology and produces a new form of idealization. This is the issue of Chapter 4, '¿*Bién Sonados?* The Future of Mystical Connections in Theology'. It was necessary for a Feminist Liberation Theology to rethink the hermeneutical circle and, specifically, how patriarchalism contradicts liberation. Therefore, the 'right questioning' of liberationists is obstructed by a gender and sexual ideology, and their unveiling of ideologies never reaches beyond the conventions. It is interesting that Marx himself provides clues for this process in his work on 'mystical connections'. Therefore liberationists need only reflect again on the same sources they are already using in order to self-evaluate their praxis.

If gender was an issue for the Latin American women doing Liberation Theology, sexuality was not. When Butler wrote her influential book *Gender Trouble* (Routledge, 1990) she presented a challenge which needed to be taken up when reflecting on the theological conceptualization of gender and sexuality, and the use of the heterosexual matrix which is foundational for Christianity. Butler sees in gender a performance or teaching (almost theatrical) strategy to produce sexualities. Sexualities are seen as non-stable, non-univocal and constructed under the heterosexual ideology prevalent in our times, at least in the North Atlantic scene. There is in Butler a denial of the understanding that heterosexuality is a given, that is, a natural sexuality, while homosexuality, lesbianism and bisexualities, for instance, are deviant sexualities. Using Althusser's theory of performativity, Butler has deconstructed sexuality in a way that may be reminiscent for many Latin Americans of the liberationist discourses on social identity under capitalism. What happens is a spectacular paradigm shift in terms of the construction of the subject and the understanding of the self. Suddenly it has become evident that gender is not a category deep enough to destabilize patriarchal theologies. Using the old structuralist phraseology, we could say that gender is a category of surface analysis. Sexuality takes us into a deeper level.

Feminist Theology also took up the challenge and, instead of gender, sexuality became a new paradigm in the feminist theological discourse. Of course we had already realized that the feminist liberationist theology was based on a heterosexual discourse. That has been the pioneering work of Gay and Lesbian Theologies, through the work of theologians such as Elizabeth Stuart, Lisa Isherwood, Gary Comstock, Mary Hunt, Robert Goss and I. Carter Heyward, among others. Moreover, we have been suspicious that heterosexual ideologies were part of the problem not only in the ordering of identities in society and theology but also in the economic implications of the heterosexual ethos and capitalism. Heterosexuality is, after all, a way of thinking. Therefore, searching for a different standpoint for theology, I searched for a different epistemology, that is, a different way of thinking sexually. Being a liberationist, my task was to use marginalized sexualities, such as bisexuality and fetish practices. As my community has always been an urban, poor community basically made up of sexual dissidents, sexuality and politics provided the point of rupture in a Latin American line of doing a very valuable Feminist Theology, but without sexual suspicion. By taking on board the concept of indecency in Latin America as a positive, subversive one, the concept of normality is also challenged. Such heteronormativity in theology means that we are still working with idealizations (as is discussed in Chapter 4) instead of doing a theology grounded in critical reality, including sexual critical reality.

Chapter 5, 'On Wearing Skirts without Underwear', is part of this early thinking on how to use a different hermeneutical circle in order to produce not only different questions but different answers. It seems somehow that we have come a long way from the dialogical style of doing theology that we saw in Chapter 3. Chapter 5 is also about a Christology, but one done from a space of (hetero-)sexual dissidence. It has been precisely that mismatch between the alliance of heterosexuality and Christian theology that has produced an uncritical theology. Indecent Theology is produced by that element of sexual dissidence, rooted in class analysis and the reality of the life of the poor in an urban mega-city such as Buenos Aires, mixed with the complexities of issues of race, sexuality, economic exclusion and elaborate gender rituals. However, sexual dissidence among the poor became the catalyst element of the process. And could Christ not be seen and conceived from a different sexual perspective? Moreover, if heterosexuality is an ideology, could it be that we need to claim the use of different forms of knowing (or love/knowing[1]) in order to think theology?

Chapter 6, 'A Woman's Right to Not Being Straight: *El Derecho a no ser Derecha*' deals specifically with this issue. The key issue in the shift from a Feminist Theology to an Indecent Theology lies precisely in this location of knowledge. It is important to think and to act theologically from a displaced position, since to accept the central tenets of theological argumentation and methods means also to accept the central authority of heterosexual patriarchalism. Indecent Theology as a theological project would like to challenge this in a style of theology which becomes truly *marginal*, that is, from the margins of sexual and economic exclusion, without trying to adapt (or adopt) those marginal ways of thinking, feelings and experiences to discourses of authority.[2] In denouncing the 'fixity' of (systematic) theology, we also denounce the pornography of its methodology.

The right not to be normal and to be able to rethink Christ from a sexual dissident position is the right to claim what Michael Warner calls 'the trouble with normality' (Warner, 1999). This normality is in reality entirely abnormal: it disenfranchises the real life experience of people by forcing them to adapt to an idealized discourse. As it is on earth, so in heaven: theology becomes a distorted praxis which, far from liberating, itself enslaves even more. However, Indecent Theology is also a *caminata*, and to continue walking in this theological praxis requires us to forgo any claimed stability: we must be prepared to accept challenges and self-evaluation. 'A Woman's Right to Not Being Straight' is in this sense a revision of the revision of the hermeneutical circle of *¿Bién Sonados?* It emphasizes the need to unveil sexual ideologies in theology and to contribute towards an effective analysis of the continuous changes produced by globalization processes and social exclusion.

---

[1] For the use of the concept of 'love/knowing' in Feminist Theology, see for instance my essay 'Indecent Exposures: Excessive Sex and the Crisis of Theological Representation' in L. Isherwood (ed.), *The Good News of the Body: Sexual Theology and Feminism* (Sheffield: Sheffield Academic Press, 2000).

[2] I have discussed the need for a theology *from* the margins, remaining in the margins and not just co-opted to central discourses of theological power, in my article 'Grace and the Other' in E. Van Woelde and T. Radcliffe (eds), 'The Bright Side of Life', *Concilium* 287, 2000/4, pp. 63–9.

4

¿Bién Sonados?
The Future of Mystical Connections in
Liberation Theology

Bién sonados. A slang expression from South America which means 'disaster struck us', or, 'we have been defeated'. People grow up with the slang expressions of their communities, as I did with the familiar phrase that every so often comes from the lips of people in my country, Argentina. *Soné,* or *me sonaron* may mean 'I lost my job', or, 'I couldn't pay the rent of the boarding house this time.' Or it may mean 'I am pregnant and on my own', or 'I am ill but I cannot afford medicines', or refer to any difficult situation which we may face without many options or hope of improvement. In my own neighbourhood that expression even meant the threatening presence of the police. Although *sonar* (which literally means 'to produce a sound') is an ironic expression of acceptance of the hardness of reality it also recognizes the responsibility of people's actions in the circumstances of their life and does not imply resignation. The life of the poor is a life of struggle against circumstances which cannot be controlled, but which are recognized as carrying no social stigma, precisely because of the deep understanding of structural sin that poor people have. The expression *sonado,* as when facing sudden material losses, refers to that understanding of the web of structural sin and the human sacrifices that it produces where one can just be a casualty.

'Liberation is a historical and not a mental act.'
Karl Marx in Marx and Engels, 1976, p. 38

Is there such a thing as a theology from the poor? Moreover, is there such a thing as an *epistemology from the poor* which could act as the legitimate foundation for a theology from the poor? How do the poor know, and how do knowledge from poverty and faith knowledge relate to each other? Karl Marx, who was a man with the gift of doing philosophy as a second act and epistemology as an action-reflection process, once reflected on the life of London shopkeepers. That was

Marx, more than a century ago: the poor man as a philosopher, a man struggling to feed his family on a sack of potatoes per month, reflecting on knowledge, poverty and shopkeepers while sitting in a poor room of a rented house in London. Probably, as the letters he addressed to Engels seem to show, his theory of ideology as historic illusion was nurtured by his life as a poor man; the business of the shopkeepers he needed to pay; his problems with the owner of his rented house and the impossible cost of medicines for his children. It was from that experience of everyday poverty that he recognized the structure of ideology as a methodology, and, by contrast, the fundaments of an epistemology from the poor. Ideology here can be defined as a combination of conceptual frameworks, particular ideas and pre-assumptions as well as established forms of social representation. However, following Marx, we understand that ideologies are epistemological systems based on social existence, although at some point dislocated from that experience. The main characteristic of ideologies is not that they are not grounded in historical contexts, but the fact that they do not reflect back on their own origins: a sort of Frankestein's monster which remakes its master in its own image; a disowning of origins; a usurpation process.

Liberation Theology joined Marx in doing philosophy as a second act, if by that we mean that the 'reality first' principle is the foundation for doing theology. First, we would say, come people's historical experiences and their needs; the consideration of their struggle for human rights (and the right to eat is the first of these rights), and everyday life should provide the epistemology from poverty as foundational for theology. However, there is a difference between 'epistemologies from poverty' and 'ideologies of poverty'. We have seen these ideologies from poverty in many theological projects from the past, when poverty becomes independent of people's experiences (Marx and Engels, 1976, p. 62), and is configured as a structure made up of values and attributed agency in which the experience of the poor needs to fit. As Marx would say, always when ideas come first, historical experiences do not even come a close second. They are erased and alienated from philosophy, theology and economics, and from the nation's memories too. But ideas and experiences are always in tension in theology. It is the tension of dogma and praxis. It is also the tension between materialism and idealism. Both terms do not need to be exclusive, but the tension is unavoidable because orthodoxy and orthopraxis are not stable terms. Sooner or later dogmas get stabilized and theology tends to impose itself as an ideology. This happens when we grow comfortable with definitions and visions of the world. Even Liberation Theology may have been becoming ideological and losing its foundation of reflecting on the concreteness of life. This may have happened as Liberation Theology kept working as an issue-based theology. There is no argument about the selection of issues such as poverty, globalization processes and exclusion, but the problem may have arisen in the way liberationists developed their reflections methodologically. Once again, a theology from exclusion could become an ideology from exclusion too. Ideology is a method, and if there is something such as a theology based on an epistemology from the poor, it must differ methodologically from other approaches, and not just by a change of issues.

The point is that historically ideologies differ among themselves and may have even been in contradiction to each other, except for one thing that they always keep in common: the methodological process of ideological formation. This process contributes to the structuring of society by systems of ideas originated in historical experience but which later become detached and independent from people. That is precisely Marx's contribution to the understanding of ideology. Ideology for Marx is the methodological process par excellence of human exclusion, what he described in 'The German Ideology' (Marx and Engels, 1976, pp. 51–63) with the phrase *mystical connections*, referring by that to the illusory nature of ideology, and the ghostly authority of its truthful discourses. Truth that is not factual, but of a metaphysical nature is a mystical truth. Mystical truth, even in theology, confirms dogmas as the dictatorship of divine illusions where people tend to disappear in methods and ready-made theological responses to questionings from reality. That may be a hard truth, but no honest theologian can afford to ignore this fact.

Mystical connections

The process of ideology-making has been organized by Marx in three steps. Marx considers how the process of human exclusion from philosophical thought occurs (separation of ideas from facts).

First of all, Marx acknowledges that ideas are formed by social interactions and people's experiences. Second, that at a certain point in the development of philosophical thought people disappear, without leaving a trace of their concrete human experience. This is the moment of ideas becoming disembodied from human actions, and de-humanized (stripped from the field of experience). Third, Marx considers how, and under which conditions, people seem to reappear again in the philosophical reflection or Grand Idea and in which manner and with which authority they do so. This happens, for instance, at the level of Grand Narratives or discourses of authority. Obviously, Marx also presents us here with an interesting case of what we could consider the death and resurrection of metanarratives, and especially of Christian metanarratives as organized in theological models, including Liberation Theology. For instance, we could consider that people's experiences give birth to a theological reflection, but then, that theology excludes them and organizes itself as dogma; that would be the metanarrative which will need to die in order for people's relation with God to resurrect again. Let us consider this argument from the perspective of exclusion, that is, how people get excluded in theology and what happens thereafter.

Exclusion

The first step to exclude people from epistemological constructs (be they economic or theological) is to redistribute facts and thoughts. That means, to make a separation between the empirical conditions of thoughts and thoughts themselves and to give priority to disembodied ideas over people's experiences (Marx and Engels, 1976, p. 43). It is in this sense that for Marx, following Feuerbach here, theology is a 'belief in Ghosts' (Marx and Engels, 1976, p. 160).

Exclusion as a dynamic force

Second, and once ideas have lost all connection to an empirical reality, they must become completely detached from human experience. For that purpose, ideas are represented in a new logical order; a sort of chronology of logical development which is set a-chronologically, that is, after the idea has been selected. This process self-authorizes ideas, creating false genealogies and showing how they fit into accepted imposed patterns of conceptual ordering. This is what Marx specifically calls *mystical connections*, because ideas, in their disconnection from social experiences, acquire metaphysical significance of a social transcendental nature, by attributing them with a divine self-justified origin (as in Androcentric White North Atlantic theology).

The dynamic of exclusion produces idols

These disembodied ideas become 'persons', while real persons (who have disappeared in the midst of the abstraction process) become inanimate objects, 'things'. These 'persons' have been considered in Liberation Theology to be idols, the product of our hands (or of the hands of ideology). Let us clarify this reversal movement of ideology. Ideas become persons because they are organized as distinct entities and renamed as 'values', 'inherent beliefs', ' rules and norms', 'common sense', and also Systematic Theology, Moral Theology etc. When they work as disembodied theological systems these *persons* also have attributed agency. They are indispensable to sustain an order that they claim to have been originated beyond human circumstances, yet they are necessary for humans to live. People have been reduced to objects as depositories of these person-ideas, their desires and their assumed agency or efficacy. Of course, people are the 'things' of 'person-theologies' too. Unfortunately, and for the sake of honesty, we must admit that theology is not by definition a Freirean process of dialogical processes. Rather, theology tends to behave at certain levels as a banking process. Theology is for domestication and not for transformation when theological methods ask people to fit into them, and not vice versa.

Exclusion and redistribution of processes of knowledge

At the end of this process, these 'person-ideas' that Marx suggests are redistributed in epistemological sub-units in society. They are attributed to sources of authority as being made by the product of historical evolution or as coming from the gospel. And with this, the circle of mystical connections is finished as in a wizardly act of spell-binding. If reality does not match ideas, reality is distrusted. People for theology, and not theology for people. People for God, and not God for people. The challenge here will be to develop a theology, paraphrasing Marx, 'as if people mattered'. 'Person-ideas' are dogmas and theological conceptions which need to be kept, admitting some degree of adaptation even, but seldom a negation.

Was it in this way that Marx said that while shopkeepers were able to distinguish between what somebody professed to be and what the person really was, historiography has not understood? Did Marx refer here to the game of pretences that poor families used to play with shopkeepers, as my own family did, dressing in their finery in order to obtain credit for buying food? The value of products and their prices do not always match. When does theology profess to be what it is not? When objective theological roles appears without actors, then theology appear without people. Theology becomes a mediumistic activity when the discourse begins as in past centuries with phrases such as 'God and Man' [sic]. Or, more fashionably, with discourses ending with the phrase '. . . and the poor', or, '. . . and women'.[1] Human experiences become an addendum, or an appendix at the end of a reflection. This is a true example of the marginalization of people's knowledge, to be added to a centre of knowledge which remains normative. Liberation Theology has done this also. The discourses of women theologians in Latin America, and therefore the communities who are supposed to be presented in such discourses, are present as marginal. Reflections from women's theological com-

---

[1] Cf. for this point Dorothy Smith, *The Conceptual Practice of Power* (Boston: Northwestern University Press, 1990), p. 49.

munities are included in books and symposiums in a couple of identifiable categories such as 'Mariology' or in general as 'Latin American Women' (rereading the Scriptures, or doing liturgy etc.). Liberation Theology has not taken on board Feminist Theology as an integral part of economic reflections, questioning the androcentric construction of economy and politics, and taking non-dualistic insights or a deconstruction of sexuality and gender to the ultimate consequences of analysis. As such, the Liberation Theology in which I was nurtured and trained as a young theologian years ago has ignored at its peril the advances in Feminist Epistemology, concerning the analysis of patriarchy and Economy and also the Althusserian-inspired theories on gender as a performative act in society, for instance. At the beginning of the twenty-first century, the masters of suspicion do not need to be any more Nietzsche, Marx and Freud or at least not exclusively. Names such as Mary Daly, Judith Butler, Luce Irigaray and Sub Comandante Marcos may deserve an even bigger space among our classical 'Mediator Sciences' in the construction of our liberationist hermeneutical circle of suspicion.

This ingrained fetishist process, by which ideologies replaced people, has rendered Liberation Theology incapable of challenging the Latin American patriarchalism lying at the core of its theological, issue-based method. This is the reason why liberation theologians have been repeating themselves so much in recent years, and why so much essentialism is found, even when working on epistemologies from poverty. As a Latin American woman I always felt uncomfortable with theological reflections starting with phrases such as 'women from Latin America', 'the authentic voices of poor Christian women in Latin America' etc. Even from the time that I was a student, Liberation Theology told me *about* myself as if it was a normative discourse behaving as ideologies do, pretending to be a 'natural' or 'a given truth', and 'universal'. How many times have men liberationists said who Latin American women are, and what they need or want, and how they feel and how their desires flow? The structures of sin in theological methods not only exclude women from the corpus of integral liberation theological reflection, but forces many women to adopt a 'theological femininity' which works as a mask. Following Joan Riviere's text 'Femininity as a Mask', Jacques Lacan advances the theory of women using the constructed femininity of their times and religious beliefs as 'a mask to conceal' the presence of masculinity involved in the display of intellectual activities, while avoiding the patriarchal punishments of isolation or derision.[2] Joan Riviere alludes

---

[2] In 1958 Lacan translated Joan Riviere's article of 1929, 'Femininity as a Mask', and elaborated upon this theme in his seminar of 12 March 1958. See Laura Aschieri's analysis on Lacan and Riviere in 'La Femineidad como Máscara' in *Acheronta*, no. 8, December 1998, http://www.acheronta.org

in her article to women who were fulfilling the role of professional women, while responding to the social criteria of idealized femininity as good wives and mothers. Therefore, the structures of sin in theology tend to perpetuate femininity as a mask in women and theology too, and in this way women's theology in Latin America has so often become a 'person'. It is against 'persons' that feminist liberationists struggle. One is what is ideologically constructed as Liberation Theology (with the addendum of women's theology) and the other is women's false consciousness.

Women become things to fit the androcentric illusion of the agency of women defined by community and family patriarchal values, heavily invested in patterns of the most abstract and ideological classical theology of all times. Women's epistemology is the most challenging and original epistemology from the poor, because every woman somehow, by the mere fact of being a woman, is ontologically separate from, and materially impoverished by, patriarchal society. However, that epistemology has not informed pastoral reflections or ecclesiology or Christian ethics or church history at the roots of Liberation Theology. Had it done so, we might now be enjoying a theological revolution flourishing like the 'Intergalactic Flowers' of the Zapatistas, who have made of sexual and gender transformations an issue of political revolution. If Liberation Theology could have overcome passé views of social constructions embedded in theological method, a complete alternative and truthful theology may have transformed Latin America and the world, beyond words and declamations of justice.

The epistemology from the poor, which ideology veils, needs to be an epistemology of the struggle and not just a contribution to make theology as ideology picturesque. If not, Liberation Theology cannot become a postcolonial theology, even if it seems to be looking 'more native' than the former theological models we had from the West. There cannot be liberation without decisive departures, but will Liberation Theology reach the point of decisive departures from ideological methods?

Mystical connections in Liberation Theology

Religion, once formed always contains traditional material . . .

(Engels, 1935, p. 55)

If ideology is a methodology based on a sort of disappearing act or 'escapology', as I say elsewhere,[3] Liberation Theology has not been

---

[3] See a further elaboration of this point in Chapter 9.

excepted from that. Mystical connection may be an intrinsic part of the process of doing theology itself, and as such it may be useless, as Marx himself has claimed. Or it may be reformed through a materialist method, as Feuerbach and many liberationists have claimed. That in itself is something still to be resolved. However, theology works by ex-centricity and by eviction, and the challenge to abandon those premises is what will take us far beyond the so-called hermeneutical circle or theological suspicion of the 1970s. It will take us to reconsider the whole basis of our theological enterprise of liberation, but this time the liberation of theology would be costlier than in Segundo's reflection during the 1970s. It could be a liberation which may kill theology, or at least empty theology of ideological methodologies and therefore transform its message deeply. A *kenosis* of theology. Who knows, but perhaps we are only going to know if theology is more than ideology when and if this *kenosis* happens. As a Freirean educator who has worked in conscientization processes even in Scotland, I know that processes of transformation require risk and an acceptance of failure too. However, as a liberation theologian, I also know that theology cannot follow capitalist patterns of production and alienation and the consequent understanding of success. What is theological success? What is the success of Liberation Theology? The fact that Latin American theologians are recognized at certain level of knowledge by the authoritative western centre of theology? A handful of famous names and well-sold books? The support and influence of Liberation Theology in the struggle for people's human rights? The success of Liberation Theology was to establish an epistemology of the *bién sonados* as a foundation for theology. However, two methodological problems occurred. One is theological ex-centricity, the other is eviction. Both are closely related to each other.

The second part of this essay is concerned with the analysis of these two issues.

The ex-centricity of the hermeneutical circle

The concept of theological ex-centricity which is usually seen positively[4] is a negative term, in relation to the hermeneutical circle. This is inspired by Ricoeur's reflection on biblical hermeneutics. By hermeneutical ex-centricity I mean the elements which enter into the Liberation Theology hermeneutical circle of suspicion from outside

---

[4] I have used this term positively in my article, 'Both Indecent and Ex-centric: Teaching Feminist Theology for Articulation or for Exoticism' in M. Grey (ed.), *Liberating the Vision: Papers of the Summer School May 1996* (Southampton: LSU, 1997), pp. 71–7.

the sensuous field of theological experience. I define the centre of theology and Liberation Theology by the circle of orthopraxis, and marginalize orthodoxy.

Consider for instance that the starting point of the circle of interpretation is people's historical experience; the material world in motion, or what Lenin called the objective reality which presents itself to humanity via human experience and perception. Consider the hermeneutical circle as a relationship of production, based on community reciprocity of tools (critical reflection, observation as principles of the theological reproductive force), goals (clarified objectives of liberation) and workforce (the community itself as a theological community). In this circle of interpretation, the reading of the Bible and the use of social sciences as mediators (from class theory to the new paradigm shift of language) may be applied in order to know and elucidate the addressee of our theological process. However, it can be proved that the circle of suspicion, as if explained by quantum physics, has brief seconds of parallel existence. This works like the theoretical experiment of Shrödinger's cat, when someone must decide if the cat in the box is alive or dead or both. The parallel existence of the hermeneutical circle of liberation flicks between the matter of things (via community as the first and primordial element of reflection) and something outside the circle (the church, accepted tradition, theological faith or transcendental 'persons' in the Marxist ideological sense we have referred to above), and patriarchal ideology which is at the base of faith and the church's life. This is why the circle is ex-centric because its claimed 'materialism' needs to decide in milliseconds where it stands: with idealism or with materialism.

Can Christianity ever be the material faith of material prophets and messianic figures such as Jesus and Judith, entering Jerusalem on donkeys with people acclaiming them as true prophets of God while dancing in the streets? Or is Liberation Theology condemned to follow the path of idealism because God cannot be thought of outside structural mystical connections? Deception occurs when ideas are disembodied or attributed to genealogies of grand authority, and all this happens by the laws of reversal between facts and ideas, or peoples' lives and Systematic Theology. Of course, we are talking about a theology whose epistemological locus is the *bién sonadas*, women whose lives are already marked by deception and disillusion at economic, political and religious levels. But how much can Liberation Theology confront itself as a fetish which can and must be questioned beyond the approved traditions of the church and dogmas?

What if some Latin American women cannot approve of the role of Mariology of Liberation, a church which refuses to ordain women and a hierarchical exclusive order of family and ways of being church which apparently cannot be reformed but should be dismantled? This is what has stopped Liberation Theology as a movement: Marcos is miles ahead of us. Mexican women sociologists and writers are miles ahead of us. They do not have respect for patriarchal structures any more. They do not want to adapt them, or reinterpret them as we do in Liberation Theology. They created new ideas, organizations and institutions. Meanwhile, no matter how many Basic Ecclesial Communities have been created and dismantled in recent years, this has only been cosmetic surgery, a face-lifting operation in the life of the church.

If it was not for the ex-centricity of a circle of interpretation which is clinging desperately to systematic western patterns of doing theology and the keeping of church traditions which are irrelevant, nothing could have prevented the militant Latin American church producing a 180-degree turn in ecclesiology and theology by rupture and creativity. But no. We are still putting new patches on old wineskins. To have taken a feminist paradigm could have transformed the lives of millions and produced a deep rethinking of economics and politics. But no, the epistemology of the rebellious poor has been evicted from the circle of interpretation. This has been the case of theological evictions.

On theological eviction: people with suitcases and furniture on the pavement of Christianity

I was an adolescent when my family faced eviction. We were given 24 hours to pay overdue rents or leave our house. When the police arrived my mother and myself moved out our few belongings on to the street: some bags of clothes, a box with tea and rice, two chairs. The neighbourhood stood still as if in mourning for yet another eviction; another family put out in the street with a few suitcases and a couple of chairs. Economic mystical connections evicted us. In times of hyperinflation and liberal economic experiments, my mother and myself ceased to be people. Economic theories became people, and evicted us because somehow we became things that did not fit their scheme. The economic system was never evicted; only my mother and myself. As political economic systems evict people so does theology. It is easy, and in the same way as the police in my story did it, theology has literally been putting people out on the pavements of the church for centuries. Of course, these were the poor. Women in theology are the androcentric ontological representation of poverty: poverty of reason; poverty of spirituality; poverty of independence; poverty of divine gender representation. Systematic Theology also made me and my mother and my grandmothers homeless.

However, women are not just evicted from theology, they represent borders, the frontiers between logical theology and what has been called a more 'experiential' theology. Women are expected to work theologically around the domestic, private area of life and they have done so well. No male liberation theologian can write the books that women liberationists do, based on reflecting dialogue among women in community, respecting others' opinions and almost disappearing themselves as theologians in order to allow other voices to come through clear and strong. The problem with that is that women have become ghettoized, and their voices are not heard questioning serious issues on the construction of the Trinity or Christology, as I myself have done. As a consequence of that, Liberation Theology allows the addendum, the women's theological notes on issues considered by men to be women's theological issues. There is no attempt to incorporate these voices into Systematic Theology. It is a complacent liberation of theology indeed that, in this day and age, has not stopped to consider, for instance, whether the Trinity is based in a homosocial conceptualization rooted in conceptions of the economy of family production or whether it is possible to talk about a God who is society, as the late Segundo did, without analysing the patriarchal roots of concepts such as society, community and even solidarity. Is it enough to add to the Trinity the addendum '. . . and women (or the female *Ruach*)'? Still we are in the realm of ideology, detached from reality because evidently we cannot change our lives by playing with theological imaginary, although we may if we change structures of work and reflection such as churches. If not, Christianity may be considered the doctrine of the Pure Land of Ideology.

People get evicted by theology as a method, but not only people. Do you remember my earlier example? Two women were evicted but also two chairs and a box with rice and tea. Liberation Theology has evicted more than just women in its circle of interpretation; it has evicted non-dualistic patterns of thought; non-hierarchical structures of thought and alternatives to non-reproductive and repetitive male epistemology. That is the real difficulty. Liberation Theology has a colonial nature which works by incorporation or assimilation from the margins to the centre. If that were not the case, Liberation Theology would have rejected the ideological principles of the centres of theology such as those concerning its own production process.

How Liberation Theology evicted people and replaced them with ghosts

Theological illusions in Liberation Theology may be seen as following Marx's schema of the main characteristics of the process of illusion-building (also referred to by Marx as 'ghosts').

Theological sources

Theological illusions arise from concrete and well-defined sources of theological production. The sources of production in theology include *capital* (theological traditions, Systematic Theology, Moral Theology) which does not come, as Marx says, referring to German philosophy, 'from heaven', but on the contrary, from earth first, and, second, is promoted to heavenly status.

Theological capital is already the result of exploitation and, of course, of struggles against the market exploitation of souls, such as during the Reformation battles against excommunication for economic debts, or money given for the liberation of souls in heaven. If the invisible exploited people of theology are women, this happened because the objectification of women in certain sexual and gender status was beneficial to keep the deep sexual principles of theology intact. Theology is a sexual subject; obsessively sexual in its interpretation of God's birth and parental relations; of men and women and their sexual ordering in society. The objectification of women is based on the ideological processes which always imply reification, and theological understanding made by those mystical connections. The exploitation of women in history is the invisible basic resource upon which the high sexual content of theology and Liberation Theology is developed, that is, the sexual and gender roles which determine relationships. Economy is just a perspective on human relationships. Liberation Theology stands up for the poor but not beyond these mystical connections; and in any way, not beyond reformism.

Of course, people are the source of theology. So, if women are evicted from theology in the multiple co-ordinates of sexuality, race and gender, so are men too. The ghosts which have been taking the place of the real persons of theology are the constructions of 'the poor', 'the Latin American women', very much abstract categories in which people are expected to fit. From the empty pews and the unpopularity of the popular church we learn that liberationists are confusing the ghosts of systematic theological expectations with the real people. At least I can say that myself and a community of women that I know in Latin America born and bred in Liberation Theology are not there, because the ghosts of women in theology are too narrow, too restrictive and obey patriarchal logic and not that of life.

Theological un/reflections

The second characteristic of theological illusions is that although they develop from the structures of society, they also remain unreflective on them. Liberation Theology has never produced a reflection on the roots of the sexual exploitation of women in the church and in theology, beyond the already passé paradigm of equality which never asked the 'equal to whom?' question. By exploitation we refer here to what Marx described as 'the merging of all . . . relationships of people in the one relation of usefulness . . . [and these] relations are subordinated in practice to the one abstract monetary-commercial relation . . . namely that I derive benefit for myself by doing harm to someone else' (Marx and Engels, 1976, p. 409). The point is that in a way Liberation Theology still subordinates itself to patriarchal understandings, which are useful for the purposes of keeping hierarchically minded ecclessiologies and a systematic theological thinking in accordance with its own rules of importance. Consider for instance the Basic Ecclesial Communities. BECs have been and still are valuable but peripheral activities, as Leonardo Boff recognizes when he claims that the dismantling of BECs has happened in recent years due not only to the New Right policies of the Vatican, but to the fact that BECs were never included in canon law. This means that to say 'We are the church' is not enough; that this needs to be reflected in the church law too. Also liberationists are subordinating their reflection to western Systematic Theology. Could they not have gone into A-Systematic Theology, and created in community a new legal understanding beyond orthodoxy? Original and inspired thinking such as 'structural sin', 'God in history' and 'structures of human sacrifices' were meant to be the beginning of a new Systematic Theology and not just the refashioning of 'sin', 'grace' or 'the sacraments' in liberation style. Moreover, new themes were meant to be not only new issues, but new points of theological orthopraxis; new starting points for reflections based on a new way of doing things. For instance, instead of 'God the Father', a 'God *La Compañera*' (female comrade), written from the perspective of, for instance, unmarried sexually fulfilled militant women in Latin America (as the *Insurgentes* from Mexico) should have become more legitimate and might have become a foundation theme to develop and supplant that old patriarchal/parental metaphor of god-fathers (which by the way, reinforce a colonial mentality too).

That could have led to a militant theology from the guerrilla women of Latin America, for instance, and not a mystification pretending to be real like the androcentric economy of god-father. A theology of liberation in memory of Tania, who died with Guevara in Bolivia, has more to say about women, compassion and images of God than parental patriarchal ideologies.

Magical theological steps

The third aspect which concerns us in Liberation Theology is the ideological step of formation characterized by spontaneous configuration of thought and ideas (Marx and Engels, 1976, p. 61). This constitutes a case of un/reflective theology behaving as ideology: in our example of the god-father metaphor, first comes the centuries-old metaphor for God, second, people must fit into it. Third, theology reclaims people back, reorganizing the experience of the poor into the centuries-old metaphor which has been so destructive for women and colonial in its spirit of dependence related to mother churches. It is also one of the main culprits of women's alienation in politics and economics, by re-presenting their childhood assumed nature once again in sacred laws. Do god-father images have anything positive? Yes, they may have. Even the slaves in their compounds heard that God the Father was compassionate; that is not a novelty for liberationists. Moreover, patriarchy excels in its art of divine contrast: God is meant to be terrible and compassionate; jealous and full of understanding, and similar contradictory metaphors which woman-ists called 'speaking with forked tongues'. So women in patriarchal Latin America will never be liberated with any reflection based on benign fathers. When theology tries to liberate by putting people back in the existent ideological theological constructs, we are into adapta-tion processes. In the end, the people are re-absorbed in this process by an interpellative process, and the ideological construct appears as 'natural', 'fresh and new' and almost spontaneous truth. In this way, *Tata Dios* (Father God in Quechua and Spanish) becomes an original and grounded piece of popular theology, when it is simply an ideo-logical interpellation.

The other thing to consider here is that the discourse on the poor as the locus of theological reflection, although grounded in experience, is not exempt from false consciousness. At that point, it is easy for theology of liberation to produce interpellation processes, where people tend to recognize themselves, although the only thing that they are doing is recognizing the internalization of their own oppres-sion. Unfortunately this justifies saying disparate things such as 'Latin American women only care for their children', or, 'the poor have a simple faith and want to remain in that simple faith'. If these things were true, Christianity would not imply a change of conscious-ness. Christianity would then be revealed even more clearly as ideol-ogy. Ideological reflections create this aura of spontaneous reflection, of ideas not consciously related to their mechanisms of production. It is the same with a popular theology such as Liberation Theology, which enjoys the spontaneity of patriarchalism and never distrusts its own dualistic and androcentric epistemology because it is taken so much for granted.

Theological inversions

We arrive now at the moment of theological inversion or the *camera obscura* effect produced between theological reflections and life. Theology of liberation has been under the illusion that the best of Christianity expresses people's needs and struggles. In reality, this is an inversion of the fact that the best of the liberationist approach to Christianity is not Christian at all. It is in fact the way that people traditionally live in community, the courage and resistance of Latin Americans under oppression and their intelligence in the strategical consideration of the struggle.

It is interesting to notice that the main task of liberationists has been to remove Christian passivity and attitudes of resignation which were precisely brought to our people's lives by centuries of Christian theology. Therefore, if the world has enlightened the church and not, unfortunately, vice versa, one of the main difficulties with Liberation Theology may lie in the fact of believing in the camera obscura effect. In fact, for a theology which claims to be a theology from the political, one must reflect on the fact that it was Eva Perón who gave women the right to vote in Argentina in full opposition to the church and Christian theology. Since then, the issue-based Liberation Theology which likes to reflect on politics and economy has not advanced into issues of women and politics in Latin America, but perhaps will one day be illuminated by the work of secular thinkers. Many women like myself feel more identified with Latin American feminists than with theologians representing an undemocratic church, whose androcentric consciousness is stagnant. This means that if our struggles could find a point of appropriate theological reflection in Liberation Theology, it would happen only after Liberation Theology, as a second act, learns more about its own androcentric spirituality, and perhaps even then it will not be able to reach many women in our continent. Theology is a limited affair, and only accepting this point, perhaps, we must be able to liberate theology from its ex-centricity, towards a true materialist circle of interpretation. 'Religion, once formed, always contains traditional material', said Engels (Engels, 1935, p. 55), and not even biblical exegesis can save us from the effect of that.

Class-motivated system of theological deception

The fact is that we are always, in one way or another, worshipping systems of production disguised as sacred systems. Liberation theologians struggle for forms of socialism and participatory democracy and therefore try to produce a theological reflection reflecting those ideals. However, the continuous allegiance to church structures which are western inventions, obeying particular economic patterns of exploitation and conceptions of humanity, has damaged or partial-ized this project. Basic Christian Communities remained as part of the picturesque scene of the Latin American church, in the sense that they were unable to redefine power. It is very romantic to say that 'BECs are the church'. If that was really the case, nobody would have recog-nized any power or authority outside the BECs, including women's ordination or changes in the hierarchical ruling of the church. In the case of women's historical struggle for liberation, Liberation Theology has become dangerous because it is more of an obstacle than a help in such a struggle. If women in Latin America need to come back to reread their Virgin Mary every so often, their awareness-raising process would not advance very far. Liberation Theology also produces false consciousness among women because of the limitation of its dialectics. Christianity, as in the camera obscura example, needs to present itself as the first and best of the human rights struggles. If women claim their human rights, the same as gays, lesbians or trans-vestites, we need to find these struggles first of all represented by Christianity, and this cannot be the case. Even the historical Jesus had a limited historical consciousness; he was not outside the context of his time, language and culture. He may have been advanced for *his* time, but not necessarily for ours.

In this last point we reach the core of our questioning process to Liberation Theology. If theology is a second act even in Liberation Theology, then the struggle must have taught liberationists about a Latin American society built upon heavy patriarchal systems of sub-mission and mastery; of violence in the domestic and public realms; of intolerance and authoritative regimes based upon heavy androcentric hierarchies. And liberationists may know by now how the pastoral letters they write every so often in relation to, for instance, family issues, rely on a concept of family which is immoral, since it is still based on property values, and leads to violence and abuse as also to poverty: not only material poverty but the poverty of being which threatens women in patriarchal cultures. For many women like myself, the worship of the Virgin Mary, with all its rereading and energy-wasting process of reinterpretation, stands against the life of many Latin American women. Idealist theologians can be quick rescuing *images,* pictures and historical insights and exegesis here and there in relation to Mary and issues of women and power, but materialist theologians go to life. Rereadings cannot answer for 500 years of women's oppression in Marianist Latin America.

¿Bién sonados?

Probably yes. Probably we are going to be sooner or later *bién sonados* as a church in Latin America if our discourses continue betraying a materialist circle of interpretation and following instead a method of ideology-building. Liberation Theology must avoid the pitfall of becoming the remake of the Jesuitical missions, where Latin Americans, especially women, needed to embrace that childlike quality that colonial discourses adore. That which domesticates and finally evicts us exists in theology as ideology, and as such it is the enemy. Even among the poor communities false androcentric consciousness exists, and its demythification should be a priority for liberationists who fail to see the links between exclusion, globalization processes, neo-Liberalism and patriarchal epistemology. For many faithful Latin American people, the struggle has involved leaving the church and its alliance with the oppressive state. As painful as it is, it seems the only option when theology has become a damaging ideology. For many Latin American women, in search for really alternative political, economic and religious systems apart from old Latin American patriarchy, Liberation Theology may also become the enemy because after 30 years of praxis-orientated reflection the changes produced are too superficial and too slow. It will not do for our daughters.

The right to insurrection

Carmen Bullosa, the famous Mexican writer, has a beautiful story in which she contrasts the life and fate of a hill and a centuries-old Roman Catholic cathedral in the middle of Mexico City.[5] Bullosa tells us about their significant location: opposite and facing each other, the Catholic cathedral is falling apart from old age, while the hill keeps growing with animal and natural life. The cathedral, Bullosa points out, is surrounded by contractors propping up its walls and supporting its roof and pillars from the danger of collapse. Meanwhile, the hill which was the site of an old Aztec temple demolished during the *Conquista* has been growing again after the destruction of its trees and life. Growing in size year by year and also growing in life. The hill keeps flourishing, its vegetable nature seems to be unstoppable. Meanwhile life has been leaving the cathedral. People have left and few newcomers are expected. The congregation has been reduced,

---

[5] See Carmen Bullosa, 'El que gira la Cabeza y el Fuego: Historia y Novela' in Kate Duncan and Electra Caridis, *Beyond Solitude: Dialogues between Europe and Latin America* (Birmingham: The University of Birmingham, 1995), pp. 180–96.

and there is a feeling of things becoming too old and fragile. However, on the hill, life is bursting out: flowers and birds, and all sorts of insects and animals grow there now. Lovers meet there too. The hill is back with a passion for life that by the justice of time has prevailed against that theological model which came to our continent to kill life and to distort people's quest for the sacred with a modern theological ideology.

This metaphor from Bullosa says in a nutshell why we are going to be *bién sonados* if we keep propping up and introducing cosmetic surgical alterations to the theological monuments of the past. There is an epistemology from the poor, and from the thinking, reflecting and dissident poor. That epistemology, like the Mexican hill, has been flourishing with the disorder and chaos of life that theologians fear so much: the epistemology of women's movements, of lesbian and gay human rights in Latin America, the epistemology of Freire and Sub Comandante Marcos, of Augusto Boal and Marta Lamas, of Pichon Riviere and Alfredo Moffat teaching beggars in Buenos Aires to become psychotherapists and work in their communities under the bridges. Years ago, J. Severino Croatto taught me that the key hermeneutical principle of Liberation Theology was just that, 'liberation'. Now, I would say that it is 'insurrection'. It was Unamuno who claimed that Christianity was a desperate way out towards hope, but without the right to insurrection from Systematic Theology and its ideological methods it becomes another form of escapism. The only way out towards hope in Liberation Theology and in Christianity in general is to recognize and work with an epistemology from the poor as it is presented in feminist epistemology, non-dualistic, non-hierarchical and relational. Only then, when marginal epistemologies become central, do the suppressed margins become central too, and theology becomes marginal in its desire to serve the centre by default. Only then will the real lives of ordinary Latin American women become more important than Mariologies and Trinities. And ideas will become ideas again, and people will return to being people. And this would be a liberation of theology from the false processes of personhood assumed by the idealism often called theology, and the end of mystical connections of theology and politics.

5

On Wearing Skirts without Underwear:
Poor Women Contesting Christ

Disputing decency in Christology and in Liberation Theology

Any sharing of differences concerning our life and experiences as women has always been an integral part of a feminist hermeneutical strategy that includes the margins of dialogue without using blanket terms and broad assumptions about the life of the poor, or of women in Latin America and everywhere.

I am concerned with the necessity of hermeneutical strategies for the restoration of the female tragedy lying at the core of the process of building a Christology. My perspective is that of a *Teología Indecente* (an 'Indecent Theology'), as a positive theology which aims to un-cover, unmask and unclothe that false hermeneutics which considers itself as 'decent' and, as such, proper and befitting for women espe-cially in sexual matters. Such a process of theological unclothing, at the end, could produce the stripping off of men's underwear too, in order to develop a theology which will uncover men's spirituality outside patriarchy.[1] From the images of the Peruvian Coya women in Latin America, who do not wear underwear under their colourful skirts, comes the metaphor of a Latina, feminist approach to herme-neutics. Coya women kneel in the church mixing the odour of their sexuality with their prayers, while their babies sleep on their backs wrapped in an apron. The Coyas' sexuality, their children, their Christianity and even the baskets of produce which they sell in the market accompany them when praying to Christ. And that is a start-ing point for a Christology done from women's bodies. The fact is that the christological process starts not with the first meetings of church councils but with the construction of the Christ, the Messiah, a process that depends on the interrelationship between a man called Jesus and a community of women, men and children. What today we call Christology shows only one main feature: the historically persistent

---

[1] See, for instance, the pioneer work of James Nelson, *The Intimate Con-nection* (London: SPCK 1988).

adaptation of an omnipresent, divine heterosexual system through different economic and political conceptions supported by theological discourses. Liberation Theology, although producing a methodological rupture in Christology, has been and still is part of the present hegemonic discourse. It has never discussed the 'ex-centric' hermeneutical assumptions that pervade Christianity and Christology, but has tried to harmonize those basic colonial assumptions, such as the construction of sexuality, in a discourse of economic and political independence. The historical patriarchal nexus has not been broken. Liberation theology is mainly a quite decent discourse, allowing women rebellious but decent claims, that is, inside the heterosexual structures of love and economics. I am defining 'heterosexuality' as a political compulsory institution which affects modes of production and identity both for women and for men alike.[2] What has been confusing is that the discourse of Liberation Theology in Christology has had important successes in its marginal theological circulation by joining the periphery of popular praxis. The classic argument here is that the Christ of the poor is the Christ of the poor communities, and that includes marginalized women. However, what we call popular praxis is, for women, a mixture of blessing and curse at the same time, because it tends to subsume women's particular oppression into the struggle of the poor. The Christ of the poor and the worker can be portrayed as kneeling in front of a miner while washing his feet. If I want to particularize that image and see Christ kneeling in front of a woman domestic servant, while touching her feet, this will have other implications, perhaps even sexual ones. The Christ of the Basic Ecclesial Communities is depicted as embracing workmen with naked torsos but not women without underwear. The Virgin Mary can be portrayed as a poor peasant mother, but if I want to represent her as the poorest of the poor among women in my country, it would need to be not as a devoted mother, but rather as a child prostitute in the streets of Buenos Aires or Sao Paulo. If as the liberationists claim, Christ is neither male nor female in the sense that Christ represents the community of the poor, then Christ should be portrayed as a girl prostituted in Buenos Aires in a public toilet by two men. Obviously, such a portrayal would be considered indecent, because we are bringing to the surface the hidden face of the sexual oppression of women, but for that very reason it should be seen as a true theology. Following that consideration, the differences between a liberationist and an Indecent Theology seem clear.

An Indecent Theology and a post-colonialist hermeneutics have in common a de-hegemonization process (stretching the patriarchal

---

[2] For this concept of heterosexuality, see for instance Adrienne Rich, 'Compulsory Heterosexuality and Lesbian Existence' in *Signs*, vol. 5, no. 4, 1980, pp. 631ff.

nexus), but although this goal may be shared with liberationists, they differ in their hermeneutical strategy. The commonality between post-colonialism and Indecent hermeneutics is that women do not claim essentialism and neither does the colonial subject want to do so. However, women cannot find a time or location for traditions of non-patriarchal spirituality or a different economic system. We do not have a women's language or a women's alternative system to refer to and contrast with the colonial model, although we do have our own suppressed cultural, political and religious traditions similar to but also different from the western patriarchal system. With Liberation Theology, the differences are basically in the area of decency. Decency/Indecency is a dialectical praxis based on the following elements:

1. that sex is a given, natural phenomenon, and not the product of a naturalization process.
2. that God's sexual story according to the Christian Grand Narrative is normative.

Therefore, God has sex with young Mary without a meaningful relationship, and Jesus is conceived by male and not female desire. That sexual immaturity attributed to the Big God called 'the father' is extended to the construction of a Christ unable to understand or develop human sexuality in the context of a loving community of equals.

Definitions of women's boundaries and ritualistic reinforcement through liturgies accompany the political and economic structures of women's oppression. *Lo indecente* (the indecent act) is to cross these boundaries, the political and religious boundaries of oppression that have developed for women. To fall into indecency is to fall outside the tenuous definition of men respecting women's lives, so it is also a dangerous affair, especially for poor women.

In the end the dialectic decency/indecency is at the root of theological control of the religious behaviour admissible for women. This dialectic mediates and legislates everyday life in the Latin American society. Indecency carries within itself the power of disarticulating a theological male elite discourse such as Christology, to the extent that the Theology of Liberation cannot do.

Liberation Theology is still patriarchal and as such notoriously unsuspicious of given sexual structures of thought and Christian spirituality. At best, Liberation Theology's discourse is one of equality but not of difference. Therefore, it fails to answer the questions that women are asking about the male-constructed Christ.

The first question concerns the entirely God-male affair accentuated by the Israelite boy born to be God whom Jesus has come to be. No matter how much the Hebrew grammar tells us that the Holy Trinity is composed of one female (the *Ruach*) and two males (father and son), such epistemological curiosities are hobbies for leisure pursuits. Historically speaking, Christ is part of a male Trinity.

The second question is about the lack of dialogical perspective in the construction of Christ by the church's theologians. Their classical Christology shows a conceptual Christ brought down from heaven. The liberationist Christ instead shows a Christ from the poor, but fallen from the platonic world of a heterosexual construction of reality. There is a basic idealism permeating liberationists' theology in their acceptance of sexuality as a given. Therefore, the Christ of Liberation Theology cannot compete with the late Paulo Freire when the Brazilian educator was 30 years old and working in conscientization processes. Between that Christ and Freire, many of us would like to choose Freire, who had more awareness, consciousness and critical strategical thinking than the constructed un-dialogical Christ of current theology, in spite of the fact that Freire was not a messiah. The problem is that liberationists are guilty of making women suffer a split personality syndrome, encouraging them to engage in political critical thinking and ideological critique but becoming uncritical, unsuspicious and even dulled when thinking of Christ. If Christ was the product of interactions among messianic expectations and needs in a community, then women made Christ, some from their own alienation and others from the denunciation of their oppression through their passivity and acceptance of the limitations of their lives (as in the case of Mary, accepting sexual intercourse with the invisible god). Many women in the Gospels are portrayed as claiming justice but in a private sphere, without challenging the religious political system which oppressed them. In relation to women, Christ never went further than a compassionate empathy. He never challenged the pollution laws of women's menstruation, for instance, or discussed the patriarchal institution of marriage. If that was beyond his historically limited consciousness, as I believe was the case, then we need a new understanding of Christ's messianic role for our times, from the dialogue with today's women.

It is important to acknowledge that Christology should not be considered only as the stumbling-block of patriarchal Christianity, as post-Christian theologians may rightly claim, but it is also the point of departure for a de-patriarchalization of Christianity. If such a project were to be viable, Christology would need to acknowledge its own process of dialogical construction in which women participated in the 'making of a Christ' process. This is crucial for the coming out of the closet of women's spirituality, even if that public disclosure will threaten at the end what is today called Christ and Christianity. Christology from an Indecent Feminist Body Theology ('without underwear') needs to be understood as an ongoing task in which Christ as a personalized Messiah cannot undervalue the historical community of women surviving the web of cultural, racial, political, sexual and theological oppressions. There are issues of domestic violence in Christology; there are issues of epistemic violence inherent in the construction of Christology in Liberation Theology too. From the perspective of Indecent Theology (which is a sexual theology arising from postcolonial studies in feminism and theology), we can see the alliance between Christianity and the patriarchal traditions in our traditional Latin American cultures. Colonization constructed our cultures in terms of illegality in relation to men's structures of social and political productions, while indecency has been the sexual structure in which the configuration of such reality lied. *Indecencia* is the colonial female Christian category par excellence in Latin America. It works as a sophisticated machinery which pervades the public and private spheres of life for women, affecting women's economic lives and sexual lives. Obviously, it also affects men and the whole community. The symbolic construction of economics and politics in Latin American society are based on the naturalization of sexuality following a western Christian notion of 'decency'. Therefore the task of feminist postcolonial hermeneutics is similar to the objectives of an Indecent Theology of interpretation by subverting, or making indecent, that ideological sacralization of a sexual economic oppressive construct which kills women and makes them into the fetish of a disconnected ontology and an exploitative form of production.

Some key hermeneutical indecent proposals

First, I am claiming that an Indecent Christology is the product of the experience and reflection of poor women. By 'product' I mean that Indecent Christology is the outcome of critical action/reflection into the complex relations between women's work and modes of production, including reproduction, and considering 'reflection' as part of the mode of patriarchal colonial production called 'thought'. This also includes modes of theological production from which women are historically and traditionally excluded. For instance, following Marx's reflections in his 'Grundrisse', we can see that women are poor, independently of their economic means and without denying the differences in the lives of women in the North or in the South. Women's poverty is their ontological deprivation of the self–other relationship and sense of connectedness which challenges the objectifying, dualistic heterosexual system in which we live, work and believe in God.

Marx defined capital as a fetish (an idol image) because of its property of hiding the absolutist construction of capital. Male ontology and linked epistemology also work as a fetish, including the fact that such an 'Absolute' (the narratives of Christ, God the Father, capitalism, the structures of women's decency) is in fact the result of 'unpaid work' or the accumulation of surplus value. By this we say that women's ontological and material poverty is the consequence of their objectification and use in society. In other words and as an example of this, in the metaphor that establishes that God the Father is almighty, we tend to forget that in fact the narrative tells us he could not reproduce Godself. In order to do such a reproductive act, God needed to acquire a property, a gadget called 'woman who is the servant of *the* Lord. Let it be with me according to your word.' I emphasize the hegemonic, univocal construction of authority in the phrase 'the lord/master' and its masculinity. However, Mary (or 'woman who is the servant of *the* Lord') disappears in the process of Christology by the appropriation of her unpaid messianic reproductive work by the male religious community, and Christ becomes the fetish of Christianity because he represents the absolute discourse of patriarchy. The material and ontological deprivation is followed by yet another construction of religion where women are impoverished. However, as women's domestic contribution is the affective/sexual production of labour force (understanding here the Messiah as religious labour force), the construction of Christianity takes a curious twist. Women *feel* a connection between the affectivity of Christ and their own. As Christ is not represented as a mature, sexually active man, and Mary is supposed to have conceived without orgasm, women identify Christianity with love but not with sexuality. The point is that we tend to read from that perspective and with that hermeneutical clue in mind: women as the hidden producers of affectivity and reproduction in that frame, but not as women producers and in control of their sexuality. Instead of that, we could consider:

1. a more realistic, non-androcentric anthropology, where women are in control of their desires and pleasures, and in complete freedom to express themselves sexually with their own bodies, with other women, with men or both;

2. that this has spiritual and economic consequences in the way we interpret the sacred in our economic life;

3. that such a hermeneutic needs to provide indecent praxis of liberation to women. For instance, the classical 'mediator sciences' used for the Christology of Liberation Theology (such as sociology, anthropology and so on) should also include Nancy Friday or Susana Finkel in female sexual research, done among ordinary women in the USA and in Argentina;

4. that the moment of praxis of such Indecent hermeneutics needs to consider also the need to disentangle women from the sufferings produced by the theological confusion created between love and

sexuality, which makes love more important for women's fulfilment than sex, and ends homologizing love and sexuality.

From Indecent proposals to Christology: the nitty gritty of an Indecent Theology

An Indecent hermeneutic whose objective is to reread Christ from an indecent, subversive and pleasurable female category, needs to start by asking what does women's sexuality tell us about Christ? That is the project of doing theology from women's sexuality which could enlighten us to see new models of thought and economic systems too. The indecentist categories that can be used are those coming from women's experience, including the realm of women's fantasies, which is important because it denounces the prohibitions while announcing desire through images of transgression. In a christological indecent project, we need to consider, for instance, prostitution, sexual options and the case for women differentiating sexual pleasure from affect-ivity.

Prostitution is already a hermeneutical although undisclosed cate-gory of interpretation. Basically any activity declared sexually illegal makes of a woman a prostitute. In Buenos Aires, people use the phrase *la puta que te parió*, or *la puta madre* as common interjections for expressing a vast range of emotions, from surprise to insult. The expression *la puta que te parió* means 'the prostitute who gave birth to you'. *La puta madre* means 'the prostitute mother'. These expressions are so common in daily usage in Buenos Aires that people of any class affiliation, gender or status in society use them in everyday conversa-tions. Of course, in a patriarchal society the biggest insult a man can give is to query the woman-property of another man. Christology is built around these patriarchal assumptions based on laws of inheri-tance but also of control over female desire. Growing up in Argentina, these two categories of decent, sexually lawful woman, and indecent (which includes anything outside that control, including separation and divorce during my generation) were and are still part of the indoctrination of women and men. However, the theological con-struction of Christ (including Liberation Theology) has made Christ participate in the female identity's definition of being either a *puta* or a decent woman. It is extremely interesting that Christ does not represent male sexual categories, at least among Protestants.[3] Christ

---

[3] The Orthodox and Roman Catholic discussion on Christ and sex could show some similarities with this analysis. For instance, the tradition of male celibacy works by excluding women from their spiritual universe. Basically, all women are potentially *putas* from whom men need to protect

represents for women the female sexual categories of renunciation of sexual desires which are at the base of the female identity and of the sexual construction of spiritual and material universes. In Liberation Theology's words, one would say that not being a *puta* (a whore) Christ represents the renunciation of the praxis of sexual action and reflection, crucial for women's ontological and material historical quest. The point is that Christology was written with nothing in between an indecent and a decent woman, and this pervades episte-mological and economic as well as religious frameworks of action and thought. It conveys a powerful distorted sexual message to women and men, and it lacks reality. Simply, it is not a grounded materialist Christology. It has not changed men's sexuality based on men's alienation from their bodies and their association between sex and violence, and no substantial challenges to capitalism or globalization processes can be done from there. Therefore Christ has become Christ-the-decent-woman, making of our concept of God a perma-nently crippled dualistic shortcoming.

Ritual prostitution

We also need to consider ritual prostitution as an economic category built around Christology. In the narrative of Luke 21, we have a case of a poor woman economically sustaining the Temple, on which we should reflect. 'Widowhood' in Israel was at that time an economic category, applied even to women who had husbands who could not support them financially. According to this narrative, a poor woman was supporting the Temple through the sacrifice of her well-being (her physical nourishment). She sacrificed her body in order to sup-port the religious institution of her time. Moreover, considering what we now would call her unpaid domestic work, she even contributed to the well-being of another institution, that of her society and state. As a woman, and as a poor religious woman, she was sacrificed by a set of sacred rules which objectified her and gave her an uncontested patriarchal identity. It was Baudelaire who wrote in his diary of the concept of prostitution as 'a lack of options'. I find this concept of prostitution closely related to Marx's idea of the worker who has nothing to offer except him- or herself, the 'strength of the worker' as the merchandise that can be sold to the market because in the end, the worker needs to sell his/her own body.[4] The Scriptures portray what

themselves. A masculinized Mariology supplies the idealism in the construc-tion of the imaginary woman to whom they could relate.

[4] For this point, see Karl Marx, 'Teoría del Plusvalor' (Mexico City: FCE, 1980), vol. III, pp. 403ff.

I call the ritual prostitution of women in the sense that women are presented as emotional and economic sustainers of religion without challenging structurally the epistemological order to which that ritual prostitution belongs. Traditional exegesis cannot challenge it because it recognizes the need for such sacrifice, but Liberation Theology does, although only in a private capacity. By this I mean that the case of the widow is confined to a denunciation of Christ in relation to Christ taking over such a structure and building the temple of the spirit, but that it is not enough. In practice, Christ-the-decent-woman cannot challenge the ritual prostitution of Christian women which still exists. That ritual prostitution works by obscuring options that women have from the economic and religious times in which they live. The fact that women may accept a constructed Christology which diminishes them, and speaks in terms of universal male experiences and conceptions of Christ, submits them to the system of sacrifice which is ritual prostitution. The problem is that, in fact, Christ did not stop the widow from sacrificing herself. Christ is presented in the narratives as compassionate, but it is not what we would call a revolutionary compassion, transforming women's oppression by an awareness-raising of the patriarchal epistemology of his time.

Therefore, the challenge for constructing Christ today is to work with the category of ritual prostitution and its final consequences, but the scope of the project is vast. Even Mariology is based on the ritual prostitution of Mary, who in reality did not have options because the reproductive rules of her society were to be accepted and not to be challenged. We need to think of a Christ from reality, and from women's reality that may also challenge the heterosexual system which we have been brought up to believe in as a God-given norm.

Contesting the body acts of Christology

Christology is based on the interpretation of the body acts of Christ, yet it has its shortcomings, mainly in the construction of Christ-the-decent-woman when it comes to sexuality. It is a known fact that most men masturbate even if Christianity considers it sinful. Theologically decent women of my generation have been ignorant in sexual matters, including menstruation and the lack of knowledge of their own bodies' physiology. That ignorance was considered 'decent'. Perhaps *putas* masturbate and know their bodies, but not decent women. The discovery of a woman's own body is a lengthy and difficult process, full of guilt and religious pressures. It makes difficult the process of doing a Feminist Theology which may deal with issues of embodiment (incarnation) from a community of women who do not know their bodies or feel that their bodies are good. In that sense, we can also identify Christ's portrayal of alienated sexuality more with women than with men. However, when it comes to the crucial question that post-Christian theologians have posed, such as the masculinity of Christ, we are still resolving it by the dualistic assumption that Jesus could be born either male or female. The assumptions about Christ's masculinity are based on a biological confusion between gender and sexuality. But gender roles are behaviourally shaped by culture.[5] Christologies based on Jesus' masculinity as a given role are in fact political categories assuming power relations in public and private spheres of life. The point is that we cannot read in the narratives Jesus' sexual options, if he had them, because probably he was also like a ritual prostitute selling his given, fixed construction of masculinity to the religious movement he belonged to in order to be accepted. However, we can proceed to construct a Christology from an indecent perspective by analysing the way that the Messiah was imagined by the community, including the genderization of his sexuality. To this, we need to add our own communities too, in order to construct a Christ who will go beyond the limitations of Jesus' historical consciousness. This is part of the process of dehegemonization in Feminist and Postcolonial Theologies, which consider that the politics of unity (heterosexuality) are not strategically or conceptually desirable. Liberation theologians in Latin America know the price of compulsory beliefs, such as the Christian ones imposed during the exploitation of our original nations 500 years ago. It is compulsory unity that produces fragmentation and stagnation of praxis; acknowledging the reality of sexual diversity in humankind, on the other hand, gives space for the freedom where social transformation may occur. A Christology for our present times of bankrupt epistemologies and religious symbols that may be becoming irrelevant to many women requires a Christology from the margins, but not from our central, doctrinal thoughts adapted to the margins. For that Christology we need to consider the power of women's sexual storytelling, the kind that exists in the intimacy among women and more recently has been researched in cultural and sexual studies.[6]

From sexual story-telling studies we learn from the voices of women and men how the system in which we live is organized by making the unusual usual, that is, by enforcing gender constructions considered normal by legislative means, in order to disrupt and tame the different manifestation of sexual behaviours in society. Christology has done the same. If we consider the highly unusual personality of a man who was constructed as divine as God's son and in unity

---

[5] For this discussion on the construction of gender, see for instance A. Oakley, *Subject Women* (London: Fontana, 1982).

[6] See for instance Ken Plummer, *Telling Sexual Stories: Power, Change and Social Words* (London: Routledge, 1995).

with Godself, it is interesting to notice how Christ has been made a normal man, beyond his exceptional degree of compassion and courage, features that may be found anywhere in the history of humanity. The social order and its possibility of changes rely on the political role that sexual stories give to reality. Traditional Christologies tell us that Christ comes from God's own sexual story with Mary, but many of the elements of that sexual narrative of the gestation of Christ are the defining ones of human sexuality. Although familiar with the reading of the angel and the pubescent virgin, still the elements of ambiguity, potential chaos and disorder permeate that story. Therefore, how can we assume, as traditional Christologies have done, that Christ's heterosexuality was natural? Only when we locate ourselves in an unquestioned heterosexual epistemology can it be so. It would be more natural to think that Christ assumed all the sexual potentials that a human being has when born, before being moulded into straightjackets of patriarchal man or patriarchally defined woman. There cannot be a new order, not even an economic one, unless new questions arise, or as liberationists say, more suspicion is brought to the texts of the Word and the world. The deconstruction of a heterosexual Christology is by no means its dissolution but the beginning of taking away the process of legitimacy built into Christianity by patriarchal ideology. It can be done from the poverty of women who hide their spiritual, affective and intellectual richness. From the sexual dreams and fantasies of poor women in Latin America we hear about the desire to love other women, and how fulfilling it is, how peaceful an experience it is for women harassed in the *machista*'s Latin American system. Dreams of having more than one man, of loving different men, also expresses the need to cease to be sexual property and grow sexually with different experiences in their life. Poor women from El Salvador are speaking of finding lesbian lovers and becoming themselves after a life in which they were married in early adolescence, had many children and then suddenly realized that they have an option. They are not ritual prostitutes for church or society any more.[7] As important as it is that Christ may be identified with a miner or with a peasant man in Brazil, it is also important to build a Christ to surpass *machismo* in a structural way. As Foucault has argued, sex roles only have coherence in a set of normative rules. These rules we may claim to be also active in the documents of the International Monetary Fund. For instance, the implementation of free-market policies and the Structural Adjustment programmes in third world countries are not gender neutral as

---

[7] From the Revd Isabel Ascencio, founder of the 'Independent Christian Women' movement, which brings together women who have left the church structures in recent years, working on issues of politics, community-building and solidarity.

they may pretend to be. At the core of such policies is the assumption that women have certain roles in society different from men. Christology has made of Christ a limited messiah if he obeys the rules of the limited masculine spiritual universe, but such limitation can also be applied when defining women's work and gendered distributed wages.

The process of thinking of Christ today is complex. We must unravel the construction of the Christ as a real man, sorting out the spiritual/sexual doctrine of Christ-the-decent-woman, but furthermore, we need Christ in a lesbian love story, or homosexual or bisexual, even among the transsexual people of our society. This is reality. It may sound very indecent, but that is precisely the point. The point of critical reality is where poor women can end the Christian split between body and spirit in a drastic way, or God will continue to be thought of as a sort of 'illusion of substance' or idealist starting point which feminists and post-colonialists alike have renounced together with the master's authority. As Indecent Theology sounds scandalous, so is life. However, for some of us more interested in orthopraxis than in orthodoxy it is clear that the right questions from reality need to be taken seriously for a hermeneutics written by women who might stop to reflect, at least symbolically, without the constrictions and forgetfulness of desire that underwear produces. Such a process would be inspired by the Peruvian Coya women, who can pray to God and participate in the economic struggle of their daily lives without wearing underwear, thus revealing ('unclothing') the reality of being a woman at prayer and at meal times, and at the moment of sexual pleasure as well.

6

A Woman's Right to Not Being Straight:
El Derecho a no ser Derecha:
On Theology, Church and Pornography

'That was a kiss', he said.
'Was it really?' I asked in disbelief with my eyes still closed. 'I didn't feel anything.'
'There are many kinds of kisses.'
'What kind was that one?'
'Doesn't matter. We're talking mathematics here.'

James Cañón, 1999, p. 79

Sechem, the prince of the country, but a slave to his own lusts, took her and lay with her, it should be seen not so much by force as by surprise . . . See what came of Dinah's gadding: young women must learn to be *chaste, keepers at home*; these properties are put together, Tit.ii.5 for those that are not keepers at home, expose their chastity.

Matthew Henry, 1892

On pornography and theology

Think pornography. Think about a pornographic image defined as offensive due to its quality of being static and detached. For instance, a woman's body used for advertising a brand of alcohol fixes and objectifies not only a body but sexuality too. Such fixity is almost of exegetical quality; it is the body interpreted because reification is an interpretation in itself. Even if pornographic images are in movement, like in an X-rated film, there seems to be a sense of confinement and stricture of sexual relationships. As with the protagonist of the story from Cañón, heterosexual ideology makes sure that in pornography kisses are reduced to a certain fixed order or taxonomy of desire. Any free, unprogrammed kiss will never be a kiss. There are many kinds of love and desire, but, reflecting here on pornography as a heterosexual art, we can say that what is offensive is the repetitive mimicry presented of one stereotypical desire. Unfortunately, the same can be said of Christian theology, which mimics the prevalent heterosexual ideology while excluding any epistemological attempt which challenges its dualism, hierarchies and institutionalized gods.

Are there any free kisses in the church or in theology? Christian theology proclaims the grace of God as a gratuitous love given to human beings and creation. Yet, the free kisses from God seem to be reduced to the private aspect of faith more than to the public one. That is, sexual dissidents do not feel deprived of their communion with God, but with the churches. This happens because theology in an alliance with pornography as a method tends to work, like capitalism, with a hermeneutical circle of inverting identities. Marx has denounced in his critique of ideology as a method that ideas come first (in the sense of being valued and given pre-eminence) while people as the real protagonists of history seem to come second. The hermeneutical circle of ideology makes of people followers of ideologies, instead of actors of history.[1] The point is that while human bodies became devalued things, and thus lovers in theology became devalued, high value and respect are given to things such as marriage for profit.

Pleasure is profit in theology for bartering purposes. For instance, there is a long tradition where pleasure is bartered with godly recompenses in Christian ethics. This is part of the exchange circle of forgiveness and the industry of confession. Hence the need to construct the loving bodies as motionless bodies, that is, outside meaningful non-heterosexual relationships from which lessons of love can be learnt and more about the love of God can be discovered.[2]

According to Andrea Dworkin, pornography is an art of territorial occupation.[3] In theology, we may also be talking here of the politics of non-consensual heterosexual ideological interventions in the name of universal salvation. Yet, like in the unfortunate biblical commentary on Dinah by Henry, in heterosexual theology bodies easily become occupied territories, to be portrayed as faulty or sinful. If Dinah did not go out, she would not have been raped. By the same criteria, women who are not heterosexual should remain in their closets. The theo/logic here is one of claustrophobia.

---

[1] This point was discussed in more depth in Chapter 4.

[2] For a reflection on the contribution that lesbian theologies reflecting on love and relationship can make to the churches, see Elizabeth Stuart, *Just Good Friends* (London: Mowbray, 1995).

[3] See Andrea Dworkin, *Intercourse* (New York: Free Press, 1987), p. 133.

On churches, capitalism and not being straight

We reflected briefly on pornography, and now we need to reflect more on theology. Capitalism, colonialism and pornography have many things in common with some kinds of theology. At least in the past they have had in common the essential characteristics such as the objectification of women, sexuality and the valorization of exploitative profit, such as when the family becomes abusive and women are discouraged from breaking their legal contracts in the name of God. Capitalism, colonialism and pornography always formed in a sense an ecumenical community, with territorial occupation as a goal and as a strategy. Today, with the global expansion of capitalism (*mundialización*) such adjudicated sexual roles in society may have changed, and even the hierarchical ordering of the world may have changed, but they still have a god-father in common; that is, the politically ever-expanding patriarchal god who does not recognize any kiss which has not been approved. For instance, in the present collapse of the Argentinian nation, the IMF has imposed economic laws for Argentina as a requisite to help the country in the extraordinary economic crisis which it is currently suffering. However, people know that such laws are only going to bring more hardship for a country where even pensions have been cut and old people are left to find food in rubbish tips. Therefore, they are organizing themselves in workers' co-operatives. Factories that have been closed down and abandoned have been taken by workers who organize themselves into co-operatives. They have not only succeeded in repairing the abandoned machines and distributing equal salaries among the workers, but they also allocate part of the monthly economic surplus for the benefit of the local communities. Yet, old-fashioned workers' co-operatives seem to be unapproved kisses for the IMF because they can lead my country into economic success but also a different political system. But global capitalism does not admit difference.

In the same way that workers in Argentina are looking for different ways in the economy instead of adapting or reforming the old ones, we can say that it is not that women need to claim their human rights in the church for the church to be reformed, but for the church to be radically transformed. Such transformation needs to be away from a way of thinking of God and the world which sexually and politically abuses people, and even God. God is the first casualty in theology if God becomes a puppet of heterosexual ideologies.

The combination of a sexually explicit position and that quality of fixity or immobility of the heavily conceptualized body may define a picture from a magazine or a text in the Bible as pornographic. Similar qualities, translated into an economic frame of thought, are also the characteristics of the IMF. However, these are ecclesiologies that seem to have more in common with the policies of the market than with the alternative society project of Jesus Christ. The market, for all its discourses on free competition and mobility, works on principles of presupposed immobility by trade agreements and regulations which allow exploitation to exist and to generate wealth for the empires. In Christianity, the heavily sexually restricted body of women seems to have produced the primordial ethos of theo/social confinement, that is, the theology which has been done for the preservation and control of the imperial ideologies in power. In order to work, they require the immobility of women in sexual confinement, but such immobility is a heavily sexually conceptualized order. It is obvious that to talk about human rights and women in the church we need to start by querying if women have human rights in the church itself, but it is less obvious (but not less important) to consider which rights these are. For instance, are we talking here about rights of equality? And equal to whom? The right of *no ser derecha* or not to be straight[4] is not a human right based on equality but on difference; this is the right of the Other, the right of people to be themselves, even if the doctrinary corpus ignores them. The time has come to recognize that a whole apparatus of pornographic, immobile definitions and fixed conceptualizations is responsible for the anthropological Babylonian captivity of the church that not only reduces people's lives and their vocation to no more than ideological definitions, but that also reduces God. If God is to be found in human relationships of economic and loving orders, it is obvious that the right not to be straight in a capitalist society and church has the goal of liberating God.

However, blessed are the humble, for it takes nothing greater than the small gesture of a woman inclined to love another woman more than doctrines to destabilize the pornographic network of theology, based on the immobilization of identities and the reification of love.

Exegeting women's bodies

In theology we deal with pornography every day by working with texts depicting the sexual immobility of women and men in time and space in restricted, uncomfortable positions of a sexual and economic nature, as are found in many doctrinal positions. The woman's body, as depicted in theology, has constituted what we can call an exegetical body of women, that is, a body subjected to complicated exposition of origins and meanings of ideological heterosexual interpretation, basically an essentialized body subject to theological desires. This

---

[4] In Spanish, the word *derecha/derecho* can be translated as 'right', and also figuratively as 'straight'.

exegetical woman-body is problematic, not necessarily because it has usually been built around the faulty biological construction of female identities from previous centuries, racial conceptualizations and different cultural understandings. Women, and Other women (women from other races, cultures and time), are not the problem. The problem is not that the exegesis of women's bodies, of their desires and pleasures, is fixed in the Bible, but that it is caught in a heterosexual gaze which has been highly sacralized. More than the Bible, it is the eyes of the reader that are responsible for the construction of the imagined Christian woman's body, the illusory exegetical body of interpretation of what a woman is, fixing, as it does, how that woman gets fulfilment in life. In this context the claim of so many women in the church, denouncing the brutality of patriarchal praxis has often been equivalent to the discourse of a 'no' meaning a 'yes'. The claim of a woman's human rights becomes a claim to be recognized as human in the church, but in order to succeed she would need to lose her faith in the church sexual ideological system. It is not the right to be a woman (as heterosexually defined) that needs to be claimed, but the right to be. It is interesting to consider that heterosexual women can only be liberated in the church by liberating the church of its sexual ideology. The right to 'not being straight' is the first to claim.

To reflect on issues of human rights in the church today means in a way to recognize the pornographic nature of Christian theology, and its characteristics of colonial expansion: bodies are occupied, identities fixed, women are objectified and the reflection on God deals more with ideology than with critical reality. Women as the actors of history and the actors of theology disappear as mere commodities of theological exchange. They become useful categories to organize a systematic theology around. For instance, in colonial theology, grace, faithfulness and redemption were redefined upon the background of a dialectic of imperial purity versus a sinful Other. The Other as the scapegoat of the sin of the masters was darker, more sinister, more sensual and lazy and less masculine, emphasizing by contrast the abundant virile virtues of the Christian imperial power. The Other was feminized. In a similar reversal mechanism, women's domestic drudgery became a theological virtue in the church. Immobilizing women in the church according to patriarchal criterias has produced a tradition. The work done by theologians such as Elisabeth Schüssler Fiorenza[5] has an anti-pornographic nature. It destroys fixed, bound

---

[5] Schüssler Fiorenza's original work has been precisely to restore the 'sense of movement' that women have in the history of the church, showing the instability of our concepts of women's submission and passivity in the church. See for instance, *Discipleship of Equals: A Critical Feminist Ekklesia-logy of Liberation* (London: SCM Press, 1993).

bodies of women in history by uncovering the movements and struggles of women in history.

The point is that women's bodies are prophetic not only because
historically they denounce their confinement and announce the possibility of the alternative in our churches and society, but because they
uncover the hidden spaces of theological struggles. Such spaces are
sexual and economic ones. Women's exclusion or restricted inclusion
in the churches and the economy are fundamental for the functioning
of theological structures in control, such as racial and national claims
and supremacies, and also economic configurations. From this perspective, it is not that the Bible is a pornographic text per se. Even
allowing the pornographic language and violent sexual imaginery of
a book such as Hosea, what is pornographic is the theological mechanism that has not allowed the text to move on. Texts are not fixed
because readers keep moving, and even strong pornographic texts, as
Hosea is, can be read not for the purpose of making an apology, but to
destabilize it in order to find the core pornography of religion. Then,
by a process of intertextuality, we could be reading to find, for
instance, religion without heterosexuality. That is to say, that the
church's eye is a pornographic eye which fixes the text of women and
impedes not a rereading but a rewriting of Hosea. For in order to use
a non-pornographic reading, the text needs to recover its mobility and
the contesting thrust of the bodies historically pinned down by sacred
forces in theology.

Women's rights and faith in sex

The point is that the church can never address issues concerning
women's rights in the secular world until the doctrine of sex which is
sustained by a pornographic theology has been declared illegal, and
unrecognized kisses have become, by contrast, canonical. Until now
the church has, no doubt, been supporting women's human rights but
only according to the limitations of its own heterosexual fixed theological landscape. Churches vary in that: from women who cannot be
ordained as priests, to women who still need to declare to their priests
when they are having their periods in order to avoid polluting the
sacrament of the eucharist; or the exclusion of non-heterosexual cou-
ples – there are many degrees and complexities of disrespect for
human rights that only women know. Women's destinies and call to
be more are daily aborted in many churches. One must not presup-
pose, though, that losing faith in the church's sexual project is a desirable project for lesbians, transvestites or bisexual women alone. On
the contrary, considering the heterosexual appeal of churches and
Christian theology alike, it should also be the task of heterosexual

women to question the normativity and construction of women's identity in the churches and their 'fixity' in pornographic theology. As I have written elsewhere, the problem is that women (and especially poor women) tend to invest in the heteronormal project of the church in order to gain respect by default. The necessary and costly respect that those who are not free need.[6]

Prophetic bodies

I would like to refer again to that seminal article from the Brazilian theologian Nancy Cardoso Pereyra on the body of women and prophecy in the Hebrew Scriptures.[7] Cardoso Pereyra makes the point of finding prophecy in the Hebrew Scriptures through the language of women's and children's oppressed bodies. For instance, the hunger of the poor becomes a prophetic voice denouncing the injustice of a society which did not distribute its resources equally. Women's bodies are also prophetic in the abuse they suffer. For instance, raped bodies speak of sex as dominion while a poor woman's body, such as that of Ruth's servant in the Hebrew Scriptures, speaks of power and affection through her relation with Ruth herself. The violation of women's rights in the church are and have been historically denounced by the prophecy of women's bodies.

Women's suffering as prophetic seems to act by de-ideologizing sexual dogmatism in Christian theology. This is an important point, because what we are saying is that women's agency is not necessarily the conceptual understanding of triumph but that there is agency in exclusion. This happens especially when the excluded women's bodies surprises the church with their stubbornness. For instance, women loving women, or women challenging the heterosexual mythologies of contractual love between women and men, have been making it more and more difficult for the church to claim God as a hetero-ideologue of the oppressed. Claiming the right not to be straight is a contribution to the church and Christian theology because it uncovers the fact that many theological disputes are somehow disputes about women's bodies. If we agree with Paul Ricoeur that the concept of evil itself in Christian theology has been elaborated upon judicial and biological concepts of debt and inheritance,[8] we could

---

[6] Cf. Marcella Althaus-Reid, *Indecent Theology* (London: Routledge, 2000), Ch. 2.

[7] See Nancy Cardoso Pereyra, 'La Profecía y lo Cotidiano: La Mujer y el Niño en el Ciclo del Profeta Eliseo' in *Revista de Interpretación Bíblica Latinoamericana*, 14 (Santiago de Chile: REHUE, 1993), pp. 7–23.

[8] Cf. Paul Ricoeur, *Le Conflit des Interpretations* (Paris: Ed. du Seuil, 1969), pp. 265–82.

start to consider how the conceptualization of women's bodies may be closer than anything else to the conceptualization of doctrinal bodies. How to think theology without pornography is the challenge that the question of women's rights in the church presents us by demanding that women's bodies cease to be doctrinally immobilized, stripped of their freedom and dignity and determined in their loving religious horizons.

At the core of any discussion on sexuality lies the threat of destabilizing dogmas and ecclesiologies which have made of God a resource of heterosexual authority. That requires the courage to find God outside sexual ideologies and ideologies of race and class. Sexual ideologies in particular are crucial in sustaining political ones, and women's rights inside and outside the church, as well as God's rights, depend on how we confront them in what needs to be an alliance for more than one truth 'out of the closet' for heterosexual and non-heterosexual people alike. Meanwhile, God remains hidden by ideology. God also remains in the closet as a prisoner of the orthodoxy of theology and pornography, claiming for *el derecho a no ser derecha*, the right not to be straight in a church where the orthopraxis of love should be more important than its orthodoxy based on an uncritical position rooted in a heterosexual ideology.

This chapter was originally published in The Concilium Foundation (eds), 'The Rights of Women', *Concilium*, 2002/5 (London: SCM Press), pp. 88–96.

Part Three

Postcolonialism, Feminism and Liberation

When Liberation texts are wrested from their native contexts and introduced into the comfort of a First World environment, they become commodities.

Sugirtharajah, 2003, p. 166

Only one thing I would like to say to you and to the venerable and holy priests. Why didn't you show up in our defence when the white (men) were killing us? . . . And now you remember that there is only one true God? Didn't you know that there is only one true God at the time when they were killing us?

Letter from the Mayan Chief Francisco Caamal to the Christian Church
González Navarro, 1970, p. 309

R. S. Sugirtharajah, one of the most important voices in Postcolonial Theology, has made one of the few perceptive comments about Latin American Liberation Theology from outside Latin America.[1] Reflecting on issues related to liberation and postcolonialism, Sugirtharajah finds that the discourse of Liberation Theology usually falls into one of two categories: either a liberation-focused theology or a cultural-sensitive theological reflection. Obviously, Sugirtharajah is well aware that there are risks of over-generalization in his statement. It would not be right to forget, for instance, that both cultural and politically based theological styles might, at some point, fruitfully interact.

---

[1] The two most important critiques of Liberation Theology in the past decades have been made by Sugirtharajah in his book, *The Bible and the Third World* (Cambridge: Cambridge University Press, 2001), and Alistair Kee's still remarkable book, *Marx and the Failure of Liberation Theology* (London: SCM Press, 1990). Kee's comment was related to the lack of radical engagement of Liberation Theology, and, while Sugirtharajah's emphasis is on the lack of postcolonial awareness, both have a criticism of the hesitant radical stance of Liberation Theology. That is, the difficulty that liberationists had to engage in a more critical reflection on the colonial roots of the church and theology in Latin America.

Yet, Sugirtharajah is right, and I would add to this that both theologies have lacked a postcolonial consciousness in the sense that little internal criticism of Christianity in itself has been produced, although there have been criticisms of the way that Christianity has been used to oppress and subjugate the people of the Americas. However, the problem remains and Christianity has been and still remains the religion that was imposed on the Other. Christian theology and the organizational structures of a European church have been imposed in Latin America in the 'cross and sword' alliance of religion and state, creating a complex web of law and order which has perpetuated ideologies of colonial power. Such an alliance may still continue in many nations of the continent, in different ways. However, the 'First Wave' liberationists tended to ignore that Latin America has its own great religions such as Maya, which is still alive, not to mention traditions such as Santería, Candomblé and Umbanda, which are part of the spirituality of millions and practised alongside Christianity without apparent contradictions. Not only are we talking here about different religious understandings but also different ways of conceiving of society, social relationships such as marriage and friendship and a system of values related to issues such as land, the market and labour.[2]

As I have personally heard many times in my own country, Argentina, many people are still asking, 'How could the religion of the oppressors ever bring liberation to the oppressed?' At this point feminist liberation theologians have something to contribute to an almost intuitive engagement with a postcolonial criticism of religion. The issue of gender in Latin America, as we saw in Chapter 2, goes deep into the problem of the gendering orders imposed into Latin American cultures by fifteenth-century European Roman Catholicism. This is not to say that patriarchalism did not exist in Latin America before the *Conquista*. On the contrary, some military cultures such as the Aztec culture were known for their deep misogyny. But we can still claim that the genderization of society and gods before Christianity was different and open to other possibilities. The problem with Liberation Theology has been that it represents a theology which has never had hermeneutical suspicions about its own colonial identity. It works from the idea that if only Christianity was correctly interpreted (as a path of liberation towards freedom, or the Kingdom of God) and the church was allowed to co-exist with popular movements (such as the Basic Ecclesial Communities), then Christianity would not be contradictory in a land which had other religions, other cosmovisions and other traditions of being society and people. It was

---

[2] For this point, see for instance my book, *The Queer God* (London: Routledge, 2003), especially Ch. 7, 'Popular Anti-theologies of Love'.

thanks to the work from feminist liberationists and a Theology of Liberation made by women who, by the mere fact of being women, are strangers in their own (religious) land, that the first elements of postcolonial critique were introduced. The aforementioned article from Aurora Lapiedra '*Yo Siento a Dios de Otro Modo*' ('I Feel God in a Different Way') was a pioneer article written by an Andean woman speaking with a different voice and a colonial critique of theologically approved vocabulary and expectations. For the first time, an indigenous woman outside the theological and ecclesiastical circles in Latin America was able to question the alienation of gender, Christianity and culture without apology.

Three main questions which concern us here are the following:

1. How does the political and economic framework of *Conquista* still interfere with the production of theology? This implies certain definitions such as what is a 'church (or theological) market' and how such market forces need to be challenged so they do not define what theology is needed, and which voices are the proper (or decent) ones for purposes of teaching and research.

2. How did Liberation Theology become commodified in the North Atlantic market, and how did the selling of theological books and fashion become the death of a theology originally done with courage and risk? In this, there is almost a process of 're-colonizing' Liberation Theology by converting it into an exotic product for the North Atlantic academic market.

3. Finally, we need to try to rescue elements from the authentic voices of women, like the example of the women from El Salvador, who produced a popular yet critical theology at different levels of politics, economy, culture and (neo-)colonialism. More relevant still is to find this critique in the voices of women from the struggle of those such as guerrilla women or religious sisters active in the militant churches, and to hear them without intermediaries.

The three chapters which follow reflect these points at the intersection of a postcolonial encounter of Liberation Theology, feminism and the commodification of theology through processes of neo-colonization. Chapter 7, 'Does the Church Need Theology or Vice Versa? A Materialist Analysis Concerning the Current Theological Industry and Its Church Market', is concerned with theology as a product. The concerns here are about the market of theology and the fact that it dictates what we can call 'a metaphysics of accountancy' to the church, organizing the production of church praxis under the banner of marketable success. However, Liberation Theology has a different vision which may consider that de-centring the church and marginalizing Christianity is more in tune with the option for the poor and the building of the Kingdom than with making Liberation Theology a successful brand.

Chapter 8, 'Doing the Theology of Memory: Counting Crosses and Resurrections', comes from a reflection upon the recollections of a group of women from El Salvador after the war. 'Memory' is a key element in Feminist Liberation Theology, as women remember and re-member their communities, by continuing the traditions of giving testimony and of assuming their responsibilities as witnesses of the tragedies and struggles of our continent. Through their theological memories, we find the presence of a Bible actively read 'outside the Bible', not in texts but on events of liberation, and the subversiveness of traditional liturgical customs such as the *rezadoras* (prayer women) who use the rosary during communal parties to conscientize the people. A whole theology of memory from women in El Salvador shows us that there was a postcolonial political, cultural and religious consciousness among these women who fought together with their men in the hills yet were relegated to the kitchen by the church and their husbands after the war ended. Yet, still is a hermeneutical circle here made of resilience and memory; of witnessing and struggle, which refuses to accept the colonial establishment of church and theology while announcing a different and more authentic way of doing theology from women's political lives.

Chapter 9, 'Gustavo Gutiérrez goes to Disneyland: Theme Park Theologies and the Diaspora of the Discourse of the Popular Theologian in Liberation Theology', is a reflection in depth on these issues: the process which made of Liberation Theology a commodity and the investment of exoticism in its work which was one of the selling points of Liberation Theology as a theological bestseller in North Atlantic bookshops. From there, we reflect on the marketing of 'the popular theologian' as the projection of 'a lack' among North Atlantic theologians. Therefore, 'the popular theologian' (as a colonial concept) was distributed in the North Atlantic market in relation to the native portrait of the Latin American Christian: poor, humble, grateful, faithful and innocent. It was an image which satisfied both the local priest and/or academic in their search for meaning in an increasingly secular North Atlantic society, but which was helpful in terms of contributing towards the formation of a European (or North American) Christian identity. The processes which contributed to issues of identity and Christian representation during colonial times and Christian mission have been proved to be more persistent than was thought. Far from disappearing or to be relegated only to fundamentalist activities, they continue actively by processes of nativization and subordination of the Other, and they may have contributed to neutralizing Liberation Theology by subsuming it into categories of exoticism and essentialism.

7

Does the Church Need Theology or Vice Versa?
A Materialist Analysis Concerning the Current Theological Industry and Its Church Market

This essay is concerned with the alleged mutual need between the churches and theology and vice versa, but more basically with making a critique of the need to produce theology as a consumer good. From this perspective, it is as if the temptation is for theology to come from a current theological industry composed of the academy and the structured church. Having said that, this does not mean that we must follow some cynical premises concerning the political place of church and theology at the end of the twentieth century, but rather try to establish a basic geopolitical position in theology, that is, to take seriously the material concreteness of our theological discourse. Of course, this cannot surprise anybody after more than three decades of pursuing materialist analysis in theology from the pioneer work of Fernando Belo, unmasking idealist readings of the gospel to the lucid work of perhaps the greatest Marxist theologian of our times, Enrique Dussel. Unfortunately, the problem is that the idealist reflection which comes from classical North Atlantic theology, and which we thought, together with capitalism, to be in a dying state, has come back in a sort of monstrous resurrection. Just like capitalism, the beast of theological idealism we thought decapitated has come back with more than one head, and no doubt it would consider itself fit to reply to questions about mutual needs between theology and the church from the perspective of a transcendent discourse on God. Such a perspective is familiar to most of us, because it disguises itself even in the discourses of Liberation Theology. For instance, we could consider a theological discourse centred on the movement of the Holy Spirit throughout history, interpreting through its movement the necessary conceptual changes which challenged the human structure of the church down the centuries. At the same time, we could reflect on an ecclesiology made in theological defiance, considering that the body of Christ (the believers) is God's geography where the Holy Spirit is incarnated in everyday life. Therefore, we could either say that the alleged crisis of the church is a theological crisis or that the opposite is true; the theological crisis exists because the church has remained fixed to superseded structures of thought, and to a style of reflection which Christians cannot identify with any more. All these reflections come from a dualistic style of thought which divides church/theology, and which is all-pervading (and perverting) in the western mentality. Liberation Theology challenged this to a point, but never enough. To overcome this, it would be more useful to reflect on the mutual dependency of church and theology in terms of forces and relationships of production. In this way we acknowledge that there are three and not two partners in this dialogue: the church, theology and the current political system with all its far-reaching ideological implications. From this perspective we must, first of all, define what 'needs' are and then how the relation of theological production relates to them.

Who needs 'needs'? Necessity in the rhetoric of capitalism

What do we understand when we talk about 'necessity'? The concept of necessity can be approached as a question arising from the rhetoric of capitalism. 'Needs', when thought of from a more sensual discourse, with a sense of concreteness, tend to be self-defining. In capitalism, needs are the force of the market, the ontological definition on which freedom is built. Needs are a subject of constant re-creation and re-definition. People need to need. In this context it is important to realize that the current economic discourse is not primarily about currencies, goods and labour distribution, but about human relationships defined in need. Institutions such as the World Bank are utopia-makers because they determine the dreams and visions of humanity through determining needs, objectives and desires. They do it through the regulation of human relationships through economic systems which fix the borders of *Being-in-Need* through history. It may well be that the deepest questions from ontology and theology concerning the meaning of life obey this limiting economic geography, which does not allow many excursions beyond these limits. This is important in theology and in the life of the church too. How churches and theologies organize their discourse around the *Being-in-Need*, reflects in how they organize their mutual need. Historically, when the discourse on need has been materially challenged in the church, it has also been contested theologically, but in these cases the main revolt has been of an ideological, not a theological, nature. Once again, we are dealing with three, not two, partners, and the ideologies of the time are much more important in fixing the work of the church and theology than anything else. When theology and church cross boundaries, it is important how they do it. How we present these crossings (e.g. the black church against apartheid, or the Roman Catholic seminarians against church and dictatorship in Argentina) speaks about power relationships and needs. For instance, since women are outside the symbolic system of the economy, church and theology can only present discourses in relation to women inside the present system. What Christian women need is not so important as what the market needs, in term of a genre discourse which is particular to the industrial society. Church and theology have been talking about humanity in relation to God in terms of submission, starting from the embodied metaphor of economic submission which are women. Submission is also a demand of the capitalist structure. These things happen because God can only be envisaged by us through human relationships, that is, economic relations. Can theology or church then go beyond being mere instruments of economic models? In this example, and unfortunately it is not unique, theology is a lackey of an ecclesial structure, which is a mini-model of a political system. Theology and church do not support each other but rather they support the system together. They do not have independent life outside it. This still happens at different levels. For instance, if the Latin American militant churches challenge political and economic structures of oppression but they do not question patriarchal epistemologies, they still work as lackeys of the system. There is nothing so radical as to consider what the needs of people are outside the constructions of the new world order of globalization, and outside the needs of the church and/or theology. Moreover, theology has entered the international market producing fashionable goods. Liberation Theology used to be a designer label until a few years ago; it does not sell much nowadays, and its critics say that it is not original any more, therefore new combinations are being tested on the market: gospel and culture without class analysis; Liberation Theology 'with women's eyes' without taking the serious challenge of feminist standpoint theory; liberation-cum-Pentecostalism, while Pentecostalism lasts. One of them could be the successful product in the North Atlantic supermarkets.

Engels and the division of theological work

The problem is that when genuine theological reflection comes, even if it is grass-rooted, it cannot determine if the ecclesiological product (the praxis which comes from the reflection) is appropriate or not, because something has happened during the process; that is, a division of labour has already happened which makes it difficult to control the act of 'doing church'. The following analysis comes from Engels. Engels and Marx not only considered the alienation of the product from the makers, but the fact that structures are very close to such processes. Thus Engels says: 'The hand [of the worker] is not only the organ of labour, it is also the product of labour' (Engels, 1981, p. 152). This has been paraphrased by liberation theologians when considering that the definition of who is a theologian is as important as definitions of what is theology. Theology in itself does not exist, because it is an abstraction of a historical economic relationship between human beings and their official (and subversive) under-standings of God. The church in itself may just as well be an illusion or commodity produced for the exchange of the real necessities of human existence such as food and love, for a theological 'good' which explains why food and love are difficult to obtain. Many Christians have understood that salvation, as a transcendental idea of a divine good exchanged for concrete needs, is a sacrificial act of humanity. Salvation has often been a luxury article circulating among poor hands, the hands of the poor who pay dearly for this created spiritual need. Let us remember that before colonization processes people did not need salvation as presented in Christianity, and the market sold them these needs in exchange for the domestication and submission of the colonized nations. The grassroots communities may well be doing their own theology but once the product is formed it is alien-ated from them. Clodovis Boff speaks openly about the role of church traditions in the hermeneutical process, but do common, illiterate people know or care less for such traditions or superstructures? He is afraid of losing the rigour of the theological enterprise (Boff, 1987, pp. 33ff.). This would mean theological decline, and it is a crucial question, because it implies the intellectual, theological needs of the academy are in tension with the more pragmatic or ecclesiastic needs (measured, I am afraid, in terms of growth per capita, that is, how many people per church per Sunday, etc.). It touches the dualism con-structed between people of action and thinking, as if thinking was not the symbolic of action and the living metaphor of a possible history. Some years ago, an Argentinian bishop asked me the following ques-tion: 'Do you think that in the present moment of the church we need more people to sit and think, or more people to stand up and act more?' When such a question is presented it is because we have reached a crisis. The concept of 'thinking' is erroneous because it assumes that every process of thinking is rooted in idealism. That was the time of dictatorial regimes in Argentina, when the official dis-course humiliated sectors of the population called 'the intellectuals'. The universities were closed and the intellectuals were the laughing stock of the media. The church of theology of liberation assimilated that discourse although it opposed the dictatorial regime. It was particularly cruel to women because the militant church did not give more space for women to work than the rest, while women theologians felt under the accusation of being mere intellectuals. In the idealist discourse, the crisis of both church and theology is defined by a capitalist analysis, based on the simplistic terminology of a free-market discourse. The crisis of the church is reduced to a challenge for chartered accountants. It is, in fact, a metaphysics of accountancy. Success is defined by 'more' in the accountancy books of the church. More people, more money donated, more churches being repaired, and more ministers, better paid. If we were talking about the theatre we would say bigger audiences, more tickets sold, greater success for actors and the authors of comedies and drama. But the church is not a theatre, although it is an industry. It is an economic space for human relationships ruled by theological models which are metaphors of known models of production, or in contrast to such models but rooted in them. Church and theology find it difficult to structure their praxis outside, for instance, models of the western medieval family. This model of the family as an economic unit has been projected into a moral, divine structure, and even 'read' in the biblical texts! Our issue-based theologies never thought that starting by challenging that structure, a whole more transformative praxis of the church could follow.

The Radical Reformation was a revolution against church and theology as structured at the time, but more than that it was an economic revolution. That was the problem. The ideologues of this world care very little about presbyteries and elders or popes and bishops per se. What they care about is that economic thought is not de-sacralized. Traditions in theology have much to do with this system. However, in recent years, Liberation Theologies have become the enemies of the success model of the capitalist churches. Militant churches are made up of minorities, and even if para-ecclesial structures such as Basic Communities exist, they do not necessarily contribute to the prosperity of the structural churches in people or in finances. Theologies from militant churches do not establish dialectics, church/theology, but they are rather people-centred. They are closer to producing a *kenosis* approach, a self-emptying of industrial categories in theology and in the church. It is a marginal discourse which does not exchange goods of metaphysical well-being for hunger and discrimination, and it is not concerned with the survival of the church as institution, but rather with its de-institutionalization. From this perspective, church and theology may be working not to support each other but to undermine each other in order to make space for a second coming of different forms of working together, challenging systems not from within the system but from its margins, and remaining there. The mutual needs of church and theology are their need to survive and support ideologies in power, and if in struggle against them it is curious how easily they lose the proper definition of churches and theology. Thus a Feminist Theology, a Liberation Theology, a *Sista* Theology are not the proper marketable thing, and even if sold to a European market as novelties, they are sold as oddities. In the same way, six neighbours organized in a Basic Community are not really a church, because outside the system there is no salvation. Churches need theologies and theology needs the churches and both need and are needed by an ideological system. To stop this vicious circle will simply require another formulation, that is, the churches need to be people-centred (and not vice versa) and theology needs to be people's praxis without the expectations of the theological market. It is only by excluding themselves from the logics of the market that theology and church can work together, not around their mutual needs but around the needs defined by those who used to be considered the clientele of churches. They are the excluded of our society and discourses of God refer to them from centrally based assumptions of what faith and the church are. The church, as an institution, is doomed to extinction because institutions do not survive the ideological discourses which made them. Theology as part of the systematic discourse of western philosophy is, thank God, much contested. Indeed, these old forms of being church and doing theology need each other, but nobody else does. God herself has been marginal to this debate and, paradoxically, to put her back will demand decentring and marginalizing the debate, changing the partners in the dialogue and their power relations. That will be 'a second coming of the Spirit' in the disruption of the present theological industry and their creating needs and selling goods of salvation. Then the church will not need theology, nor vice versa, but people defining needs and relationships in their own terms and from the margins.

8

Doing the Theology of Memory:
Counting Crosses and Resurrections

Resurrection as a community issue

How do people resurrect? In a future moment outside history and with trumpets and angels coming from heaven? Or in the tension of the present, but 'not-yet-among-us', Reign of God?

Latin American art and poetry are full of images of resurrection. The popular painters from Nicaragua depict the resurrection of the body, with the familiar faces of people killed during the revolution leaving their graves. They are wearing jeans and shirts, smiling at each other, and giving us the impression of a community resurrecting from death. The fact is that Jesus' resurrection was also a community event: women and men witnessed how he came back from death, walked among them and continued the dialogue which existed before his crucifixion. Every death changes the life of the survivors, because some humanity is removed from them, so it is legitimate to think that, starting with Jesus' resurrection, a whole community of people who suffered his loss when he was crucified came back to life again. Their eyes were opened in the sense that death took on another meaning; the resurrection became the paradigm showing us the durability and indestructibility of life and justice.

Nobody resurrects alone: we all resurrect in community

We were reading the Bible, praying and reading the newspaper at the same time, in the disorderly fashion so typical of small community groups in Latin America. Someone had brought a brief editorial article written by Gustavo Gutiérrez called 'News of the Cross and Resurrection', in which the Peruvian theologian reflected on the death of the martyrs of El Salvador: Segundo Montes, Amando López, Joaquín López y López, Ignacio Martín-Baró, Ignacio Ellacuría, Juan Ramón Moreno, Julia Elba Ramos and Celina Ramos.

From El Salvador we have received news of the Cross . . . from a country with such a meaningful name ('The Saviour'). The Jesuits and the two women were threatened and killed because of their testimony to justice. From El Salvador we also received news of resurrection, materialised by the strength of the Holy Spirit. The good news of the resurrection.[1]

After this reading an old woman said that perhaps we do not die alone, because we are all part of a community; whenever someone dies in the community, the community also dies a little. In fact, El Salvador died every day with every brother and sister murdered. Things cannot be the same again after a death in the community, but as the death is shared, so, the hope is, will be the resurrection.

The contribution of the Theology of Memory

The women of El Salvador exemplify what it means for Christian people to be the witnesses of the cross and the resurrection, and this is one of the most important contributions to the action and reflection process of Liberation Theology in Latin America. This is a Theology of Memory, counting crosses and resurrections, and it is being developed by poor women in Latin America. Theirs is an obstinate exercise in the belief in life amid death squads and the politics of hunger and dehumanization, which produces infinite forms of little everyday deaths in the life of the poor. Dead dreams and plans for a better future are resurrected by a community of women remembering. They are part of a wider community of Latin American women who are still claiming the bodies of their dead, such as the *Madres de Plaza de Mayo* in Argentina and the widows of Guatemala. Even their white head scarves have come to characterize 'the ones who remember'. But remembrance is also memorial and celebration, three elements which are closely associated in the Scriptures as belonging to the communitarian creed of the people of God.

Towards a collective women's Theology of Memory

The stories shared by the Salvadorean women are about the essentially collective act of doing theology by women survivors of the years of war and pain in El Salvador. It has elements of remembrance, but as part of a reflection which is projected on to the future, to the utopia of the Kingdom that is created from everyday life, with its tragedy but also its simplicity. By calling it a 'collective women's theology' we

---

[1] Cf. G. Gutiérrez, 'Noticias de Cruz y Resurrección', *Páginas* 100, Lima, Dec. 1989, pp. 6–7.

engage in reclaiming the theological validity of the praxis of the poor, in this case poor women of El Salvador. Basically the Theology of Memory is a methodology, a walk which starts with the silenced history of the poor women in Latin America, finds in them 'that of God' present (what we can call resurrections, that is, the presence of God in the memories of life and death) and continues the path begun by Liberation Theology. The sources of reflection are life itself from the perspective of women living under political, socio-economic, domestic and military violence. The reading of the Bible is done 'outside the Bible', through the search for motives, motivating life events, and what have been called 'events of liberation' which coincide with other events of liberation in the Scriptures such as exodus or the resurrection event, for example. This women's popular theology is basically hermeneutical; that is, it interprets the word and the world simultaneously. At the same time it is dialogical, because it is done in a participative way in community, and has elements of openness to new understandings which have become part of processes of social and spiritual transformation.

A Theology of Memory becomes a theology of blossoming

A poor person blossoms when they feel they count for something.

(Ernestina Rivera[2])

There are two kinds of 'popular theology'. Both are pertinent to the life and needs of the poor, but the theological subject differs. There is a popular theology developed with the poor by professional theologians, rescuing key issues from their lives as a basis for a theological reflection related to their everyday experience of deprivation and suffering. This type of theology requires a serious commitment on the theologian's part to what Leonardo Boff has called 'a call to evangelical poverty', that is, becoming poor as part of a theological option.[3] The results of such theological processes are usually politically mobilizing and transformative; the elements of denunciation of injustices and the annunciation of the Good News are an important part of the ongoing conscientization[4] which this theology carries with it. Sisters

---

[2] From Maria López Vigil, *Piezas para un Retrato* (San Salvador: UCA, 1993).

[3] Cf. L. Boff and C. Boff, *Introducing Liberation Theology* (Maryknoll, NY: Orbis Books, 1987), pp. 48ff.

[4] Concientization is a concept developed by the Brazilian educator Paulo Freire which refers to processes of awareness-raising among the poor, as part of literacy or post-literacy campaigns. These processes include a questioning of the reality from political, sociological, cultural, religious and anthropological perspectives. Cf. P. Freire, *Pedagogy of the Oppressed* (London: Penguin, 1993), ch. 2.

Peggy O'Neill and Jean Ryan are an example of that kind of conscientization work done with the people. This includes a biblical reading that it is discussed with people and guided reflections.

The other type of 'popular theology' is also transformative and *conscientizadora*, but it is not developed by professional theologians choosing poverty as an evangelical option. Instead, it is worked out by the poor themselves. Such a theology usually presents a challenge not only to structures of oppression, but to Christianity itself owing to its critical stance arising from the historical experiences of the poor in Latin America. In other words, this is a critical Theology of Memory done from the underside of history. This is the theology which 'makes people blossom', because it restores the principle of the authority of the believers, and respects their right to express their particular experience of God in their lives, according to their cultures, traditions and political circumstances. This 'theology of blossoming' is the one lived by women in El Salvador.

'Blossoming' is the metaphor for a women's theology characterized by changes, growth, transformation and, especially, for a corporeal theology born out of women's bodies and their suffering during the war. Memories blossom and produce new actions and reflections, going from the crosses women have counted on mass graves to the annunciation of the community resurrection. The characteristics of this theology of blossoming coming from the reflections of the women in El Salvador are:

1. the distinctiveness of the theological subject of reflection, which is women, and communities seen through women's eyes; the theological focus they use for their reflections, and the theological method where 'memory' is a key category;
2. the 'action–reflection–action' circle, and the efficacy of this theological process: for instance, the consequences of their reflections in terms of a new ecclesiology, that is, a new way of being church.

Women of El Salvador: their theological focus

What, then, are the theological resources used in the circle of action and reflection illustrated by the women of El Salvador? Some distinctive elements are how they use the Bible and the new way of interpreting old traditions of the church. However, it would be interesting to consider whether the Bible has been used by all the women or by an educated minority under special circumstances, for instance, under the leadership of priests or religious sisters.

The testimonies on the use of the Bible

Sister Mark spoke about the situation in Gotera, Morazán, during the days of the war and the lack of opportunities in formal education. For instance, a woman called María confessed that she did not know how to read or write, and joined the Bible study group only to hear the readings and to write the Word of God 'in her heart'. Another woman, Lucía B, comments that she cannot say much about the Bible because she is not 'well educated'. In Latin America, for poor communities who are illiterate in Spanish, the reading of the Bible is perceived as exclusive to the educated priesthood, and carries with it the authority and prestige of the well-off people with education. When Mercedes Cañas talks about the miserable conditions of life of women in some regions of El Salvador where they 'sit on a stone, with another stone in their hand, crushing olive stones one by one', because after the war their poverty is even more extreme, she is indirectly questioning Christianity as well as raising issues of extreme deprivation. Therefore, is it legitimate to ask what is the place of the Bible as a theological resource for these women?

The question to ask is how representative the reading of the Bible could be among illiterate communities struggling to survive because, as Cañas says, 'from salt upwards everything is a problem'. How can the woman in Nuevo Gualcho find time or energy for Bible studies after her long day of washing in the river and grinding corn to make tortillas for her family? Yet it seems that the Bible has a place, although different groups use it in different ways. Educated or not, the key point is that they all start to 'read' the Bible first of all 'outside the Bible', that is, from their *realidad*.[5] Their lives become a living text where God manifests Godself, and, from there, the events of liberation in the Scripture are rescued and reflected upon in a circle of '*realidad*–Bible–*realidad*'.

Reading the Bible 'outside the Bible'

The Base Community of San Antonio Abad is an example of women doing theology through Bible study groups, which also includes the reading of texts such as selected documents from the Roman Catholic Church. Sister Mark and Sister Jean followed Carlos Mesters' approaches for their study programmes, that is, a dialogue which includes people's experiences interwoven with the experiences of the poor in the biblical texts.[6]

---

[5] *Realidad* is a concept that in Spanish goes beyond the English translation of 'reality'. *Realidad* includes the notion of the present situation but also the historical developments which have contributed to it.

[6] See Carlos Mesters, *Defenceless Flower: A New Reading of the Bible* (London:

The *rezadoras* ('prayer ladies'), such as Rosy, use the Bible in their rosary prayer meetings in a radical way. Rosy has developed a popular liturgy which includes praying with the Scriptures, understanding how to relate the texts to the *realidad* and using her guitar and music as vehicles to communicate with people beyond words. The fiestas are occasions to dance and sing. They became liturgical when Rosy asked people to join her in the prayer of the rosary while reflecting in their reality of their country. Rosy called for a political reflective rosary prayed in community.

Their *realidad* was the *realidad* of the war: fleeing from the massacres through the mountains, and experiencing all sorts of suffering related to their attempt to escape their pursuers, leaving behind their homes and villages. This was called *la guinda,* and became a theological focus for a reflection on death and resurrection.

The guinda[7]

The *guinda* seems to be a real-life example of the biblical paradigm of exodus. Lucía O, sharing her experience of the *guinda* from Cuscatlán to Santa Ana, never mentions the Exodus paradigm, although the story reminds us of the flight of the Hebrews pursued by the Egyptian troops. A professional theologian could have related the events described in Exodus to the flight from Cuscatlán: the pharaoh's soldiers would be represented by 12,000 soldiers sent to kill the people from Cuscatlán in the 'Guazapa 10' Operation; the leadership of Moses, by the *muchachos* (boys) who asked the community to leave; the presence of the pillar of cloud and fire would become the constant words of the *muchachos*: 'Keep going, keep going . . .' However, the community which escaped through the mountains reflected theologically not on exodus but on death and resurrection. They took the story of Luke 8.42, because the community experienced death, and yet they were spared. The theology of blossoming seems to find in 'life' a permanent focus of theological reflection and renewal. The old memories of liberation in the Bible find new meaning among the poor. The women from El Salvador understood their experience of the *guinda* in the light of the miracles of the New Testament, passing from death to life, in a paradigm of community resurrection.

CIIR/Orbis Books, 1989), where he recounts the methods used in Brazil to read the Scriptures with the people.

[7] *Guinda* is the name given by civilian Salvadoreans to the escape they made into the mountains when persecuted by troops or paramilitary.

The living tradition of the church

The text of the Bible is read not only in relation to life, but in a permanent elaboration of the traditions of the Roman Catholic Church. These women stress the living tradition of the church, by the way they reflect on their faith in relation to the war. For instance, the prayer to the saints for protection, characteristic of the popular religiosity of the poor in Latin America, becomes a prayer and reflection on the lives of the contemporary saints who have laid down their lives working for the Reign of God, through the pursuit of justice and peace.

Bernarda gives testimony of how she prayed to the 'blessed blood of Monseñor Romero' for deliverance from the massacre of Amatitán. As part of the process of reading the Bible 'outside the Bible', the blood of a just man appeals to God for justice. In this case, the Abel of Genesis 4.10 is Monseñor Romero whose blood cries out to God for the crimes against the people of El Salvador. This blood from Romero protecting Bernarda and her child is then a visible sign of justice and, at the same time, a sign of the resurrection of the martyred saints among the people.

Another example is the story of the alcoholic helping at the graveside of the woman 'who never failed to give him a tortilla'. Here solidarity has also become a sign of living faith in Christ. The tradition of the church concerning miracles becomes tangible in the life of the community through the testimonies of solidarity and hope. The historical testimonies of miracles in the life of the church are not remembered because for these communities 'God is a God of the living, and not of the dead' (Luke 20.38).

Solidarity as part of the living tradition of the church produces the development of popular organization. Popular organizations renew the traditions of the church structures. In Base Christian Communities and in popular organizations such as the Widows' Group formed by Dolores or the Women's Group of Andrea in Usulatán, the reading of the Bible goes together with the reading of the *realidad* of a country at war, and the conviction that God wants God's people to live a life where their human rights are respected. 'Human rights' becomes, then, a theological focus of reflection and a very important part of this living tradition of the church.

Theological method

The key theological category used by these women is 'memory'. Memory functions as the element that orders the hermeneutical circle of interpretation of the Scripture and also as the project for the future. Memory is used to relate to the past, to interpret life in the light of faith and past experiences; to the present, to make meaningful an existence with such a deep knowledge of suffering; and to the future, to think about the utopia of the Reign of God in terms of what is known about the actions of God in their recent history. Lucía recalls how, in the flight from the Cuscatlán massacre, many in the group 'saw God', that is, they knew God in a concrete way, as if God was also in the *guinda* with them. Memory, then, provides us with the following theological aspects:

1. Memory gives women a community identity and a religious identity. They remember who they are through key issues such as their gifts of organization, courage and the obstinate faith which refused to accept the power of war as superior to God's power.

2. Memory provides women with concrete focuses of reflection. One of these focuses is on women's bodies. Women are the ones who suffered their wombs being opened, as María Julia F tells, and the cruelty of torture directed against their sexuality. Suyapa remembers how women fled to the mountains with their children. Lucía flees with her mother-in-law and her baby born two hours before the escape through the grass, without food or water. Violence hit the whole community, but women's bodies were hit even harder through hunger, torture focused on their sexuality and sufferings related to maternity. However, Doña Isabel reminds the community that, after the war, 'women are raped even in their own homes', and now they organize themselves against domestic violence.

3. Memory, as a key for the simultaneous interpretation of the Bible and the *realidad*, produces an ethical reading of culture, religion and ideologies. In the same way that the writers of the Scriptures reflected theologically on their historical events, and discerned from them the ways of God in their life, the women of El Salvador identified issues of culture such as *machismo* which they found un-Christian; they also criticized patriarchal church traditions. *Machismo* is a key element identified in their reflections, in relation to structures of power (ideology) and the construction of religious belief in Central America. Julia and her community read Isaiah 58 and Hosea 3 from that perspective.

The action–reflection–action circle

The main areas of the action–reflection–action circle are found in the development of a new spirituality, liturgy and community ethics.

Spirituality. The spirituality has been described by Nelly del Cid as 'nomadic'. Nelly considers it a spirituality on the move, not settled, with elements of expectation and discovery in this walk with God which is their theology. If the Theology of Liberation has been described as a *caminata* (a walk), then its spirituality should also be constantly moving forward. For Nelly, this is an essentially feminine walk, because she sees the Holy Spirit as the feminine presence of God, constantly challenging the church and Christianity. Sister Patricia Farrell from Suchitoto also considers that we are now living in the age of the Holy Spirit, which is essentially free, and gives us back the feminine face of God in a new way of being church in Central America. 'God came with these women', says Lucía O in her theological remembrance of the action of the religious sisters during the war. The solidarity and courage of the sisters gave the people the concreteness of the presence of a living God among them. Moreover, this is the presence of the feminine face of God manifested through the faithfulness of religious women.

This spirituality is then reflected in a new ecclesiology, described by Mercedes as a non-hierarchical and democratic structure of the church. This new way to organize the church takes from the feminist movement a horizontal, participative nature, which is identified as the work of the Holy Spirit in our time.

Liturgy. The liturgy which accompanies this new ecclesiology has 'fewer words' and incorporates women's experiences such as breast-feeding, as in the liturgies developed by Sister Patricia Farrell with her community. The courageous attitude of women during the war, challenging the 'principalities and powers' of the time, was inspired by a Jesus described as a 'big mouth' denouncing injustices and announcing the Reign of God. The prophet of the Hebrew Scriptures has been described in popular terms as the rebel who refuses to shut up when confronting injustices. Interestingly, this also has liturgical consequences. Doña Isabel tells how fasting in the church has been incorporated as part of a living tradition of the church, and a liturgy for justice. The fasting she describes produced a transference of land that the community reclaimed, and also the formation of a committee to investigate murders committed. Since liturgy is the celebration of the presence of Christ among the people, praying and fasting now become part of the liturgical life of the persecuted, crucified church. However, the fasting and praying are not only done in the church. The *guinda* also includes a form of 'fasting' when whole communities fled without food, and sustained themselves by prayer and solidarity. The liturgy of the church has given way to the liturgy of life. The women share their ministry with their communities, celebrating life by refusing to accept death without resurrection.

Community ethics. Finally, the community ethics elaborated by these women concentrates on issues of violence, *machismo*, undemocratic structures in the church and in the government and on family issues. *Machismo* is denounced as the main ideological root underlying domestic and state violence, and in the hierarchical, non-participative clerical and governmental organizations which obstruct the reconstruction of El Salvador after the war.

Family is an issue of increasing interest in Central American theology.[8] Families were divided during the war, and in some cases a member of one's own family could become an enemy. Some women even left their families, losing their support during critical times when their vocation of solidarity for their people became a religious vocation too. Paradoxically, their religious community did not always become a family either. The family then seems to begin to be redefined in what constitutes it. The vocation to join the people's struggle is a vocation of love for a family which exceeds the links of blood and membership of an organization, because the links of compassion and the prophetic vocation to follow the 'big mouth' Jesus are stronger.

The future of the theology of blossoming

This is the case where the past is the future. Sandra reflects on the subversive memory of the people as the key for a future dreamt by the women during the war. A future where women and men could work together in community, and solidarity would flourish against individualism, lack of hope and indifference. A future where hope will overcome the disillusionment produced by the fact that, after the war, so little seems to be gained in terms of the right to a dignified life, and greater security for women who are still threatened by the ghost of old *machista* values, taken for granted before the war, but not any more. Nidia Díaz has said, 'I don't want to go back to making tortillas', because the tortillas they made during the war were of a different kind. Those were tortillas of theological, political and cultural praxis for change. Their ingredients were courage, faith, strength in the organization of the community and a critical awareness concerning the role of the church in Central America. They also gave as a gift to the world a way of doing 'real theology' (as Sister Peggy O'Neill called it, because Liberation Theology always has its starting point in reality), which may encourage women of other continents to do their own theology of blossoming, to go with them in their everyday lives and to transform Christianity in this, the *kairos* of women, and of poor women of Central America. A *kairos* where people see God 'coming with those women' who showed their obstinate solidarity during

---

[8] Cf. for instance, 'The Pastoral Challenge of the Latin American Family' in *Latin American Pastoral Issues*, CELEP, Year XVIII, 1994.

the war, and keep showing it afterwards, in the struggle to remain faithful to the example of Monseñor Romero and the multitude of anonymous saints of Central America. A *kairos* which is telling us that resurrection and theology are community issues and women's issues among the poor but wise women of El Salvador.

This chapter was originally published in M. Best and P. Hussey, *Life out of Death. The Feminine Spirit in El Salvador* (London: CIIR 1996), pp. 194–206.

9

Gustavo Gutiérrez Goes to Disneyland:
Theme Park Theologies and the Diaspora of the Discourse of the Popular Theologian in Liberation Theology

In [Latin] America, the theologian is defined by her/his knowledge of the processes of liberation . . . It is very difficult in Latin America to conceive of a theologian reflecting at the margin of some engagement in the struggle for liberation, as has happened in Europe.

Diez and García, 1989, p. 56

Six men play the leads in the grand opening of Haiti's incinerator. The six are burning as a punishment and as a lesson. They have buried the images of Christ and the Virgin that Fray Ramón Pane left them for protection and consolation. Fray Ramón taught them to pray . . . and to invoke the name of Jesus . . . [but] the [natives] buried the images because they were hoping that the gods would fertilise their fields of corn, cassava, boniato and beans.

Galeano, 1995, p. 69

So where have all the 'natives' gone? They have gone between the defiled image and the indifferent gaze.

Chow, 1993, p. 54

Transversal definitions

By 'Liberation Theology' I refer in this essay to the classical Latin American theology of liberation, with its universalist tendencies, as developed from the 1970s. Such theology is defined as a theological orthopraxis of economic and political liberation, contextualized in the experience of Latin American political and economic oppression and the struggle for social transformation and liberation. Traditionally, Liberation Theology had a limited hermeneutics of suspicion, although more recently cultural, sexual and racial elements have been incorporated. However, such incorporation seems to follow the conception of a linear theological journey, without the disruptions and fluctuations that a postcolonial hermeneutics would entail.

By 'Postcolonial Theology' I refer to the criticisms of that way of theologizing imposed by the western world as theology. The postcolonial theological project shares elements of the liberationist one but problematizes such categories as 'the poor' and 'indigenous theology' because it is distrustful of the continuation of the western ontology as the theoretical subject of theology.

By 'Diasporic Theology' I mean the postcolonial discourse that emphasizes the displacement or the erring in Liberation Theology as a sort of meta-postcolonial discourse characterized by identity in instability and geographical conflict. This is the place where we can discuss the conceptual joint construction of Liberation Theology from Latin America and the North Atlantic as a metadiscourse on the politics of deviancy in postcolonial Liberation Theology. Latin America is not the destiny (by geographical determination) of Liberation Theology but one of the many sites where the promiscuity of a disseminated theological discourse travels.

In this essay my aim is to engage in these three standpoints transversally, that is, opening up borderline points of agreement and departure and seeing how conceptualizations sometimes co-exist even if in opposition. My objective is to reflect on the 'popular theologian' as the interpreter of the Bible in Latin America from a diasporic perspective, questioning the construction of his or her identity outside the colonial North Atlantic discourse of theological expectations. The popular theologian is not a person in diaspora but rather the conceptual product of Liberation Theology in the diaspora of the theological markets of Europe and the United States. Therefore, it is of utmost importance to clarify and reflect on the hybridity of the popular theologian trajectory in order to untangle the postcolonial project of interpretation 'of the word and the World'.

On differences and *différance*: from liberating theology to postcolonial suspicion

The new gods of Fray Ramón Pane's story in the sixteenth century did not fertilize the soil of Abya-Yala.[1] No matter how many statues of Jesus and Mary the natives buried, no prosperity came for the

---

[1] Abya-Yala was the original name given by the Kuna of Panama to the continent called Latin America by the *Conquista*. Americus Vespucius was the conquistador who used his own name to name the continent. The emphasis in 'Latin' America obliterates the presence of African cultures, apart from the native cultures of the continent.

children of the Sun God and the Mother Earth. Unfortunately, it was only their own native blood, poured out during the genocide of the *Conquista* that fertilized the land, bringing prosperity and untold riches to the western Christian invaders. This was the sixteenth-century Gospel of European Prosperity, a gospel that the Roman Catholic Church in the renamed Latin American continent kept faithfully through centuries of alliances between church and state powers.

However, religious structures are symbolic figurations that change meaning according to the prevalent forces in the field of economic production. The crisis of the 1950s in Latin America, including the triumph of the Cuban Revolution in 1959, produced a change of consciousness in the continent's perception of both the ethos of theology and the role of the church in the continent. This was the beginning of the liberationist movement, which became prosperous in legends, because legend-making is part of the traditional way of cultural appropriation of the West. Legend-making was part of the process of understanding of the new theological thought coming from the South. Legends are made up of several stories unified by a male or female central character. The legend of the popular theologian as community theologian was drawn within a picturesque contrast involving, on the one hand, the community-committed, barefoot academic from the South reading the Bible with the poor and, on the other hand, the proper North Atlantic theologian made of books and university research. Unfortunately, the legend, wrapped with quasi-ontological myths about Latin Americans and poverty, was set in a dynamic relation with liberationist discourse and ended up hybridizing it.[2]

The tension that arises in theology from knowledge and a sometimes unrelated practical experience found a path of resolution in a new understanding of the theological role in Liberation Theology, but, once it received the acceptance of the western theological market, the figure of the popular theologian permutated its own boundaries for the diasporic needs of western academics in search of new identities. Although there is partial truth in saying that the popular theologians were opposed in their conceptualization and methodological frame to their North Atlantic counterparts, for the makers of easy discourses on liberation the reality has, unfortunately, been far more complex than this. The so-called split between liberation theologians

---

[2] Here I use the concept of 'hybridity' following Mikhail Bakhtin's idea of the 'dialogic imagination' constituted by the encounter of different linguistic consciousness. From the point of view of cultures, this thought is reflected in the idea that no theology is without transmutations, borrowings and appropriations. Depending on the context, results may be subversive or supportive of the status quo (1981, pp. 358–60).

and North Atlantic theologians obeyed a dialectic not of *différance* but of differences in mutual dependency.

North Atlantic theology and Third World Liberation Theology may have a long history of differences, but not of *différances*, because there is no deferral of meaning in theological praxis. *Différance* may have done theology with the buried statues of Christ and the Virgin Mary, while differences made an implicit theological contract based on agreements and compromises with the central (western) discourse of faith. If it is right to say that there has been an epistemological difference in theology during the past decades, given the takeover of the traditional idealism of the West by a materialist methodology, it must also be acknowledged that the differences were not substantial but rather reconciliatory in nature. The popular theologian was the key figure in this process of adaptation whereby theology was not de-centred but relocated in the context of cultures of poverty. The narratives of the 'theologian from the poor', the 'Christ of the poor' and 'theology from poverty' never de-centred Christian western theology but rather adapted it more successfully. Indeed, the very possibility of dividing theologies into two groups, such as 'bad ones' (North Atlantic) and 'good ones' (Third World Liberation), or vice versa, shows the degree of dualism in the discourse of the divine and historical scene in which this discourse is still grounded. Such dualism, in the long term, does not help the cause of liberation, because the mechanisms of dependency are perpetuated in repetitive models, Pavlovian models – a sort of resurrection paradigm of the western style of obsessive classification and moralization of ideas and behaviours.

Context: 'theme parks' of theology

Theology is returning to the hands of its true makers.

Fraser and Fraser, 1986, p. 46

Here youth may savour the challenge and promise of the future.

Disneyland, Dedication Plaque, July 1995

The discourses about the poor, with their constitutive dualism, have been contested in recent years, even within the inner circles of Liberation Theology. 'The poor' as the subject of Latin American theology functioned as a Metaphysics of Presence or abstract authority obliterating the contradictions that gender, sexuality and race introduce in the analysis of the poor masses. A metatheological discourse is now limiting universals while opening the liberationist understanding of reality. This metadiscourse is a form of postcolonial theology with elements of a diasporic theological critique which acknowledges that the conceptualization processes of Latin American Liberation Theology have never been as stable as the constructions done from western academic circles wanted the public to believe.[3]

Postcolonial Theologies go further than liberationist ones because their quest is to dehegemonize multiple bodies, such as human bodies in the discursive limits of sexuality, for instance, but also bodies of knowledge, including cultural and economic knowledge. Liberationists share partially in the dehegemonization process of the postcolonial project. A theology done from our own people's cultures is at the root of this process, but the split comes when Liberation Theology considers western Christian faith and the systematization of theology as a natural or given in the process of doing theology. Liberationists are happy to find in the Bible Christ as the liberator of the poor but not to accept the deconstruction of Christ the subject, who, in some forms of popular religiosity in Latin America, emerges as a woman, the child of a dying mother, a corpse who walks, or even multitudes instead of an individual.[4] Moreover, there is the fact that sometimes Christ *is not*, because the constructed Christian Christ has not been able to join people's symbolic processes, to the point that it can no longer be claimed to be compatible with traditional methodological frames of understanding God. Such is the case, for instance, in a theology of the Dirty War in Argentina, as it reflects on torture and the function of eucharistic rituals in concentration camps and detention centres (Graziano, 1992). The Basic Ecclesial Communities (BECs) show that liberationists can improve the structures of the church but not replace them with traditional indigenous forms of community religious organization or new alternatives coming from the experience of workers, guerrilla movements or popular women's organizations.

Perhaps the most important thing to understand is that Post-colonial Theologies have unmasked the fact that western theological discourse works by simulation. For instance, to simulate spiritual and

---

[3] The issue of Latin American theological identity in North Atlantic discourse follows the same rules of any process of essentializing colonial identities. The main characteristic is bodily (or geographical) fixation, which deauthorizes any contradictory sign of the fixed identity or mutations produced. The 'Otherness' of Liberation Theology is therefore an object of codification, seldom of disruption. An example of this is the discourse of 'the poor' and the photographs and artistic perceptions of 'the poor'. One may think that the poor in Latin America use uniforms, speak the same language, have the same beliefs, and look the same.

[4] For instance, in Argentina, *Santa Librada* is a female crucified Christ. See M. Althaus-Reid, *Indecent Theology: Theological Perversions in Sex, Gender and Politics* (London: Routledge, 2000), pp. 83–7.

structural western reality among Latin Americans is a task that accentuates hegemonic divine productions, such as theological discourses. However, Liberation Theologies have been forced to participate in the simulation process in a subtle way, because their ultimate authority still lies in the central church structure of the West and in the academic centres of Europe and the United States. From that perspective, Liberation Theology becomes a sort of 'theme park' of theology, variously characterized as 'Latin American Theology', 'Indigenous Theology' or 'Latin American Women's Theology'. These are interesting theological subthemes worthy of being visited, and people in the West are encouraged to visit them as if going to a botanical garden. Such a theme park conception thwarts pluralism. It may be the theology of the poor, but it still obeys the tradition of the thinking and logic of the centre, and, although in opposition, it perpetuates the centre's discourse by default. It is the visitor to the theme park who carries meaning to the product. Moreover, the fact of being presented as a theme park accentuates the imaginary aspect of the construction of regional theologies. They highlight by their mere native presence the fact that real theologies are elsewhere, and, as such, may be called 'theologies at the margins' in more than one sense.

Liberation Theologies as theme parks function at the level of popular attractions and have done a lot for the book market of the western world, as an extension of the capitalist market of theological production of goods. Crafts, fashion, books, food, posters and a collection of popular travel anecdotes have been marketed in Europe and the United States as products of the 'theology of liberation'. All these productions work at the level of expressive symbols organized in the following way: the centrepiece of theological thinking is constituted by systematic western theology, and it is done even if in opposition. The theme parks, in the case of Liberation Theology, are divided into subthemes, such as 'Marxist Theology', 'Evangelical Theology', 'Indigenous Theology', 'Feminist Theology' – all of them with a central unifying theme ending with 'and the poor'. The true makers of the future of Disneyland ideology and the true makers of theology as seen by the Frasers share a common illusion of being equals in a dream of being different.

Capitalist codes: a key for a further analysis of theological theme parks

Liberation Theology as a theme park theology is the natural context of the popular theologian. The western understanding of productivity homologizes at a certain level the work of the popular theologian as the one who produces things with theological ideas. 'To produce things' means to continue with an understanding and approval of a system of theological production, but, since the concept of poverty used by Liberation Theology came from dependency theory, the popular theologian was defined as independent of church and state structures of control. This is the meaning of the concept of the theologian living among the poor.

The focus of this construction of the theologian's identity in Liberation Theology was political and cultural decentralization, with certain limits applied to the understanding of faith according to orthodoxy, classical church organization, and so forth. From there the image of the Roman Catholic priest or Protestant minister who lives with the poor and reads the Bible with them while engaged politically emerged powerfully not only in Latin America but also in Europe and in the United States. Stress was put on the simplicity of people's faith and community sharing of the gospel and on how the popular theologian simply reflected that. At this point, the popular theologian's reflection was never his or her own but the people's reflection. The popular theologian was a mirror who reflected images from the poor, a mirror that 'gives a visible image to the invisible people' who were outside the theological market at the time. The relation of production was thus a peculiar one.

The popular theologian became the intermediary of the free-market society, the parasite who gave 'a voice to the voiceless' as if without his or her presence the poor could not speak. That has never been the case in Latin America, but the fear of theological misconstructions lay behind the role of the popular theologians. Clodovis Boff wrote extensively about the risk of *bricolage*[5] or producing 'a carnival of meaning' by allowing poor people in the BECs to read the Scriptures without the guidance of Christian (Roman Catholic) traditions and proper methodology (Boff and Boff, 1987, p. 139). Such is Boff's terror of the voice of the voiceless that he demands that such popular readings of the Bible be done with a method he devised ('correspondence of relationship') and the continuous use of church traditional teaching and hermeneutic tradition. Therefore, the popular theologian becomes the 'punk' whose father sells the safety pins punks use in their ears.

This is not to say that popular theologians did not have any genuine commitment to and engagement with social changes. Obviously, they did and still do, but these end with reformism or, to put it in another

---

[5] Clodovis Boff misunderstood Claude Lévi-Strauss's concept of *bricolage*. For Lévi-Strauss it is a positive concept that expresses the multiplicity of materials to be used for a symbolic construction, but Boff interprets it negatively as a *vale todo* ('everything is valid'). This shows Boff's fear of multivocal theological dialogue and the failure of his liberation theological assumptions. See C. Boff, *Theology and Praxis: Epistemological Foundations* (Maryknoll, NY: Orbis Books, 1987), p. 136.

way, with the way we do the marketing of theology to include a vast public that was outside our reach. I have said elsewhere that no guerrilla group in Latin America has ever been called 'The Prophet Isaiah' or 'The Gospel of the Alternative Kingdom Movement', but rather *Tupac-Amaru, Tupamaros* or *Montoneros* – names associated with indigenous rebellious movements of no religious origin. However, this does not diminish the religious role of resistance and its importance for revolutionary movements, as far as its preoccupation is related not only to the self-perpetuation of a western-based definition of what theology is and the role of the theologian but also to the underlying methodological and logical assumptions, which in reality are productive assumptions.

Unfortunately, a touristic theological industry existed and created much confusion, in the sense that this industry became part of an academic imaginary. However, my claim is that the popular theologian has been and still is real, but under permanent construction with regard to his or her role, and that it is important to analyse the mythological shift in that construction. The popular theologian has been and still is a priest or minister, living in poverty, doing community work in a slum while teaching in a seminary or working in a parish, and reflecting and acting with the people. Eventually, they might produce a book or not. I had lecturers in my own seminary in Buenos Aires during the early 1980s who performed all these roles at the same time, for little or no pay at all. They went to jail; they confronted the military state; they disappeared and suffered torture and death.

However, at the margins of life, there is a non-coincidental discourse, such as the academic one, that builds narratives like that of the popular theologian and not always in concordance with reality. The popular theologian, as a key classical performer of Liberation Theology, is in reality a hybrid construction between native and European discourse, concerning not only the task of theology but the shifts of definitions from the modern to the postmodern paradigm. To call it 'hybrid' does not connote a pejorative meaning but indicates tensions in the construction of identity and fidelities. What we define today as a popular theologian has changed and has been transformed during the past ten years. More importantly still, this has been done mostly independently of the historical experience of popular theologians, such as Gustavo Gutiérrez. To observe and analyse such conceptual changes provides us with interpretive clues with which to understand elements in Liberation Theology that became more postcolonial than liberationist and, in the end, to identify how diasporic thought, as part of a metatheology of liberation, has challenged the scene even further.

However, we are not fully in the presence of a Postcolonial or Diasporic Systematic Theology. Postcolonial and Diasporic Theologies are of a dispersed nature, because, in essence, they are contrary to the more western notion of systematizing theology. The point is precisely one of opening borders and tunnels under the theoretical constructions of the West, not only in the content of theology but also in challenging the order of submission that lies behind Systematic Theologies. In Systematic Theology we find the quasi-anthropological compulsion of the West for classifying a theory of understanding of God as theology into neat, closed compartments or systems. Is this administrative, taxonomic and colonial order in which historical experiences of some discourse about God and humanity are comprised challenged in postcolonialism and diasporic thought? If so, a reflection on the genesis of theological theme parks should provide us with important clues to consider.

Indeed, such genesis should be seen as a hybrid process. The discourse of the church is a process of production obeying the logic of the formation of capital. Theological categories like 'salvation' or 'revelation' are not disembodied universal truths, captured by some oracular or mediumistic communication with the Sacred, but rather the fruit of labour. Moreover, such categories participate in a process of appropriation of labour and exploitation. In classical North Atlantic theology reflections have followed and have been followed by early assumptions from the industrial model.

Classical liberalism was rooted in a particular anthropology modelled after an atomistic nature. People's object in life, according to Jeremy Bentham, was a negation, the absence of labour and the following of pleasure, with pain and sacrifice to be avoided (1955, p. 341). The moving force for change was to be found only among the higher ranks in a classed society, with the individualistic rather than communitarian aspects of life to be stressed. Theology mirrored that, for I believe that political forces are stronger in modelling society than sacred ones. Thus, theological production stressed sacrifice, pain, individual virtues and, in economic terms, competition and not solidarity with the Other.

Processes of colonization, for instance, are about spiritual competence but also competition. Western Christianity was able to prove that the white race was superior in spiritual terms to other races. Western theology affirmed its identity in a discourse of 'we are the best', which also justified the pillage of the colonies and the fables concocted to explain economic dependency in the twentieth century. Economic and spiritual competition are related discourses of identity, based on perceptions of human relations as competitive. Another element to highlight is Thomas Malthus's population theory in relation with what he thought was the danger of an excessive birth rate on the planet (1981, pp. 179–81). This produced a theology of restriction of sexuality, particularly valid when used with the indigenous people. To be more specific, theology became an industrial enterprise for the production of goods of ideological sustenance as well as of financial sustenance. After all, churches are vast enterprises where capital is accumulated and invested for profit. The churches were the first place where the capital was given a sacred status.

The logic of selling more (theology) and producing less

From a Marxist analysis we can consider that capital accumulation equals the profit of production. In the unjust, exploitative market in which capital acquires a life of its own, the being of capital, as lucidly pointed out by Enrique Dussel in his essay about Marx as a theologian, is at a deeper level the being of a non-being (1993, p. 270). That non-being is that of the exploited person who produced it but became alienated from it and negated, because their working contribution to the making of the capital does not even give its value to the product. The value of a good lies in its utility and not in labour, that is, the work of the producers.

To which capital are we referring here? Systematic Theology is the capital of the church: it contains the doctrine of God and an understanding of religious consciousness. It is the place of orthodoxy. However, dogmatics is based on the historical experience of a community's exploitation and restriction of life under dualistic patriarchal assumptions. The implicit anthropology in western theology comes from an interpretive methodology that excludes the roots of human pain and suffering. Any ontology or projected theology (discourse about God) that has not confronted human alienation as a result of a patriarchal capitalist system has a Systematic Theology made of exploitation. As soon as the church's capital – that now defined as the experience of and quest for God of the exploited masses in the midst of class, racial and sexual struggles – discards its producers, it becomes an abstraction. The capital of the church's dogma is sacralized. For its preservation, multitudes have been sacrificed. Economic interests are tied to ideological ones. Theology becomes a product to sell, but not allowing new producers to come on the scene. No new creative process can occur, except those that somehow come from the original dogmatics and perpetuate its preservation. To sell more and to allow less production means to invest more directly in the capital and not in the people as producers. Thus, dogmatics becomes more ahistorical than transcendent, while method in theology follows a similar pattern.

Liberation Theology wanted to break this economic pattern of making theology as an ideological capital to serve the interest of the elite in power. This was also reflected in the structure of the churches and in their accumulation of material wealth in terms of lands, buildings and investments amid the poverty and destitution of the original producers of theology. Their product, that is, their experiences of God in the midst of a life of exploitation and degradation, was not only denied but turned against them by a theological exchange mechanism. For instance, hard work badly paid was exchanged for the promise of eternal life by the currency of humility and submission. The controllers of theological capital and the system of exchange needed to be challenged. At this point, Liberation Theology started to develop the concept of the popular theologian.

The popular theologian

This was defined as someone who could reflect theologically with and from the experience of the exploited masses in Latin America. In reality, this had started before the Second Vatican Council in a movement called ISAL (Church and Society in Latin America), which had a Marxist political background and was supported by such important theologians as Rubem Alves and José Miguez Bonino. The point was that the theologian should never expropriate the theological praxis of the poor or encourage the alienation of their experiences into a reflection based on an exchange system of immaterial goods for the currency of exploitation, as in the oppressive forms of current theologies. The popular theologian was a Marxist revolutionary, with a praxis oriented towards social change and the compassion and empathy with the poor of such revolutionaries as Ernesto 'Ché' Guevara or Fidel Castro, who did not compromise for the liberation of the people. The theologian then was thought of as the person who worked with the people and reflected and acted with them for the transformation of society. During the late 1960s and early 1970s, that revolutionary figure was based on a Freirean model: the popular theologian as a 'conscientizer'.

It is not coincidental, then, that Liberation Theology, following the Freirean conscientization methodology based on the experience of work in rural areas, started to use a topographic vocabulary. The terms used were 'grass roots'; 'doing theology from below'; 'from the base'; 'with feet on the ground'; 'down to earth'; 'underdogs of history'; 'underground theology'; 'indigenous theologies' (referring to the so-called 'Indian' population of Latin American natives). This was due to the fact that liberationists started to define their work mostly in relation to the Latin American peasant population. This happened at a time when agrarian reform was high on the agenda of the programme for independence. However, if the popular theologian had been defined from the reality of the urban poor, then it would have used border vocabulary: 'margins', 'slums' (*barriadas marginales*), 'street level', and terms associated, for instance, with factories and industrial life. This may be one of the reasons why the popular theologian could not survive ideologically or physically in the cities, and, as in the case of guerrilla movements, was only successful in rural areas. The early Movement of Third World Priests working in cities was persecuted and exterminated, leaving little scope for the continuation of the *guerrillero-priest* role, except in the mountains, as in the case of Camilo Torres. Nevertheless, the priest in the mountains adopted more the role of a guerrilla fighter than a spiritual leader, which was not a popular model to follow, especially among Protestants, who had families dependent on their work.

The popular theologian was a man – for women theology was a forbidden area in Liberation Theology during the 1970s – working in a rural area in some form of conscientization process. However, the concept did not evolve on its own for long, since it became dependent on European theology. In Europe, as in the United States, Latin America has always been seen through the eyes of those who only see *pampas*, horses, *gauchos*, natives and jungles. The image of picturesque faithful Christian natives dressed in colourful attire and cultivating the soil while suffering much exploitation was attractive for European discourse. The faith of the simple people amid their suffering, their interest in the gospel, and the childlike qualities of the native Christian started to be exalted. This image Europe reproduced, especially through books and articles, but also crosses, posters and Christian memorabilia.

Reading the Bible

In academic circles the rereading of the Bible done in the BECs was the key element to publicize. The popular theologian had acquired by now the role of the interpreter of the poor. However, contrary to this belief, the Roman Catholic Church did not encourage the reading of the Bible in the BECs; the Bible was used sparsely, because the BECs were constituted almost completely by illiterate people and the church had not promoted the Bible during its 500 years of existence in Latin America. Carlos Mesters, one of the most honest voices regarding the truth of popular biblical readings, presents us with a picture of readings that were done sporadically and without a particular methodological option (1993, pp. 15–16). This meant that the Bible was, at times, read as an oracle to divine the future, a talisman for good luck, an allegory or literal truth. The allegorical form was approved by European academia, while the literalist forms were ignored.

In Latin America, popular theologians were conscious, as Mesters himself admits, of the risks of biblical interpretations done in a totally spontaneous way. Such spontaneity was mediated by messages received, for example, from the media, with unpredictable results. For instance, I once participated in a popular Bible study in Argentina, where a man claimed that Mary Magdalene, announcing the resurrection of Christ, was not only disbelieved by the apostles but also beaten by them. The minister intervened to read the Scripture again and to prove that this was not the case: Mary Magdalene had not been beaten. However, it transpired that a television drama based on the Gospel had presented a scene where Mary Magdalene was slapped in the face by disbelieving apostles. Even if the Bible did not say so, people were adamant that 'they saw it happening'. When the minister intervened to say that God did not approve of men beating women, people counter-argued that perhaps the Bible was saying that it was fine to beat a woman only if she was considered to be a liar. Just as these interpretations were common, so there were also other forms of reading the Bible among the poor that were more of a dialogue regarding issues of daily life, with an occasional quotation from the Bible by the leader to illustrate the point.

There was little analysis of the role of the media among the poor and marginalized. The problem was that these Bible studies were 'too loose' to be shown as examples of popular interpretation. Liberationists wanted popular readings that could be displayed as examples of the exegesis people could produce. Exegesis obviously depended on many factors, including the literacy level of a group, but the best examples, those that resulted in actions of liberation in the community, were, in general, not worth publishing. In other words, they could not pass the test of western academia. Therefore, in academic circles, the popular theologian needed to be refashioned again as a leader, a guide in the process of people rereading the Scriptures, although books and articles written at the time as 'authentic exegesis from the people' tended to obscure the intervention of the leader and stress spontaneity.

In Europe, that spontaneity was admired. Western academia saw the popular theologian as a benevolent father dealing with ignorant, although sweet and well-disposed, native children. Two discourses, one Latin American and the other European, started to produce the imaginary of the Latin American popular theologian, but in Europe that image was naive and simplistic. No wonder many Europeans tried to use this image to work in their own communities without result. However, it was stressed that the Latin American context was different because Latin American people were different. In popular biblical studies done in Europe, the Latin American native was, then, sadly missed. The European poor were not as simple and as grateful faithful Christians and did not produce the original exegesis of their

Latin American counterparts. Many Europeans would have liked to have submissive, faithful Christian natives in their parishes, instead of real people. In Latin America, however, the discourse was more prudent. Excesses were only the product of confrontation with Europe and the necessity of self-affirmation. In Europe it was thought that there were thousands of popular theologians working with the poor – statistics that were obviously exaggerated, as Gustavo Gutiérrez has pointed out (Gibbs, 1996, p. 369). The BECs did not have the elements to make a Disneyland film of them.

The popular theologian: a new definition

Clodovis and Leonardo Boff produced a book in the late 1980s to help clarify this point. The popular theologian was not to be considered any more the guerrilla priest. At the time, the guerrilla movement had been defeated and dictatorships in Latin America were giving way to a democratic transition. In their book *Introducing Liberation Theology* (1987), obviously aimed at Western students, popular theology is defined as a tree with three main branches: while the roots of the tree consist of the communities of the poor, theological reflection is carried on at three levels – the professional, the pastoral and the popular. It is interesting to notice that at the professional level theological discourse was defined as 'detailed and rigorous', while at the pastoral and popular levels it was considered to be 'organically related to practice . . . diffuse and capillary, almost spontaneous' (1987, p. 13).

Although the Boff brothers make the point that all three levels reflected on the same issues and that their work was interrelated, it becomes evident that the book was an effort to stress that the so-called popular theologian should not be confused with the trained academic, who used, according to the authors, 'the logic of erudition', while the popular theologians used 'the logic of life'. Even the location of the popular theologian needed to be specified. During the 1970s, with the use of conscientization styles of work, the locus of the popular theologian was the BECs; now, this location was contrasted with the academic, as new theological institutes based on Liberation Theology were opened in Latin America. This shift in the conceptualization of the role of the liberation theologian came at the time of the critique of dependency theory. Gutiérrez, in his revised edition of *A Theology of Liberation* (1988), reflects on the impossibility of keeping the categories centre and periphery, as they are too simplistic and ignorant of the complexity of the struggle, but in practice the shift was being produced in order to incorporate the liberationist discourse into the proper realm of western discourse.

Meanwhile, in Europe a number of books written by European

theologians doing their required tour of Latin American BECs illustrate this incorporation while trying to keep the image of the popular
theologian as the prophet of the natives. For instance, Christopher
Rowland and Mark Corner, in their book *Liberating Exegesis* (1990),
present images from slides produced in Brazil under the title of
'Parables of Today'. The popular theologian emerges as the link
between the sufferings of the community and the world of politicians
and paramilitary forces. The context is the state terrorism of Latin
America during the 1970s.

In the slides, the popular theologian assumes different presenta-
tions: a young white man ('the parish priest') and an older, white,
European-looking man called 'the Bishop'. The bishop is responsible
for ordaining a man from the community (who looks racially ambigu-
ous, but more on the side of a white Brazilian than a black one). The
bishop and the priest show how they are able to perform more roles
than reading the Bible with the poor, such as helping people out of jail,
but they look very erudite, serious and well educated (Rowland and
Corner, 1990, p. 9). Both bishop and priest use glasses (probably to
show that they know how to read) and are power figures. There is
almost a coolness in the image of the bishop, in contrast to the community people portrayed. Bishop and priest show knowledge and
political influence; they are almost western academic figures who
command multitudes not by producing books but people – people
whom they organize in popular demonstrations after they have
taught them the meaning of the gospel. Even the political forces of the
country bow to them and seem to release prisoners at their sugges-
tion.

Rowland and Corner do not exercise any hermeneutics of suspicion
in their reading of biblical interpretation in Latin America, especially
from a postcolonial perspective. They do not step outside the theme
park theology, perhaps because outside the land feels uncomfortable and contradictory. Basically, Liberation Theology in action has
always been diasporic and unsettled, more in tune with Chaos Theory
than with North Atlantic Systematic Theology.

The prophetic model: problematic

All this reflects the 'prophetic model', which followed the hierarchical
and authoritarian tradition of the church. This was not, of course, a
new model for the church in Latin America, which is the church of the
'cross and sword' and the sustainer of political, cultural and religious
western imperialism. How can a theologian be popular in a church
that was authoritarian even in its propheticness? During the 1970s,
the continent was living under the harshest forms of dictatorial

powers, whose authoritarian claims could not be challenged or discussed. Part of the Roman Catholic Church confronted human rights violations, but did so through another authoritarian discourse, the prophetic one.

Liberationist discourses acknowledged cultural, economic and political domination from the West, but ignored the way domination was structured theologically. That is the point of prophetic models: they do not challenge theological structures to their root. Liberationists analysed the forms of theological discourses of oppression but ignored the structure of western theological thought. Thus, the popular theologian, for instance, reverted to a discourse of theological efficacy without analysing which theological givens, or epistemological assumptions, were obstacles to such efficacy. For the church, the Christians who died in the struggle became martyrs. Thinking in terms of martyrdom is another example of theological western incorporation in Liberation Theology. The central model was still that of North Atlantic theology. Martyrdom was testimony, but there is a conceptual difference between 'martyrs' and *guerrilleros heroicos* (heroic guerrillas). In popular Catholicism, martyrdom participates in the category of resignation and sacrificial needs; it is not as positive or mobilizing as heroism. The point is that, while political militants tried to find models in a Latin American culture based in role models from the *Conquista*, Liberation Theology was busy re-adapting the teaching from the centres of western theology.

The systematic discourse of popular theologians

The problem was that the aura of illegality surrounding the liberationist process, as it organized a hermeneutical theology around Systematic Theology and capital formation, fascinated North Atlantic academia. Both Europe and the United States became romantically involved with the forces of production of Liberation Theology, which can be defined as the BECs and the gatherings for the popular reading of the Bible. North Atlantic theology behaved as a paterfamilias, either disputing the insufficient knowledge of the natives or finding their childlike faith enchanting. In one way or the other, North Atlantic theology did not let liberationists go their way freely.

Liberationists, meanwhile, wanted to be recognized as adult on an equal footing with their colleagues abroad. This was the moment of apologetics – a style very much overdeveloped by the Universidad de Centro América (UCA) in El Salvador, still in vogue today. Indeed, some published work, such as the *Mysterium Liberationis* and the *Systematic Theology* of Jon Sobrino and Ignacio Ellacuría (1993, 1996), show the desire to be seen as equals and not different in the sense of *différance*. Both books claim that Liberation Theology is a proper Systematic Theology and, while different methodologically speaking, comparable in the end to North Atlantic theology. And that is precisely the problem with a theology that was generated from a borderline, subversive edge, but was unable to transgress that border.

For the western academic, this may be an example of Rey Chow's claim that desire is always located in the Other (1993, p. 32). The western theologian projected a 'lack' in the making of the theme park of theology and the construction of the popular theologian. The hard movement of pushing frontiers in theology became an entertainment for a European public looking for novelty in the religious market but also for meaning. Theologians were looking for a meaningful framework of praxis for their lives, and through the alliance of a transverse conceptualization between Latin Americans and North Atlantic academics the theme park of liberation was produced.

Christianity is a utopia, and the actual process of utopia-making is basically diasporic, made of identity shifts at different levels but basically at the level of differentiating desires. The so-called decline of Liberation Theology at the moment, as assessed by European academics, may be no more than a decline in the market for the selling of books on Liberation Theology. But more than that it may be that the entertainment is over, because the constructed utopia of liberation is not, in the real world, the coherent narrative that theology wants. When westerners sent Gutiérrez to Disneyland, they also became liberation theologians, traditionally dressed with their colonial vision of the poor in Latin America and the role of popular theologians.

Meanwhile, the real poor in Latin America have become totally excluded by the globalization processes and refuse to continue supporting BECs and popular Bible studies. A tremendous diaspora of whole communities living in the streets, under bridges, desperately trying to cross frontiers looking for a job to give them food and shelter or to save their lives as people in Chiapas, cannot remain in any confined space of theology. This diaspora is not an exodus: the point is one of multiple trespasses, over borders of economic, philosophical and political systems to understandings of sexuality and genderization of power and authority. This is not Liberation Theology but Post-Colonial Theology, with a clear vocation for diasporic instability and sympathy for subversion more than for God. However, the challenges of theological hybridity are devastating for church and theology. And that is the good thing, because a Postcolonial Theology is not one that asks for the right to give a voice to the voiceless but that challenges the 'small voice' of western theology in Liberation Theology as structurally part of western Christianity and a discourse of the centre.

The Theology of Liberation is a hermeneutical theology. The reading of the Bible from a materialist perspective has been dependent on an understanding of the role of the popular theologian as part of the communities of the poor. Diasporic studies are crucial here to help us to discern the colonial dynamics of our third world theological reflection. For instance, such studies can help us to denaturalize the whole theological enterprise, allowing us to see third world theologies in their ambivalence and reflective bifurcations, which come not only from people's diasporas but also conceptual diasporas. The diaspora of the popular theologian is both internal and external. It challenges us with issues of the representability of the culture of poverty in theology and the translation process that is at the core of liberationist thought, usually expressed with the phrase 'to give voice to the voiceless'. However, Gayatri Spivak has warned us against benign representations of the subaltern in colonial thought and the validity of representation once the subaltern has moved to the area of representation at the cost of their alienation (1993, p. 90). The popular theologian is the 'alienated intermediate' figure in the reading of the Bible, representing the interface between Occidental Theologies (North Atlantic) and Oriental Theologies (third world).

However, the concept of the popular theologian shows fluctuations and degrees of incoherence during the course of its development that can be encouraging, if we consider that the subversive force present is the one resisting systematization. The subversive power is present by the mechanism of exaggeration and negation. The theme parks of theologies are a diasporic product based on this dialectic of 'negation/exaggeration'. What is exaggerated in the North Atlantic shows the degree of 'colonial enlargement' in the limitations or lack thereof regarding community life in Latin America. Typical of this discourse is the affirmation by negation present in such common phrases as: 'the Latin Americans are communitarian people, not individualists like us', 'they are faithful, not secular as we are', or, 'these people are humble and not competitive as we are'. What is exaggerated in Latin America also shows exaggeration but based on a mimicry of European theology. This mimicry constitutes our colonial souls, arising from a process of identity based on negation of the non-colonial. This is the discourse of the children of Wesley and Calvin, not of the indigenous Christianity of the continent. From the contradictions and fluctuations that a diasporic reflection throws into the construction of the popular theologian, we rescue its phantasmatic nature as a crucial site of subversion. The popular theologian had been made to mediate between negations and exaggerations, but it is not more than a phantasmatic figure. It is a spectre of the 'something else' needed in western theology, but also a domesticator of our colonial souls and a new colonial border of theology. This is a point of resistance and delegitimization by the deconstruction of the negation/exaggeration paradigm.

Finally, to discern the genesis of the popular theologian and the spectre of her/his reality would always be a major contribution to popular biblical interpretation in Latin America and a key point of reflection on the colonial tensions of our more autochthonous theological discourses, even if it is no more than a place of resistance. Paraphrasing Régis Debray in his interview of Subcomandante Marcos in Chiapas, the end of utopias is not a surrendering, but resistance must not cease (Debray, 1996, p. 137). Resistance in Latin America is always the privileged site of a return to the essential of our Latin American discourse on politics and biblical interpretation in the diaspora of a theological discourse that went to Europe and came back to us as a hybrid product of different dreams and struggles.

Part Four

Indecent, Radical, Queer:
The Future of Feminist Theology of Liberation?

Introduction

The challenges that Lesbian and Gay Theologies have presented both
to Liberation Theologies and to Feminist Theologies cannot be under-
estimated.[1] Women in Latin America decried the essentialism of the
liberationists, the assumption that 'women' are a homogenous group
sharing common identities and needs. In the same way, lesbians and
gays challenge the essentialism of orthodox theologies: sexual identities could not be homogenized. And yet, according to Elizabeth
Stuart, the problem of sexual ideologization tends to be pervasive
and is present even within Lesbian and Gay Theologies (Stuart, 2002).
How? By assuming a fixed sexual identity in non-heterosexual
people. Why? Because a heterosexual ideology, as a central discourse
of authority, extends its perspective on sexuality and relationships
even to non-heterosexual identities. It is at this point that Indecent
Theology links up with Queer theory.

Queer theory is an umbrella term encompassing diverse sexual
identities. Queer is a word which originally meant 'transverse' or
'oblique' and it is used in a positive way. Queer theory celebrates
diversity, the crossing of borders and imprecise frontiers. It liberates
the assumed reference of theology and therefore liberates Godself
from assumptions and ideological justifications.

Liberationists were modern in their hearts, challenging Christianity, the churches and the Scripture from the perspective of political
analysis and the unveiling of class ideologies, but indecent theologians have gone further. It is not artificially unified identities, homogenous understandings or common-sense definitions that Indecent
Theology seeks, but diversity, possibility and the sense of irreduci-
bility which comes from the experiences of people at the margins and
the margins of theology itself. To talk about God and Queerness

---

[1] See Elizabeth Stuart's analysis of the interface between Liberation
Theology and Gay and Lesbian Theology in her book *Gay and Lesbian Theologies. Repetitions with Critical Difference* (Ashgate: London, 2002).

means to try to demonstrate how Queer theory gives to theology a new understanding about the crucial importance of sexual thinking in traditional theology which, although it is denied, seems to have been fundamental for the church and the Christian understanding of life and faith. Theology is a sexual art, but a Queer one. Chapter 10, '*Rejunte*: A Theology from Excluded Love', uses an epistemology derived from circles of poverty and sexual exclusion to interrogate theology from a different perspective of love and a different understanding of Christian salvation. What is important here is to dare to dislocate that specific given-ness of love as an epistemology which grounds Christian theology. The intention is to reflect on a new hermeneutical circle or methodology which is Queer and radical, sensuous enough to ground a theology engaged in the transformation of structures of oppression yet spiritual enough to allow us to keep discovering the face of God among us. '*Rejunte*: A Theology from Excluded Love' reflects on love in times of globalization. What can we learn from the patterns of promiscuous love, extended families of lovers or communities of impoverished people such as transvestites? The love-solidarity of the excluded and the affective understanding of the people who live under the bridges of large cities such as Buenos Aires have much to say to a theology which cannot love any more. *Rejunte* is a slang word from Buenos Aires which literally means 'a new gathering'. It works as a *bricolage* in affective and economic terms. That is, in *rejunte* extended families comprised of ex-lovers and children from present or previous partners can be closely related, dislocating the monopoly of monogamy in favour of the solidarity of the poor. Using a concept from Deleuze and Guattari in *Anti-Oedipus Capitalism and Schizophrenia*, *rejunte* represents the dynamic of love outside the law. For Deleuze and Guattari, schizophrenic thought celebrates the parts and the creativity of fragmentation and freedom, while paranoic thought represents authoritarianism and closed systems of understanding. Curiously, Deleuze and Guattari associate schizophrenic thought with freedom, while paranoid thought is linked to fascism. Applying this analysis, *rejunte* is even more significant if we consider that the people who suffer extreme poverty in Argentina are the victims of fascist political thought, past or present, especially if we think of the IMF as an extreme form of the paranoid institution. *Rejunte* represents a challenge to patterns of relationships and affection coming from the excluded, while at the same time contributing towards a significant spiritual dimension. This is what a *rejuntada* means and in theology it represents a spirituality of exclusion which is diverse, changing, unstable and in tension with institutionalized forms of religiosity, especially of institutionalized Christianity. *Rejunte* Theology is Queer Theology under the bridges.

Chapter 11, 'A Profane Book of Saints: *San La Muerte*', continues the reflection on *Rejunte* Theology by focusing more on the Queer spirituality of sexual and economic exclusion alluded to in Chapter 10. The popular forms of worship such as *San La Muerte* (St Death) present us with a Queer sense of holiness, a Queer God of the poor who is recognized in the provisionality, transversality and instability of their own divinities. In the end, a Queer God of the poor appears more generous, more in solidarity and more unruly, upsetting the patterns of Christian marriage and the economic understandings which create exclusion and suffering. The worship of *San La Muerte* is typical of the spiritual systems of inversion by rejection which come from the marginalized people of Argentina. It is a product of hybridity. The worship of *San La Muerte* comes from migrant rural populations from Paraguay and the north of Argentina, drifting into large cities such as Buenos Aires. These forms of worship denounce political corruption by inverting the orders of social sanctity: the bandits become honest distributors of justice among the poor and death becomes life. Jesus the Lord of Life is now hailed as the Lord of Death, and yet it is in this death that solidarity, justice and reciprocity become relevant to the life to the poor. *San La Muerte* works outside binary systems, dislocating the genderization of worship spaces. There is no public (male) space of worship for *La Muerte*. Its worship is of an intimate bodily nature, frequently a bone inserted under the worshipper's skin or hidden in a room. A Queer popular form of devotion can be identified in the worship of *San La Muerte*. As such, it is part of a *Rejunte* Theology and it helps us to understand the revelation of God among the excluded.

Chapter 12, 'Scenes from Queer Cruci/Fictions: *Matan a una Marica* (They Killed a Faggot)' is another search for the Queer God, through a Queer Jesus. By scrutinizing the texts of Mark and John, together with the text of a Queer Argentinian writer, we attempt to produce a bi/reading (bisexual reading) of the gospel. The writer, Néstor Perlongher, constructs an almost messianic narrative based on the headlines of the tabloid press in Argentina, concerning the killing of a transvestite. I have developed the idea of reading the Scriptures together with Queer texts in my book *The Queer God* (Routledge, 2003).

There I called such a technique 'permutations'. In this case the permutation consists in the juxtaposition of the text of Perlongher's story *Matan a una Marica* (They Killed a Faggot) with the texts describing the killing of Jesus. This produces a reading of Gethsemane and Golgotha transversally from the perspective of the life and death of a transvestite on the Panamerican Highway of Buenos Aires. A permutative reading is not a comparative reading: it is a mingling of the text of the reality of sexual and economic exclusion with the text of the gospel, to disruptive effect. What we are doing is bringing to the reading the voice of a different reader. The effect of this is to make of the reader a 'second reader', who becomes a witness of a different exchange in the production of the meaning of the text. The first reader who is then introduced in the permutative reading is a Queer one. In this case, it is a poor transvestite whose death and anguished life informs our reading of the passion of Christ.

As a result of this the figure of Christ gives way to the figure of the Queer God as the stranger at the gate of churches and theology. This is a Queer God who is found in the transversal encounter between the sexually excluded transvestites in Buenos Aires and the excluded God, whose divinity is made redundant in the cruci/fiction scene of the gospel. An unloved messiah, marginalized and diminished ends his life as a rejected, unnecesary God. That Queer God starts to appear in the many deaths and resurrections of Jesus during his lifetime and in the continuing struggle of the Queer Christ to bring resurrection to our lives in times of deadly exclusion.

In a way the permutative reading of the life and passion of a poor transvestite from Perlongher's story with the life and passion of Jesus is also part of the *Rejunte* Theology of the poor. It dislocates and problematizes the compartmentalization of love and decency in a western theology which is fixated with monopolies of an affective or economic nature. The subversion that *San La Muerte*, as a popular worship from the excluded in Buenos Aires, brings to theology is also the subversion of bringing the voice of a different reader to Christian theology. It is not just, as in classical Liberation Theology, the harmonic voice of a suppressed reader who may add or reinterpret a text or the revelation of God in his/her community with a particular application, but the voice of a reader who is a wholly (and holy) Other.

And that is the challenge of this theological *caminata* or walk, which I have called 'From Feminist Theology to Indecent Theology'. What informs this *caminata* is the desire not to make of God an occasional and compassionate visitor to the margins of the margins but to rediscover that God is a truly marginal God. This is a God who has never left the marginal because this God belongs to them. This is not a God of the metropolitan centre who, like Kierkegaard's king, graciously spends a day with the poor before returning to the life of glory, abundance and security, leaving them to their lives of destitution, illness and vulnerability under the bridges. For the Queer God is the God who went into exile with God's people and remained there in exile with them. Indecent Theology is still Feminist Theology and Liberation Theology, but more marginal and perhaps even more messy, as the life of Jesus was marginal and messy. It is a theology of those who still want to keep reflecting and acting during these difficult times of globalization and social exclusion.

10

Rejunte: A Theology from Excluded Love

Cities of hell

When reflecting on the lives of the original nations of Latin America such as for instance Andean communities, we frequently observe the integration of mystical, affective and economic issues. In the cosmologies of Latin America, love and the sacred are in constant interaction with issues of land and economics. We are referring here to the poor of the continent and to the original indigenous peoples, still exploited and increasingly oppressed (as if that were possible) by further exclusion from society. The migration of peasant populations to the large capital cities, seeking work or the possibility of education for their families, creates changes not only in their patterns of relationships but also in their place in the original mystical universe. There are traditional patterns of loving reciprocity in institutions such as *compadrazgo*[1] or in the *ayni*.[2] These arrangements manifest the ways in which people relate to each other by co-operating in their agricultural work, without expecting payment, or by becoming part of the extended family with responsibilities towards children. These patterns have been taken to the life of a large city such as Buenos Aires by migrant families, but they have been adapted to the difficulties of living in urban centres where reciprocity patterns are more open to abuse. Reciprocity patterns can also be found in the expectations of popular spirituality, inspired by the traditional system of divine reciprocity. The old, trusted saints who were effective in the past seem suddenly unable to function in the new situation of destitution and exclusion in which the faithful find themselves: the institutionalized forms of relations with God are simply not flexible enough. Exclusion

---

[1] *Compadrazgo* (lit. 'co-paternity') is a Latin American traditional ritual system of co-parenthood which integrates different families into a close socioeconomic relationship.

[2] The *ayni* is an institution of economic reciprocity from the Aymara people in Latin America. It is part of a festive system of labour exchange based on communitarian ritualized friendship.

can be seen as a journey to cities of hell, with different intermediary stages but without hope of any final resurrection. The old saints cannot be effective unless they too become marginalized and transformed. Like the people themselves, the saints must pass through all the rings of hell of a large city.

It was Eva Montes de Oca who some years ago carried out a study of marginalization in the city of Buenos Aires using the idea of circles of poverty. She calls them 'the rings of hell'. The first circle is constituted by those whom she defines by the loose category of transgressors in a large city (Montes de Oca, 1995, p. 15). These are the prostitutes of saunas and brothels, *gatos* (upmarket prostitutes) and drug addicts from a middle-class background (although middle class is an increasingly imprecise term in impoverished Argentina). Some homosexuals can be found in this first circle, usually closeted homosexuals also of a middle-class background. The second ring is constituted by unemployed people, poor homosexuals, children of the streets, slum-dwellers, *troteras* (poor prostitutes of the streets) and pensioners with a minimum income. In this ring there are also *ocupas* (squatters) and AIDS sufferers. In the last ring of hell there are transvestites, transgendered beggars, ex-convicts, mad people and people who live under the bridges or in the huge garbage dumps on the outskirts of the city. Montes de Oca remarks that the differences among these circles concerns their relationship to power and obligations incurred in relation to different forms of political and social regulations. In the first circle, people still belong to society, that is, they fulfil certain social duties and are recognized as citizens by the state. This is the circle of men and women who take great risks by visiting gay bars at night, the circle of closeted sexual transgressors who do not want to risk their jobs and civil status. In the second circle, the situation is more dubious, or perhaps more open, but links with society are still maintained. In the third circle, the level of alienation between the people and civil society is almost total. This is the circle of social exclusion where important reflections on forms of love-knowing and theology may enlighten our Queer quest for the face of God in human relationships.

Rejunte

The most common form of family in the slums of Buenos Aires is called *rejunte*. The word in Spanish comes from *junta*, a gathering, and in slang *re-junte* means 'a new gathering'. It refers not only to the fact that partners in a unit consisting of a man, a woman and children change several times (that would be the situation of the *juntados* – living together), but also to the fact that each time a new family combination is produced an old one may be recycled. People who are *juntados* or *rejuntados* are not legally married, but *rejuntados* are the ones who separate and form new relationships. *Rejuntes* constitute a spontaneous institution among the urban poor and the excluded (Moffatt, 1988, p. 76), but as a description it is also a derogatory term among the *burguesía porteña* (Buenos Aires bourgeoisie). To say of a couple *'estan rejuntados'* is an insult and shows a lack of respect particularly towards the female member of the couple. It can also have implications of class and race. Middle-class people 'live together' (*viven juntos*), something only very partially accepted in Roman Catholic Argentina, but very common, especially due to the fact that divorce was legalized only a few years ago. The habitat of *los rejuntados* in Buenos Aires is the *villas miserias* (slums), or *bajo los puentes* (under the bridges). It is interesting to notice that the habitat of the excluded in a major city is a testimony to multidisciplinarity and the *bricolage* style of knowledge among the poor. People come from rural areas to live in Buenos Aires, but they also come from neighbouring countries such as Paraguay, Peru, Brazil or Chile, looking for better economic prospects. With them, they carry their traditional knowledge and spirituality. For instance, they may bring a traditional knowledge of architecture; they know how to make a house with mud, or with wood, but in the city they cannot find their own materials to build. Therefore, people learn from each other traditional techniques and how to employ them with whatever materials are available for construction. For instance, instead of bricks they might use discarded car batteries to build a *villa miseria*; many slums take the name of the elements used in the constructions of the huts or from a specific characteristic. For instance, in 2003 there was in Buenos Aires a slum called *Villa Inflamable* due to the fact that it was built on land where some multinational companies had been discarding inflammable substances from their production line. People living there have been known to have been engulfed in flames by lighting a cigarette or trying to boil water, because of the inflammable substances permeating the soil.

Living under the bridges is different. Lacking the traditional heavy woven cloth of their cultures, people might use old towels to build corridors and walls when living under a bridge. There are whole houses divided and organized by rags which used to be bathroom towels. These rag walls that separate the rooms are treated like real walls. On them are hung posters and pictures, creating aesthetic spaces which can be very colourful and artistic. But people also carry with them a spirituality which, symbolically, is divided by towels and produces imaginary separations and illusions of privacy for the gods of different people. In this form of multidisciplinary *bricolage* there is a coming together of divine figures such as the evangelical Jesus and the *Pachamama*. They share the life of their followers in the ring of hell which is social exclusion.

This *bricolage* is what a *rejuntada* means, and in theology it represents a spirituality of exclusion which is diverse, changing, unstable and in tension with institutionalized forms of religiosity and especially of institutionalized Christianity.

To say that the excluded are the invisible people in our big cities may be useful simply as a metaphor of disempowerment, but in reality it is their presence and not their invisibility which challenges us. Poverty is obvious. It is not invisible. It looks like poverty and even smells like poverty. The excluded are some of the most visible people in a large city. They constitute a mass of people who can be identified simply at a glance and recognized without even speaking a word or asking for details of their circumstances. The excluded are recognized by their clothes, though not necessarily by wearing traditional clothes or particular items by which other groups can be identified, and also by the colour of their skin. The excluded constitute a culture of their own, complex, heterogeneous. Elsewhere I have recalled that the first time I visited *El Borda* (a famous mental asylum in Buenos Aires), it was not a vision of madness which greeted me but of extreme poverty: the patients were dressed in rags or in ill-fitting clothes, including shoes several sizes too large or too small (Althaus-Reid, 1998, p. 258). In addition to that there was the smell of the food of the poor, a smell of fat and boiled soup which entered the very fabric of the walls and corridors of the asylum. It was not possible at first sight to know whether the patients were mad, but there was no doubt, just by looking at them, that they were poor, excluded people. It is the same in the streets. We do not need to enquire into the biography of marginalized people. Even a brief glance from the safe distance of a passing car enables us to identify their habitats under the bridges, or in derelict neighbourhoods in houses scheduled for demolition, or in the slums around the corner from the affluent city centres. But the excluded owe their visibility to yet another characteristic of their marginalized life, that is, their nomadism.

The distinctive feature that a lack of work produces in the poor of the city is a continual search for resources. During the week there is the round of displacement caused by the opening hours of soup kitchens, while at the weekend levels of security in different areas dramatically change. This is a kind of geographical nomadism practised by family groups as well as individuals, aggravated by other forms of enforced nomadism. For instance, the authorities might dismantle a slum in a few hours with the use of heavy machinery. There have been cases of children coming home from school only to find to their bewilderment that their poor houses and neighbourhoods did not exist any more. Worse still, rooms under bridges made of towels can be dismantled in but a few minutes. There are also natural disasters, to which the habitats of the excluded are more vulnerable, since they are usually located in areas known to be at risk. The fragility of the houses makes them even more susceptible to storms, fires, floods and land slips. The geographical locations of the excluded are unstable and therefore it is common for people to move frequently, but their family (or affective) locations are also unstable. That in itself is not a bad thing. The *rejunte* as an institution may be seen as a permanent source of renewal of affinity relationships. As such it is an emotional and economic resource, a key element in the art of surviving required in a big city. That 'gathering' or family is also part of an effort to stay together: in the small space of one room whole family structures of living, eating and sleeping literally come together. These are family structures composed of a couple and their children, but frequently also including grandparents and brothers and sisters with their families. The presence of brothers- and sisters-in-law is particularly important in this fluid community comprised of stepfathers and -mothers and different relatives in a variety of combinations. It is a place of meeting in which people become acquainted, some departing and others remaining, while still others who might return need not come back to a former relationship. Sexual relationships within the group can be complicated, for instance between a brother-in-law and a daughter of the family. Promiscuity is common, as is incest, though the two may coincide less than might be anticipated since these groups are not as consanguine as more stable families (Moffatt, 1988, p. 83). Privacy is scarce: the houses of the poor do not have doors. The excluded are exposed people: their life circumstances, their bodies and emotions are more visible than is the case with any other group. Their habitats emphasize this exposure in terms of relationships. Exclusion makes families disperse under the weight of the struggle for survival but the *rejunte* allows people to come back to the family or move on to another, a recreated group organized around some members of an original group to which new people are added. People may be forgiven for old deeds and partners in disgrace may return not as partners, but as people who are in need of support.

The life cycle with its expectations of childhood, adolescence, maturity and old age is diffuse. Children start work and confront responsibilities and problems very young. Old people do not have any 'retirement' time; they depend on adult children to help them to survive or they end their lives as beggars, since they seldom have pensions or any benefit to allow them to live out the last years of their lives.

It seems unnecessary to point out here that this is the social group that Liberation Theology in Latin America has been addressing in the past decades, denouncing the social system which creates the circumstances of their lives and trying to organize a praxis of change through the church. However, the church's instinct has always been to re-order family structures by encouraging or coercing people to marry (to baptize their children, for instance), as if the idealized family structures promoted by the church were independent of the socio-economic conditions which support them. For instance, it is expected that the life of the individual or family group will include habitats which encourage privacy, homes supplied with electricity, a 'progressive' conception of time including, for example, a concluding period of retirement.

If we take the characteristics of nomadism and the recycling of family groups among the excluded of the big cities as part of a spirituality of survival, we are confronted with a theology which arises from circles of marginalization and which challenges the survival and re-organization of the traditional values of the church. Somehow the excluded elaborate a *bricolage* theology which corresponds to their own lives, a mixture of encounters with different understandings (based on the experience of the other excluded) and with the aim of surviving. This is a very concrete form of theology which reflects experiences of nomadism, changes of family and geographical structures and a dyadic affective life which is reconstituted frequently. This is a theology whose aim seems to be a pedagogy of reciprocity and a reaffirmation of the courage of defying the centralized definition of love and success, although it also identifies and makes alliances at some levels with the state and its official (Roman Catholic) theology. However, it is in the different combinations of its binary forms of religious, political and even gender oppositions that some subversive strategies can be identified. This could provide us with a theological base from which the Queering comes from the marginalized of our societies. We could call this the base for a *Rejunte* Theology.

Rejunte Theology

Sometimes an evangelical minister comes and then we women get together and he gives us each a bag with food . . .

Sometimes a car comes and brings some clothes for adult people; then I go to the church in Canning Street and exchange them for children's clothes . . .

I am evangelical so we get a lot of help, although the other church, the Roman Catholic, also give us clothes, food, things like that . . .

From testimonies of poor women from Buenos Aires, Montes de Oca, 1995, pp. 242–7

If the Queer discourse is somehow the opposite of domesticity, it would be difficult to locate it in the testimonies from the excluded of Buenos Aires. For their Queerness also participates in domesticity and the expected, in a kind of exclusion theodicy which mixes intimate experiences with approved forms of communicating them. Still, we are faced here with diglotic symbolic activities, that is, with, for instance, familiar and religious activities which, although resembling the official accepted forms, differ from them simply because some of the terms are untranslatable. The family structure of people living under bridges may appear to be similar to the one proclaimed by official theologies, but in reality they are not the same. As Herzfeld has noted in his reflections on issues of cultural intimacy and identity, the fact of living in a house, that is, of developing one's life in the framework of a solid, stable environment, produces illusions of solidity in morality too (Herzfeld, 1997, p. 20). That 'solidity' also takes the form of religious mimicry, where the domestic display of saints and offered candles looks similar to that found in any middle-class home, and yet it is different.

In this context it is interesting to notice that the women quoted above (women who live under bridges in Buenos Aires) tend to identify themselves as evangelicals, a category that in Argentina is very vague on its own and simply means 'not Roman Catholic'. However, it also means first of all belonging, a sense of identity, and, second, participation in the national myth that evangelicals are closed groups who help each other economically. This probably originated with the idea that the first Protestant churches were expatriate churches, whose members were identified as gringos and therefore economically powerful. That is to say, in identifying themselves as evangelical they also claim not to be on their own, unprotected or without any support or help, but on the contrary as having access to important people. In the case of the women quoted, as they were women living under a bridge in Buenos Aires, it also adds some respectability to them. Otherwise, and for charity purposes, nobody needs to be affiliated to an evangelical church in Buenos Aires in order to receive economic help.

What are the characteristics of this Theology of *Rejunte* in the Christianity of the excluded? Surprisingly, there is still a searching for paradigms of liberation, the interpretation of a popular, oral version of the Bible, which takes up issues of economic and social exclusion and spiritually promiscuous alliances containing themes of love, money and perceived enmities such as illnesses and disgraces.

However, the agenda of this theology is somewhat distant from typical evangelical concerns. The following testimony from one of the women quoted above gives us a sense of where she is coming from in terms of how social exclusion carries with it a particular social perception. The woman who speaks, María, illustrates her experience of 'society' by recounting that she was a poor child whose grandmother gave her to a family to be trained as a domestic servant in one of the provinces in the north of Argentina. She eventually ran away, reached the city where she met someone as destitute as herself and had four children. They married (according to her testimony) following the promise of a local governor who offered 'a house' to every poor family under the bridges who decided to legalize their marital situation. This offer of housing did not materialize and she was disappointed that she had got married:

> The political parties come and tell us that they will help us, that they will give us a house if we vote for them . . . But we have already had experience of that, because when we were living in Moreno, my husband was single and so was I. We were together (*juntos*) and they said to us that they would organize a free wedding for us . . . that people needed to get married because [the governor] would pay for it . . . Once married, they were going to give us a house, a piece of land of our own, and everything. And we were married and look where we are now. They didn't give us anything; we are still here, so I don't trust in them anymore.
>
> Montes de Oca, 1995, p. 247

Later she adds that she knows what society is, and who the people are who live in society, but she is happy not to belong with them:

> I don't complain about living in this way, because I have already been in society and I know what society means. I know who is in control of society, how people live there and how they keep themselves. I know how that system works, from the inside and from the outside . . . So the only thing I would like is to have a better house, and nothing else.
>
> Montes de Oca, 1995, p. 248

From the houses made of towel partitions and illuminated by candles or kerosene lamps comes a dis/identification of what society means. In this case María claims not to be interested either in marriage (she was tricked into it) or in belonging to the *sociedad Argentina*. Her proclaimed evangelical faith is probably also related to this alienation from institutionalized forms of religion. These are sometimes theological systems of retribution, maintained in relation to spiritual protectors. This is a kind of urban pedagogy which helps to remind people what they have in common, reciprocal forms of organization of their mythical values and also the capacity to share them with others.

All the common practices of patriarchal abuse are found among the marginalized, including extreme violence against women. Ironically their lack of civil marriage may on occasion come to their aid by allowing them to run away more easily than if they were actually married. But in addition it is interesting to notice that there are also displacements to be observed in terms of gender constructions. This is what we might call a form of heterosexuality outside *some* closet, which can be located in the displacement and even redistribution of moral systems. In Argentina morality is a heavily gendered discourse. As gender localizes morality and the perpetuation of moral values, women who are considered indecent transgress gender boundaries – and so do men. Let us consider now some evangelical habits of the excluded people and try to consider what displacements are produced and which Queer strategies are present.

Instead of what we call the Bible, those who neither read nor own books have a collection of popular sayings, many of which are apocryphal but which have passed from person to person by way of proverbs and popular metaphors. Sometimes people in Buenos Aires might claim to be quoting Jesus, retelling how he once said, 'Help yourself first if you want me to help you.' Or they might create stories which are a collage of biblical fragments and elements from their own original religiosity. Thus it is claimed that when Jesus came to earth from heaven 'one day', he met someone, performed some action and then returned to the heavens. Jesus is a common character in popular religiosity who authorizes these stories of the gospel of the excluded, as if the New Testament was moving with them into the rings of exclusion, becoming chaotic, disorganized but alive to people's understandings and needs in many different ways. Also, reference to the name of Jesus acts as a legitimation of any *other* practice outside the official Christianity of the country. The Bible drinkers are a case in point. People might cut a page out of the Bible (commonly a psalm or another text recommended by someone who knows about these things). The page is then cut into small pieces, soaked in a glass of water and drunk, for purposes of protection, empowerment or luck in gambling. For instance, drinking Psalm 23 is said to be effective against the dangers of being exposed to drug wars in the neighbourhood. Drinking Jeremiah 33.3 is said to be effective when a member of the family is lost and the family would like to make contact (Althaus-Reid, 2003a). Some years ago Bible drinking was a popular 'reading' of the Gospels by the excluded, but this type of exegetical exercise changes year by year, month by month, according to the political situation and the current crisis which needs to be managed. Some years ago, during a particular time of high insecurity in the city, a neighbour advised me to paint my house with holy blood. This was done with an imaginary bucket full of Jesus' blood and with the help of a large imaginary brush. Covering the door of my house would provide protection against intruders, providing that the door was 'repainted' every day and that a short prayer about the salvific power of Jesus' blood was also said. Any of these exegeses from the excluded can be sought out and located during a specific economic crisis of the country. 'Drinking' has long been associated with mysticism among the excluded in Buenos Aires. Pancho Sierra, a miracle worker of the nineteenth century, was called 'the cold water doctor', because his main technique for curing illnesses and emotional problems consisted in offering to the person in need a glass of cold water from the well at his home. The other dimension is of course the importance (even liturgical importance) of drinking among the community of the marginalized in the country. Suddenly alcoholic drinking, so common among excluded populations, becomes biblical drinking. In his study of popular forms of psychotherapies among the excluded in Argentinian society, Moffatt has considered how bourgeois drinking habits (more privatized and carried on in an atmosphere of guilt and secrecy) differ from those of the excluded. Among the excluded drinking is expressed in fiestas during which the whole community gets drunk, for instance, during the seasonal *carnavales* (Moffatt, 1988, p. 78). The biblical drinkers I met years ago also drank in community, as they passed to each other texts and advice from this communitarian exegesis which expressed the need to make concrete and 'incarnate' whatever may be called the experience of the sacred in their lives and the meaning of salvation.

The worship of the excluded offered to the saints of the Roman Catholic calendar also keeps that concrete dimension in incarnational theology alive. Other saints are new creations, or mixtures of old and new. Divine figures such as *San La Muerte* (Saint Death), *San Son, Los Santos Bandidos* (Bandit Saints) such as the Gaucho *Lega, Gauchito Gil* (actually shown in pictures crucified as a gaucho-Christ) together with the old *manosantas* (miracle healers) of the poor, *Pancho Sierra* and *La Madre María* exemplify the needs of different moments in the processes of exclusion in my country. They also exemplify different forms of messianic understandings which are closely related to the material practices of relationships.

Some of these forms of worship might have a starting point in the biblical paradigm chosen (or created) by the people, but then, it is the perspective of exclusion which illuminates and gives an opportunity to people to relate to that text or oral story based on a biblical passage. People read from the point of view of the *fracasados* (the 'failures' of society) and search for biblical heroes not in the more traditional Abrahams or Moses but in more humble heroes such as Samson (in a modified version which stresses strength against adversity) and martyrs and prophets identified with legends of local 'good' bandits.

They are generally represented by pictures and carvings as crucified on crosses, like Jesus. They also come from biographies of *rejuntes*: we are told that when they died (generally in a confrontation with the police force, which represents 'society' or 'the state') they left some woman behind, some poor children without protection, who died without care. In this way attention is drawn to the need to extend a family by caring for other poor people, as they do in the *rejunte*.

In the same way that Liberation Theology worked with poor people who identify themselves with the exodus paradigm as a promise of liberation, the excluded have chosen their own related themes. For instance, 'strength' is an important issue. Strength is sought and cherished through a recreated *rejunte* of biblical stories. This strength needs to be physical, in terms of good health and strength to fight against adversities or other people in aggressive environments, but also strength to have an 'abundant life', which is translated in terms of love and luck (including gambling). Several particular forms of worship address the issue of love and death in the city among the excluded, including the worship of *San La Muerte* and *San Son* (Samson). In the past decade, the death of popular singers such as Rodrigo or Gilda have also generated popular devotions, and chapels have been built to *El Angel Rodrigo* or *Santa Gilda*. In all of them, a spiritual *bricolage* made of a web of fragmented, de-centralized forms of affection and a different understanding of the presence of God among people brings a Queer sense of holiness to the discourse of the spirituality of the poor. A holiness that goes beyond exclusion, nurtured from the solidarity of a God identified as an excluded among excluded.

A Profane Book of Saints:
San La Muerte

You are all powerful, so make me find what I am searching for . . .

From a popular prayer to *San La Muerte*

During the eighteenth century and as a result of the Christian *Conquista*, devotion to divine images of Jesus and Mary, and particularly to a multitude of statues of saints, became popular in South America. In the area that today is known as Paraguay and Chaco Argentino (the Guarani region), indigenous people started the tradition of the *tallistas* or wood carvers, initiated during the period of the Jesuit missions. With the passing of the years, however, the representation of the statues and images of Jesus, the Virgin Mary and the Roman Catholic saints started to suffer problems of transmission or distortions in their identities. These distortions were in some cases the product of a desire to manifest artistically other beliefs which had been suppressed by Christianity, while in others they reflected contextual reinterpretations of the given official book of saints. Among the Tupí Guaraníes one important religious leader called the *Payé* was a priestly figure, combining the role of healer and miracle worker, who obtained special powers by acts of silent meditation and fasting. It is thought that the *Payé* was somehow identified with Jesus at some time and that it gave rise to small wood carvings of what is known today as *Señor La Muerte* or *San La Muerte*.

Nowadays this has become a popular form of worship among the urban poor in Buenos Aires, brought to the city by migrant workers from the north of the country, especially from Corrientes. There are many accounts of the origins of *San La Muerte*, but his genealogy changes from time to time and from community to community. A common biographical theme expresses a strong economic concern and offers a criticism of usury and the attempt to make profit from the poor. It says briefly that Jesus Christ came to earth and while walking about met a very poor man. He was so poor that he had not eaten for many days and had become very thin and weak. Jesus felt compassion for him and gave him a gift, the gift of healing. It is interesting that the story does not feature a man who had been healed. This would have been the more traditional story of a man who worshipped Jesus because he was himself restored and liberated. No. The story has another logic. Jesus gave the starving and sick man the gift of healing others. Therefore this thin man (represented as a skeleton), started to heal poor people in his own neighbourhood. But soon he became greedy. He discovered that he could make a good living out of healing people. However, Jesus became angry at this entrepreneurial spirit. But once the man properly repented of his actions, he was condemned to wander the earth healing people for free. He became a nomadic divinity.

Healing is here an extended concept: it refers to economic healing (from the wounds of poverty and debt to the restitution of stolen goods by thieves); love (healing from solitude and the social vulnerability related to loneliness in poor people), as well as healing from illnesses. *San La Muerte* is represented by a skeleton with a scythe and belongs to the hidden worship life of the poor, for his image should not be seen by anybody, except worshippers. Moreover, it is traditional that a small carved bone bearing the image of *San La Muerte* should be inserted under the skin, to maintain a very concrete relationship between the saint and the person in need. If not this, then a piece of cheap jewellery such as a ring, an earring or a medal should be carried about the person, provided that it is not seen by others. The bone of *San La Muerte* inserted under the skin is part of a theological sign language used by the excluded. At the same time it presents an ironic commentary, contrasting the permanent element in the worshippers' contact with the sacred and the insecurity of their grasp on their own transitory world. The habitat of *San La Muerte* under the skin is therefore permanent and secure: no demolition squad or natural catastrophe can threaten the presence of the sacred in their lives.

The Queer elements of the *San La Muerte* popular worship can be organized around elements of provisionality, inversions, diglosia and different binary allocations. The interrelation between the religious symbolic activity of the excluded and their affective activity (as in family patterns) reinforces and recreates each other in a permanent dialectics of mutuality. For instance, provisionality is a key element in the life of the excluded: their habitat is provisional and so are their family relationships, subject as they are to economic migrations. The contrast between this provisionality in their affective social structures and governmental discourses on family and national identity could hardly be greater.[1] The Argentinian state has an official discourse on

---

[1] Michael Herzfeld suggests that 'images of domesticity' and family stereotypes are widely used by the state in order to build a symbolic system which could explain and reassure people against, for instance, cases of human rights abuses and anti-democratic measures. For instance, he quotes Hastings

national identity which relies heavily on Roman Catholic family idealizations. These are the discourses of *La Madre Patria* (The Mother Fatherland), a term which grammatically might look at first sight like a contradiction in gender, although in Spanish the term *Patria* (Fatherland) is feminine. Therefore 'The Mother Fatherland' takes the Argentinian people to be *los hijos de esta tierra* (the children of this land; 'this land' replaces here the term *Patria*). The 'honour of the land' is invoked when there are international difficulties with *paises hermanos* (brother countries), that is, Latin American or border countries. It is as if this was a family discourse concerning the rape of virgin daughters.

And finally, the official discourse follows that of the church in comparing the life of the nation and the life of a family. A whole legal terminology of separations, domestic disputes, divorce and reconciliation are commonly employed in official explanations of social tensions, from general strikes to internal disagreements over government policy. Even the official emphasis on reconciliation after high-profile disagreements (the metaphorical *divorcios*) can be related to the anti-divorce policy of a state legally associated with Roman Catholicism.

To this gendered universe of family discourses of national identity we may add what Herzfeld calls the images of domesticity (Herzfeld, 1997, p. 4), conveyed by a multitude of images taken from the universe of bourgeois domesticity. In times of extreme crisis, such as the intense internal conflict of Argentina in the 1970s, the domestic discourse homologized the everyday virtues of a bourgeois home with patriotism. For instance, to speak about the country when abroad was considered an improper form of behaviour. The difficulties experienced by the country were officially explained as lack of confidence, lack of trust, not talking 'over the table' (as during a family meal) with frankness, lack of obedience (to God and to the government), and gender transgression attributed to the fact that in this 'home-country' women and men sometimes do not accept the roles assigned to them by God, that is, of homemaking (for women) and courage in public service (for men). Moreover, the political crisis of the country was equated with a crisis in the family structures of the country. Even the critics of the then military system used domestic metaphors such as Maria Elena Walsh's famous article 'Desventuras en el País-Jardín-de-Infantes' ('Misfortunes in the Land of the Kindergarten', Walsh, 1979).

These metaphors based on gender are also class metaphors, for the poor do not send their children to kindergartens. However, in con-

---

Banda, the former President of Malawi, referring to the good cause of 'Mother Malawi' in the midst of serious claims of human rights abuse (Herzfeld, 1997, p. 4).

trast to these, there is what we have called the excluded theodicy based on the experiences of other forms of family relations which have little to do with the official discourse already mentioned. Basically, they contravene the sense of domestic stability and permanency and the morality exuded by the bourgeois family's sense of security. In religious terms, popular proverbs such as *vergüenza es robar y no llevar nada a la madre* (it is a shame to steal and not take something to your own mother) can be related to the worship of the bandits, considered humble men who stole through necessity, but always shared what they got among people in their own communities. This is part of the belief that one can be an honest thief (*el ladrón honrado*). It is the political system which is declared to be corrupt, committing theft against ordinary people. The act of stealing from such criminality is now redeemed. Stealing becomes part of the accepted universe of things, but it can have an honest purpose too, for example in relation to solidarity with those who share the same fate of poverty and destitution.

Therefore, while the official Christian redemptive discourse is about identity by repetition of family metaphors applied to the community without distinctions, among the excluded, at least in this particular example, redemption comes from an appropriation of the state's sins of corruption but with a twist. In this spirit, we can read the following testimony of a person who lives under a bridge in Buenos Aires:

> There are days that I go to the streets to check the garbage bins and I find bags full of clothes; it is shocking. Could you believe that I found a fridge and a TV discarded in the streets? . . . If people knew that we are living here, under the bridges . . . We live in a country where everything is thrown away. This country is so big and yet see the [small] space that I occupy [under a bridge].
>
> Montes de Oca, 1995, p. 238

The perceived excessive consumerism and carelessness of some sections of the population is seen as sinful by destitute people who do not understand why things (in this case, discarded goods) are not shared with the community.

In the worship of *San La Muerte*, it seems that the familiarity of the poor with death in the midst of everyday life – in more than one sense – identifies the provisionality of life as the only constant experience. The people who say *basta la salud* (health is enough) and *mientras hay vida hay esperanza* (where there is life, there is hope) worship Death. The provisionality of their experience of life is inverted; death is healthy. But health is more than absence of illness in this case and it is represented by good luck in such things as the arts of popular gambling and finding affective and sexual company when one is alone, in order to better survive a difficult life. This is what is called the art of *el rebusque*, literally to search and search again for little things that can help in the emotional recycling of the life and love of the poor. *Rebusque* as a concept shares with *rejunte* the *'re'* of repetition and as such it is usually found in popular expressions which indicate the sense of struggle among the excluded. Things need to be tried again and again, from bureaucratic administrative procedures which ask people to wait and 'come tomorrow' (*vuelva mañana*), to provisional solutions in life which need to be continuously reworked. The worship of *San La Muerte* is a theological reflection on inversion by rejection: the rejection of the administrative procedures of an organized political life which is meaningless for the poor; of the institutionalized medicine and the poor health-care facilities, largely out of reach of those at the margins of society – especially at a time when medical provision is being privatized and international pharmaceutical companies are developing drugs which few can afford to buy. It is hardly surprising that statues of *San La Muerte* can be found in the *Santerías* of Buenos Aires alongside strange books promising miraculous cures for illnesses such as appendicitis, constipation or liver problems occasioned by excessive drinking. They are happily mixed on shelves displaying booklets offering advice on how to fix a TV or build your own radio. Alongside are the tarot cards of *San Cono*, the popular version of a (supposedly) Roman Catholic saint represented as a young smiling priest with a shining halo who, while praying the rosary, was told by the Virgin the secret of how to win the lottery. These are all part of the same system of theological *rebusques,* and a theology of *rejunte*.

The *Rejunte* Theology unveils the diglotic dialectic of the life of the excluded, exposed to an ecclesial theology and a state discourse which are untranslatable into their lives. The division between the public and private discourses of national identity is then relocated. The public worship of Jesus in the Christian churches is transformed into a bodily, private and hidden worship. The bone or statue representing *San La Muerte* receives a hidden blessing from the church, when according to specific instructions the believer takes it to seven different churches or is 'blessed' by seven different priests. (This is achieved by having the bone or statue in a pocket and touching it while the priest gives a general benediction.)[2] The church as well as the individual priests are oblivious to what has happened. Christianity is re-ordered as a different liturgy of open and private spaces. *San La Muerte* becomes an associate divinity, recognized and influential in

---

[2] For the worship to *San La Muerte,* see E. Noya, *Corrientes entre la Leyenda y la Tradición.* Special issue of 'Todo es Historia', vol. 7 (Buenos Aires, 1987).

the sacred Christian pantheon and able to obtain significant favours for the believer, as if heaven were ordered like a feudal court or a colonial administration in which it was necessary to have friends in high places.

Sometimes there are attempts to bring this worship within the control of the Roman Catholic Church. I have personally collected homemade street leaflets inviting people to pray the rosary in honour of *San La Muerte* in some new chapel dedicated to the saint. This might be part of a strategy towards the legitimation of the saint, but it includes a commercial element, since the people are frequently asked to give some money for the maintenance of the place of worship and its so-called administrator. Simply put, this is another economic *rebusque* of the poor. Yet all this is part of the worship of *San La Muerte* and the liturgy of his fiesta which takes place on 20 August. In honour of the saint people in the community try to bring and share food and drink. There is also singing and an atmosphere of happiness among those who believe in the saint. Sometimes, depending on the location of the worship, the celebration can be very elaborate, with clear mimetic resemblances to Roman Catholic processions and the liturgical gestures of the mass, including the central element of the sacred banquet in the presence of *San La Muerte*.

The gender dislocation of the worship can be seen in the way in which the traditional division of public and private spheres of worship is delineated. The private or the area of intimate female self-knowledge (Herzfeld, 1997, p. 20) takes prevalence over the public sphere of worship. It is also a bodily worship. In Argentina, the domestic space of worship is made by women decorating and looking after statues of the Virgin Mary, Jesus and the saints, by arranging their clothes, by bringing flowers or burning candles at their feet. The public space of worship belongs to male power represented by the male hierarchy of the Roman Catholic Church with its divine canon, to whom belong the power to forgive and decide issues of inclusion and exclusion in society. For instance male power decides if children of non-married people are bastards, if they may attend certain schools, if divorcees can go to church or not. In general male power establishes the canons of decency among the people. However, efficacy is attributed to the domestic sphere, that is, the prayers in the home in a world of novenas and rosaries. In the worship to *San La Muerte*, the public (male) sphere of the devotion simply does not exist. Everybody is their own priest. *San La Muerte* does not enquire into the legality of people's relationships but simply shows them favour. This is a divinity who acts as an intermediary between the life of gods such as Jesus on the one hand, who belongs to the life of people who are integrated into society, and, on the other, the excluded whose life is an exercise of diglotic meaning in Christian theology.

Once again we encounter in *San La Muerte* a popular religiosity which is deeply rooted in the subversion of a family order: it is therefore Queer. The subversion is partial and it is not to be seen as a model which might confound binary systems of thought, but rather in the use of such binarisms. Herzfeld is very perceptive when he claims that somehow only social usage makes a difference to binarisms. This is true in this case, as in the cases of certain Andean cultures.[3] Both in the city as in the Andean culture, heterosexuality seems sometimes to get close to leaving the closet, although it falls short of actually doing so. Yet, the different configurations of patterns of family life and the different solutions which the excluded present to a political system sustained by a Christian family discourse on identity give us further clues to add to the search for a Queer God (or the face of the Queer God), coming from people at the margins of society through a combination of class, gender, sexuality and race.

Insights: outside heterosexuality

Adding sexuality to exclusion changes the situation of people's lives considerably. Recent studies on poverty and exclusion in the city of Buenos Aires show that transvestites tend to live in community in order to receive more support and protection. In this way transvestite 'families' are to be found in poor hotels (the run down boarding houses of the poor, where rooms can be rented by the day) and even in poor houses rented with the economic effort of the whole group living there. Curiously, they claim that their best experiences of integration into society, in terms of receiving respect in spite of their obviously different sexual orientation, have been in the *villas miserias* (slums) of the city. So, one poor transvestite declares that '[the slums] are the only place to live with some respect and without being persecuted, because everybody is marginalized there' (Montes de Oca, 1995, p. 223). Prostitution is the main economic option of the sexually different poor and this is the case with transvestites. Some transvestites claim that they have a better life than gays, in terms of avoiding persecution and marginalization. But in this we are confronting the exclusion of identity, based on a theological argument which is particularly strong in Argentina, namely, that bodies are created by God and belong to God along with a kind of given naturalization of civil identities. Of course, some bodies seem to suffer more than

---

[3] I am referring here to the case of the bisexual religiosity in some Peruvian towns, and to the family structure of the Canela indigenous people from Ecuador. See for instance M. Althaus-Reid, *The Queer God* (London: Routledge, 2003), especially ch. 7, 'Popular Anti-Theologies of Love'.

others from this interdiction of creative thinking about a person's own body (as in the case of transvestism). This theological elaboration has been legalized and therefore no rights remain for a poor transvestite. The formation of community flats, or the strategies of living in the same location, provide them with a family of affinity. It is common to hear them say that they have learnt from the mistakes of others in all senses, from issues related to self-defence and protection to the selection of hormones to grow breasts. For this, in some sense, is what a family needs to be, a place of nurturing of people and sharing experiences of life: an economic unit in itself. As they experience so little protection in society, money is an important goal: economic independence is the only guarantee to any claim of rights they might have. I have personally found some forms of secular theology among them. Many hold a special reverence for Argentina's famous former first lady, Eva Duarte de Perón, 'Evita'. Evita is much revered, almost worshipped and some even claim to have some kind of spiritual contact with her, receiving guidance from heaven. Others might claim, whether seriously or not, that they are the very reincarnation of Evita. There are some who worship the Virgin Mary, but Evita, the prototype of the intelligent Argentinian woman, beautiful while at the same time a political genius of action and reflection, sadly has no theological equivalent. It is curious though that those who transgress the politics of sexuality as transvestites draw spiritual inspiration from one who also transgressed many gender borders in such a radical way.

From the life of the excluded and their affective, family ways, Christian theology has much to learn – but in order to change and not simply to adapt. First of all, the lessons of critical realism among the poor dismantle the good intentions of the theologies whose aim is to normalize the life of people into a discourse on family middle-class ideals. There are lessons on recognizing plurality and theological insights in the face of the Queer God of the poor: generous but unpredictable as life; honest in its own way, with the final aim of solidarity for survival. This is a god who rejects the economy of the market, its public worship and the exchange of money. But it is also a god who announces that Godself can represent collectively the world of people's unruly affections by re-locating the discourse of the family into a wealth of relationships of love in transition, impermanence and reciprocity.

Scenes from Queer Cruci/Fictions: *Matan a una Marica* ('They Killed a Faggot')

It was the third hour when they crucified him . . . The passers-by jeered at him.

Mark 15.25, 29, Jerusalem Bible

'A homosexual has been killed in Quilmes.' Every so often, the news about the violent death of gays came with macabre rejoicing . . . the sensationalist headlines from the newspapers.

Perlongher, 1997, p. 35

'They killed a faggot.' This is the title of one of the stories of Néstor Perlongher, the *neo-Barroso*,[1] Queer Argentinian writer who wrote stories deconstructing sexuality and poverty in Buenos Aires. This is a story of love, poverty and hope of resurrections, as the dreams of the poor. Perlongher took the words for his title *Matan a una Marica* from the headlines of a tabloid newspaper from Buenos Aires. Curiously, these words preserve a certain ambiguity. *Matan a una Marica*[2] can be translated as 'they kill a faggot', and also as a present tense functioning as a very recent past tense: 'They killed a faggot.' That ambiguity

---

[1] Néstor Perlongher was an Argentinian poet and professor of anthropology whose activism in the 'Movement for Homosexual Liberation' in Buenos Aires and his work on poverty and Queer issues won him international recognition. He called his style *'neo-barroso'*, playing with the words 'neo-baroque' and *'barroso'* (muddy) in Spanish.

[2] The word *marica* is used in the slang of Buenos Aires for gays. Originally, *marica* is an old fashioned diminutive of the female name 'Maria'. Other variations include the words *mariquita* or *maricón*, even *mariposa* (butterfly). Although this last term is not related epistemologically, it is used because of the term 'mari' present in the word. It is then the association with the name Maria which confers 'gayness' to the terms. One could argue that there is a relation between those nicknames and the influence of Mariology in the understanding of gender formations in Latin America.

of the title adds to a sense of presence and continuation of the text which is almost ontological.

Perlongher's story is centred on the news of a body being found on a road. Probably 'she' was a transvestite. Probably 'she' went with other girls to the Panamerican Highway which divides the capital city from the suburbs of Buenos Aires to engage in prostitution, or in the Sao Paulo slums, but then . . . What happened? It could have been a fight or simply that she was attacked. Perlongher describes the body lying in full transvestite regalia, now broken and dirty, as a scene from a cruci/fiction. There lies in the muddy road the love for shiny scarves and polka-dot blouses *à la* Marilyn Monroe. There you can see the refined femininity of long, colourful earrings and the high-heeled shoes adorned with ribbons. All that made her, the loving hands which sewed her blouse and assembled the earrings from bits and pieces which looked good together, and her love for life, now lying covered by blood and dirt from the road. Who killed her? Was it the Sao Paulo police, in one of their *razzias* against transvestites? The cruci/fiction style of writing of Perlongher reaches a climax as he describes the messianic panic of one policeman when looking at the quality of the girl's make-up and torn clothes: she reminds him of someone he saw on the cover of a magazine. 'Damn it!'– he exclaims as he discerns the identity of the innocent – 'The *loca* was famous' (*loca*: a Spanish term for a mad, crazy person, which is used with sexual connotations). An indecent transvestite lay there as an innocent victim of a system of sexual violence. Transvestites are *locas*; they represent something liminal which has crossed borders and has dislocated the almost spatial ideology of heterosexuality.

The transvestite, the *loca* from Perlongher, lies in the mud and blood with 'her' torn clothes, and it is by something in those torn clothes (colour, shine, transparency, the production of femininity) that she is identified as someone who was somehow a minor celebrity, and should not have been killed. Perhaps she had a brief appearance on some local television show, or perhaps she was interviewed for a tabloid newspaper about human rights and sexuality. Somehow she belonged to a small celebrity circuit. Her death may raise voices; it may not be just another killing committed with impunity. It may create questions and problems. By her death, she may succeed then in calling attention to the killing of so many 'girls' like herself. She may even contribute to the girls' redemption, and, finally, a transvestite may be able to get a job, have a decent life, love and be happy. But at the moment the preoccupation is what to do with the body. The body should disappear. And some other transvestites, some girls who were friendly with her might come and ask, have you seen our friend? Where have you put her body? But the body will never be found, for she has ascended to heaven. Like the Magdalene asking 'What have you done with the body of my beloved?' the answer will remain mysterious. The name of the transvestite will become legendary. One day the girls will be using medals with a younger and flattering portrait of one who has not died. They have killed a faggot, but she will come back. Cruci/fictions: messianic deaths.

Drag

In patriarchal Argentina, transvestites are at a crossroads of public worship and church and state tactics of extermination. They are adored when acting in public theatres as the famous and admired Florencia de la V and the late Chris Miró, but they attract police as well as religious brutality. Perlongher's narrative on the death of an innocent transvestite forms a close parallel to the scene of the crucifixion of Christ described in Mark 15. Jesus' clothes become the centre of attention. This is Jesus in drag, dressed in a royal purple cloak with a crown of thorns. He is the subject of laughter and derision, just as the transvestite of the Panamerican Highway in Buenos Aires or in the Brazilian slums attracts laughter and derision for her gender-fucking, that is, for crossing borders of dress codes and dislocating identities. And there are also Jesus' own torn clothes, muddy clothes that are taken by the soldiers, not even choosing what they wanted but receiving as the result of gambling, distributed on the throw of the dice. And then there is a Roman officer musing to himself, 'Truly this man was the Son of God!' (Mark 15.39). Or as Perlongher would put it, 'Damn it! The *loca* was famous.' Perhaps a famous dancer or perhaps a human rights activist. Or perhaps both. And her body would become the secret of the centuries to come, the *Mysterium Tremendum* of Otto, on which Derrida reflected by saying that the secret is what makes people tremble (Derrida, 2001). And people will tremble sensing the mystery of a Queer holiness.

The Queer reader and the Bible

The starting point of these reflections is the assumption of a Queer christological project such as the one developed by Robert Goss in his book *Queering Christ* (Goss, 2001) and my own work on bi/Christ, which is in permanent dialogue with Goss's own project. The basic assumptions that we are making here are:

1. Reading Christ in the Scriptures cannot be an exemplary but a revelatory reading. It is reading that unmasks that of God in Christ's own intimate chaos of love, messianic public expectations and con-

tra/dictions, that is, the voices of subversion in an otherwise well-tamed text.

2. Reading Christ should not become a conclusive task. Revelation is not compatible with the closure produced by authoritative (and authoritarian) readings of the Scripture. What we are looking for is a permanent displacement of references, a quicksand scenario as the alternative for a reading of the different of God in Jesus, beyond the ideological configuration of heterosexuality.

3. Reading Christ needs to relate to Jesus' sexual practices. By that we understand Jesus' practices of solidarity with love and a praxis of social justice, outside a dualist mind/body separation.

4. Finally, we need to read the life of Jesus with the same eyes that we read stories in the tabloids about homosexual people being killed. Unless we can locate Jesus' passion in the real life of people we will not be able to understand the meaning of incarnation nor the subversion of bodies that resurrection implies.

A gay lost his job: counting the killings of a Queer man in Mark's Gospel

One of the mistakes we may commit is to read the text from Mark as a progression: the young preacher of conversion, the itinerant healer, the prophet arrested and put to death. Surprisingly, the early manuscripts of Mark contain no narratives of resurrection after the crucifixion scenes. We shall return to this point, which in itself is hermeneutically significant, but for the moment let us focus on a different, non-progressive dynamics of reading which can liberate the Queering of this text. I should like to begin by saying that Jesus' crucifixion was not his only death, just as the transvestite in the story of Perlongher was not killed only by police. The *trava* (transvestite/transsexual in the argot of Buenos Aires), suffered in life many deaths by ostracism, by being abandoned by her family, by being denied a job, by being denied her right to her own identity and to love, and to have a good life with dignity.

Jesus' life according to Mark is also signed by a multitude of deaths. These are the deaths of a Queer man. First of all, Jesus is a man who has departed from his family. In a way, he lost his family and social location. Second, he suffers from economic death. How? He is a poor man, rendered invisible by the economic power of his time, a nobody. And finally, torture and death by crucifixion ends his messianic mission. The crucifixion made him redundant. He becomes an unemployed God, a devalued, misunderstood God outside the market. In everything Jesus did, God's abundant presence was there, but nevertheless, for society, he was a failure.

First deaths: a gay alone

The Gospel of Mark starts with action. Mark shows Jesus doing things rather than simply saying things. It is Jesus' actions and not just his words which will lead to his ruin. There are no supernatural stories of miracle births. There are no loving scenes of mother and child. Whatever happened in his childhood is omitted by Mark. The beginning of the 'good news' is his actions, not his words. The most significant passage is not the ritual of baptism, but the narrative of the temptations. Jesus is a man who seems to be making his own way alone, struggling with dark temptations. We do not know what they are, but if we include the reference from Mathew 4, they relate to many things, including even suicidal thoughts. This is an isolated man who is hungry, unemployed (the temptation of bread – he has no money to buy it, neither has he a family who will provide for him). This is a man who is wondering if anyone in the entire universe would care if he threw himself from the pinnacle of the Temple, which also seems to be a kind of religious protest. Why was the Temple building part of his obscure thoughts at that moment? Were the Temple authorities, traditions and regulations driving him mad? And finally, there is this plea for public recognition, to be part of something, loved and respected by society, present in the metaphor of the vision of the cities of the world at his feet, that is, befriending him. Whatever the point of this inner struggle, that isolation and crisis which precedes his public ministry or the kind of voluntary work he felt he needed to do to honour his own identity, was tied to a call from God in his society. Interestingly, in this story, it is not a family that is behind Jesus. It is not the stereotype of the man who with great effort must leave family and friends to become a priest. No, Jesus here is already a man who has been separated from his family and friends, whose call comes already in his inner struggle in search for his own divine identity.

However, the desert is not an image of isolation in itself, but of isolation in the sense of a location where many people who did not fit in with society were to be found. Not only a Jesus with suicidal thoughts of jumping from temples but also other strange people lived in the desert, notably John the Baptist. In any case he was isolated but not alone in the sense that communities such as that at Qumran and other unsettled spirits were also gathering at the margins of Jerusalem's authority. Interestingly, after that period of isolation and crisis, almost a nervous breakdown, we see Jesus searching for companions. He returns from these 'temptations' looking for new friends or a family – as a Queer person usually does: you go to places, you speak with some people, and with luck you start a circle of befriending and love. That is precisely what Jesus did in engaging with the four fishermen. Reading from a Queer perspective this is an uplifting text. It is a remedy for melancholy, a text of instant rapport in the kind of encountering that happens among people who recognize themselves as different. Were the fishermen also men accustomed to the isolation that happens in the lives of people when their affectivity has become religiously and/or socially repressed? Why this instant rapport, this immediate desire for togetherness that happened among them? It is like a cruising scene: one minute they did not know who they were, and the next they are walking together like old friends. Later in the text we shall read more about this man Jesus who was called a friend of sinners. Who were those fishermen? Did they know each other already from other occasions? What did these men do when looking for a moment of relaxation?

These Queer questionings are important because they help us to think about the original location of Jesus' good news from Mark's perspective. The temptation, the crisis and the meeting of new friends which resolved the crisis is then followed by a curious text concerning 'an impure spirit' (Mark 1.21–28). A heterosexual reading, obsessed with dualist assumptions and a polarized organization of the world, tends to emphasize a Jesus who is pure and meets the impure or the just who meets the sinner. However, the constructions of sin or purity used in these cases is far from clear. The fact is that what strikes us about the text is that 'impure spirits' obey him. Using a bisexual reading perspective, we find ourselves confronted here with a continuation of a narrative thread concerning a man without family, hungry of many things and now coming out. This 'coming out' is carried through with forcefulness.

Shut up and leave him alone!

The account here continues the narrative of friendship/isolation. It is located in the synagogue of Capernaum. The scene is one of transgression: an impure man is sitting in the Temple. Impurity, in the Scriptures, is a very corporeal category. That is the reason why it needs to be associated with body disfunctions, such as leprosy, blindness and of course menstruation. Impurity is without doubt what exceeds the normativity of the body as religiously constructed and it is important to recognize that 'impurity' is not a given but rather is a legal category imposed upon a person. There is a little scene in this text in which Jesus is presented in general as a scandalous young man. There are frequently outbursts, shouting, calls for explanations and heated exchanges associated with Jesus' appearances – this is no exception. The impure man reacts strongly when he sees Jesus. The words used are 'I know you' and 'Do you want to destroy us?' A

Queer reading needs to begin by setting aside any supposed intonation of the words, whether angry or ironic we simply do not know, and the mythical representation of what was declared 'impure' in that man. What we have is the following: the 'impure man' receives a response from the by now assertive Jesus saying: 'Shut up!' and 'Leave this man alone.' But who is Jesus addressing in these words? To the impure spirit who possessed the man (as in a case of dual personality)? Or to someone in the synagogue? Whatever it was, the man concerned seems to have had a strong reaction. Now he also shouts, but we do not know what he says. Did he in turn say 'Shut up yourself, and leave me alone?' What a magnificent scene of deliverance from prejudices this may be! Not only a lesson to the homophobes of the synagogue but a lesson to the man himself, who also becomes suddenly assertive. And to confirm our Queer suspicion, someone else present is quoted as saying, 'What is this? . . . Even the impure spirits obey him . . . '

Is there a link here? Is the impurity mentioned as a religious construction of the different the Queer category which links all these texts together? Is the friend of sinners the friend of impurity? In that case we need to reconsider what we call impurity in the Bible. After this, we have several stories of impurity and of Jesus loving and 'healing' the impure people in society. However, the impure of society have good relations with Jesus (Mark 3.11–12). Finally this cycle of isolation, self-discovery and the beginning of a popular movement among the impure leads us back to where we began, the scene of the man who did not have a family. This is the dramatic moment when his mother and brothers come to claim him back for his natural family: but Jesus has already found a new spiritual kind of family. These things happen all the time.

Jesus had survived the death of isolation, experienced resurrection and come back to life from his suicidal crisis by an act of taking responsibility for what was different in him. Thereafter he found many others who suffered as he previously suffered. And he found love.

The economic deaths: Jesus, unemployed

Some time ago a friend told me her story. She had been happily working in a firm, until the rumour began to circulate that she was gay. Little by little, her job became more difficult. The secretaries treated her with discourtesy. Her colleagues ignored her or made obscure but hurting remarks in her presence. One day she could not find her own desk chair! It had been removed and she had to get a chair from another office. After describing a long sequence of humiliations and suffering she finally said to me, 'And then you see, they tried to killed me.' I must have stared at her in incomprehension. To kill her? Surely not. But she continued her explanation. She became depressed and as a consequence her contract was not renewed. Having lost her job, she could not find another. As her savings were used up she moved from flat to flat, convinced that in the end she would be living on the street. She did not have a family to help her and could see no way to survive. Yes, economic killing exists, people become destitute and die.

Was Jesus also killed economically by the system at that time? The wandering preacher, the man who lives his life among the marginalized is not a man with a proper job. It is not original to say that Mark's Gospel is one of the most 'economic' texts in the New Testament. Fernando Belo, in his pioneering work on materialist exegesis, drew attention to the links between Jesus' preaching on the Kingdom of God and productivity relations (Belo, 1981). Belo's most revealing exegesis is his reading of the narrative of the feeding of the multitudes which presents Jesus as a compassionate but impoverished messiah. It is clear in this text that he does not have anything for himself and therefore nothing to share with the crowds. Jesus is not simply the presence of God among the marginalized: more than that Jesus represents a truly marginalized God.[3]

The redundant God

It may be correct to say that God in Christ was a God with an identity crisis, in all the good and revelatory meaning of the term 'crisis'. That is, a God putting Godself under judgement, a self-judgement involving a type of quest identity, for Jesus was at the same time a becoming messiah and an unfinished God. Let us reflect on two important theological points here: First, the killing of a Queer as part of an expiatory sacrifice performed in society; and second, the issue of the redundant God. Was the killing of Jesus an attempt to eliminate that difference which Jesus presented in the idea of God? The Messiah was made redundant by death on the cross. Whatever it was, God Godself was no longer needed. But was God (and God in Jesus) a Queer God?

At this point in the narrative we find Jesus more or less at the same point where he began his public life. The Queer man of God came out and somehow conquered: he conquered hearts, and his community was becoming strong enough to present a different or alternative

---

[3] I have already elaborated this point in my article 'The Divine Exodus of God' in W. Jeanrod and C. Theobald (eds), 'God, Experience and Mystery', *Concilium* 289, February 2001, pp. 33–41.

lifestyle. It was a kind of Stonewall[4] resistance which developed from
synagogues to private houses. However, and as with Stonewall,
resistance can also be violently killed. Now we see a Jesus who seems
to have lost a few friends, a Jesus without a loving companion. This is
a Jesus who is greeted with kisses and a show of affection, but who is
also betrayed, deserted and denied. The whole cycle of public humil-
iation, torture, laughter and derision ends with this poor, fragile
young God dying a miserable death on the garbage dump of his city.

Cruci/fictions: Jesus in the tabloids

Imagine a tabloid headline: 'A Queer man of God was crucified
yesterday'.

Why was Jesus killed? What threat could this man have represented to anybody? It is difficult to see. In his story *Matan a una Marica*,
Perlongher elaborated on the issue of the need of the expiation
sacrifice of the Queer. The killings of homosexuals in Argentinian
society have within them a necessity of biblical proportions, manifest-
ing the purifying rituals of the different in society. In the tabloids, the
killing of Queers is a genre in itself, designed to produce a mixture
of moralization and amusement in the readers. They are a kind of
reasoned killing, which becomes part of a discourse of 'expected
deaths', since death is portrayed as the consequence of a sexually
transgressive lifestyle. The tabloids reflect the need to provide the
public with the exemplary deaths of gays. They go to great lengths to
trivialize these crimes as part of a self-justificatory strategy. If we see
the killing of Jesus as a crime committed against a sexual dissident,
there are some parallels which we may wish to consider. For instance,
sexual dissidents are portrayed as ones who seek their own death. For
the gay man or woman to deserve their own death is not enough.
They need to be portrayed as going out looking for it. Jesus knew
what was coming. He could have avoided going up to Jerusalem, once
there he could have avoided confrontation, or having left the city he
need not have gone to a hillside where he knew his enemies would
catch him in the act with his friends. Even accounts in the tabloids of
the killing of gays tend to be so deprived of reality that they have the
appearance of coming from a comic strip. The horror of the events is

---

[4] I am referring here to The Stonewall Inn events of June 1969 in New York,
when gay people who were the clientele of the bar confronted the routinely
humiliating police practice of checking gay bars. Gays, lesbians and Drag
Queens barricaded themselves in the bar and spent three days fighting and
protesting against these homophobic practices. Since then Stonewall has
acquired a symbolic significance in the struggle for sexual rights in the world.

glossed over or denied. So it is that in the taking of Jesus the scene is not without comic elements. First there is the description of the company of soldiers creeping up the slope with a variety of swords and weapons to deal with a handful of men who apparently cannot keep their eyes open. Almodovar could not have devised a funnier scene for one of his films. Jesus himself seems to mock them for the exaggerated display of arms. And then there is the incident of the young man who, curiously, was wearing nothing but a piece of linen cloth. As the soldiers attempted to apprehend him he dashed off naked like a streaker, leaving the soldiers holding the sheet. Were they annoyed or did they all collapse with laughter? Queers can be very funny, and our attention is distracted from the true horror of the moment.

Perlongher comments how, in the gutter press, Queers seem to be portrayed as prone to do the kind of wrong things which provoke crimes against them, as when they insist on going to places where they should not be seen. Either they love someone too much, or they are too lonely to be prudent. Or too often they have simply a kind of obstinate loving behaviour which attracts fateful crimes against them. The death of a Queer in the tabloids never seems real enough. These are texts which produce lesser deaths, like Jesus' own death. Is that the reason why the cross appears so easily as inexpensive jewellery? If Jesus had been electrocuted instead of crucified, would there be a large switch on the altar? If he had been decapitated according to the custom of the ancient world, would Christians carry swords? The death of Jesus has been trivialized not by the tabloids but by the theological gutter press of homophobia.

The most important thing to remember in all this is that with this crime a Queer man of God was eliminated. The messianic position was declared redundant. This was a Messiah who announced a strange, Queer God among those made impure and outcast by the social order of the time. A God who was more than can be expressed, who exceeds all categories of definition and control is a Queer God indeed. At the end of Mark's Gospel there is no resurrection narrative. The last words refer to 'fear'. Those women who went to perfume the corpse with spices (Mary, Mary of Magdala and Salome) did not find Jesus' body. Instead they found a man who told them, 'He is not here . . . and you will see him in Galilee . . . ' But they said nothing. They were afraid.

Queering Theology, we can see that in fact Jesus died and was resurrected throughout the whole narrative of the Gospels. Resurrection is an ever-present theme. But the Queer reading of the Scriptures is not progressive: it is transgressive. We see how the category of resurrection appears every time that Jesus is made redundant. When he loses his family and place in society even the council of priests discuss publicly issues concerning his identity and his being-in-the-world, just as at the 1998 Lambeth Conference gays were discussed *ontologically* for press consumption. And, ultimately, God is declared so redundant that forgetting himself Jesus cries to God for the oblivion of the cross. In reality, the cross is the attempt to kill once and for all the multiple resurrections of a Queer Jesus, to fix him once and for ever on a stable cross so that no Queer God would do what Queer Gods do, that is, to exceed the border limits of a fatigued heterosexual foundational epistemology which has reduced religious experience and human love. But will the Queer Jesus resurrect? I belong to a community of people who think that yes, the resurrection of the Queer God is not only possible, but already a reality. The Queer God is present in every group or individual who still dares to believe that God is fully present among the marginalized, exceeding the narrow confines of sexual and political ideologies. For God comes out from heterosexual theology when the voices from sexual dissidents speak out to the churches, daring to unveil sexual ideologies from theology, and daring to love with integrity in a world where love has also become a commodity. In fact, in every community of excluded people and in every inch of the struggle for sexual and economic justice, the Queer God manifests Godself with full glory, power and grace.

Bibliography

Althaus-Reid, M. (1997), 'Both Indecent and Ex-centric: Teaching Feminist Theology for Articulation or for Exoticism' in M. Grey (ed.), *Liberating the Vision: Papers of the Summer School May 1996*. Southampton: LSU.

—— (1998), 'The Hermeneutics of Transgression: Time and the Children in the Streets of Buenos Aires' in G. De Schrijver (ed.), *Liberation Theologies on Shifting Grounds*. Leuven: Leuven University Press.

—— (2000), *Indecent Theology: Theological Perversions in Sex, Gender and Politics*. London: Routledge.

—— (2000a), 'Indecent Exposures: Excessive Sex and the Crisis of Theological Representation' in L. Isherwood (ed.), *The Good News of the Body*. Sheffield: Sheffield Academic Press.

—— (2000b), 'Grace and the Other' in E. Van Woelde and T. Radcliffe (eds), 'The Bright Side of Life', *Concilium* 287 2000/4, pp. 63–90.

—— (2001), 'The Divine Exodus of God' in W. Jeanrod and C. Theobald (eds), 'God, Experience and Mystery', *Concilium* 289, February, pp. 33–41.

—— (2001), 'Outing Theology: Thinking Christianity Out of the Church Closet', *Feminist Theology*, no. 27, pp. 57–67.

—— (2003), *The Queer God*. London: Routledge.

—— (2003a), 'The Bible of the *Fracasados*: Readings from the Excluded' in M. Oduyoye and H. Vroom (eds), *One Gospel – Many Cultures: Case Studies and Reflections on Cross-Cultural Hermeneutics*. Amsterdam/New York: Rodopi, 2003.

Anonimo (1945), *Codice Chimalpopoca: Anales de Cuauhtitlan y Leyenda de los Soles*, trans. from the Nahuatl by Primo F. Vázquez. México: UNAM.

Aschieri, L. (1998), 'La Femineidad como Máscara', *Acheronta* 8. Available on line at http://www.acheronta.org

Bakhtin, M. (1981), *The Dialogic Imagination*. Austin: University of Texas Press.

Belo, F. (1981), *A Materialist Reading of the Gospel of Mark*. New York: Orbis Books.

Bentham, J. (1955), 'An Introduction to the Principles of Morals and Legislation' in A. Melden (ed.), *Ethical Theories*. Englewood Cliffs, NJ: Prentice-Hall [1789].

Bonino, J. M. (ed.) (1984), *Faces of Jesus: Latin American Christologies*. Maryknoll, NY: Orbis Books.

Boff, C. (1987), *Theology and Praxis: Epistemological Foundations*. Maryknoll, NY: Orbis Books.

Boff, L., and Boff, C. (1987), *Introducing Liberation Theology*. Maryknoll, NY: Orbis Books.

Bollig, B. (2004), 'Néstor Perlongher and Mysticism: Towards a Critical Re-appraisal' in *The Modern Language Review*, January, vol. 99, no. 1, pp. 77–93.

Bono, S. and Kemp, S. (eds) (1991), *Italian Feminist Thought: A Reader*. Oxford: Basil Blackwell.

Bullosa, C. (1995), 'El que gira la Cabeza y el Fuego: Historia y Novela' in Kate Duncan and Electra Caridis (eds), *Beyond Solitude: Dialogues between Europe and Latin America*. Birmingham: University of Birmingham.

Butler, J. (1990), *Gender Trouble: Feminism and the Subversion of Identity*. London: Routledge.

Cañón, J. (1999), 'My Lessons with Felipe' in Jaime Cortez (ed.), *Virgins, Guerrillas & Locas: Gay Latinos Writing about Love*. San Francisco: Cleis Press.

Cardoso Pereyra, N. (1993), 'La Profecía y lo Cotidiano: La Mujer y el Niño en el Ciclo del Profeta Eliseo' in *Revista de Interpretación Bíblica Latinoamericana*, 14. Chile: REHUE.

——— (1994), 'Liturgia', *Mandrágora*. Saõ Paulo: Netmal, pp. 85–91.

Central American Kairos Document (1988), New York: Circus.

Chow, R. (1993), *Writing Diaspora*. Indianapolis: Indiana University Press.

Códice Chimalpopoca: Anales de Cuauhtitlan y Leyenda de los Soles (1945), trans. P. F. Vázquez. México: UNAM.

Croatto, J. S. (1973), *Liberación y Libertad*. Buenos Aires: Nuevo Mundo.

Debray, R. (1996), 'Talking to the Zapatistas', *New Left Review* 218, pp. 128–37.

Deleuze, G. and Guattari, F. (1984), *Anti-Oedipus: Capitalism and Schizophrenia*. London: The Athlone Press.

Derrida, J. (1994), *Spectres of Marx*. London: Routledge.

——— (2001), 'Whom to Give to (Knowing Not to Know)' in D. Jobling, T. Pippin and R. Schleifer (eds), *The Postmodern Bible Reading*. Oxford: Black-well, pp. 334–52.

Dussel, E. (1976), *Filosofía de la Liberación*. Mexico: Edicol.

——— (1993), *Las Metáforas Teológicas de Marx*. Estella: Verbo Divino.

Dworkin, A. (1987), *Intercourse*. New York: Free Press.

Elizondo, V. (1983), 'Mary and the Poor: A New Model of Evangelising', *Concilium* 168, pp. 59–65.

Engels, F. (1935), *Ludwig Feuerbach*. New York: International Publishers.

——— (1981), *The Origin of the Family, Private Property and the State*. London: Lawrence & Wishart.

Fisher, J. (1983), *Mothers of the Disappeared*. London: Zed Books.

Fraser, I. and Fraser, M. (1986), *Wind and Fire: The Spirit Reshapes the Church and Basic Christian Communities*. Dunblane: Basic Communities Resource Centre.

Freire, P. (1970), *Pedagogía del Oprimido*. Buenos Aires: Siglo XXI.

——— (1993), *Pedagogy of the Oppressed*. London: Penguin.

——— (1994), *Pedagogy of Hope*. New York: Continuum.

Friedman, J. (1997), 'Global Crisis, The Struggle for Cultural Identity and Intellectual Porkbarreling: Cosmopolitans versus Locals, Ethnics and Nationals in an Era of De-Hegemonisation' in Pnina Werbner and Tariq Modood (eds), *Debating Cultural Hybridity*. London: Zed Books.

Gadamer, H.-G. (1975), *Truth and Method*. New York: Seabury Press.

Galeano, E. (1995), *Memory of Fire: A Trilogy*. London: Quartet Books.

Garibay, A. M. (1958), *Veinte Himnos Sacros de los Nahuas*. México: UNAM, 1958).

Gebara, I. and Bingemer, M. C. (1989), *Mary, Mother of God, Mother of the Poor*. Maryknol, NY: Orbis Books.

Gibbs, P. (1996), *The Word in the Third World: Divine Revelation in the Theology of Jean-Marc Éla, Aloysius Pieris and Gustavo Gutiérrez*. Roma: Pontificia Universitá Gregoriana.

González Navarro, M. (1970), *Raza y Tierras. La Guerra de Castas y el Henequen*. México: Colegio de México.

Goss, R. (2001), *Queering Christ*. New York: Pilgrim Press.

Gottdiener, M. and Lagopoulus, A. (eds) (1986), *The City and the Sign: An Introduction to Social Semiotics*. New York: Columbia University Press.

Graziano, F. (1992), *Divine Violence: Spectacle. Psychosexuality and Radical Christianity in the Argentine Dirty War*. San Francisco: Westview Press.

Grey, M. (ed.) (1996), *Liberating the Vision: Papers of the Summer School 24th–28th May 1996*. Southampton: Centre for Contemporary Theology, LSU.

Guardia Mayorga, C. (1967), *Diccionario Kechua-Castellano*. Lima: Los Andes.

Gutiérrez, G. (1988), *A Theology of Liberation: History, Politics and Perspectives*. London: SCM Press.

——— (1989), 'Noticias de Cruz y Resurrección', *Páginas* 100, Lima, pp. 6–7.

Hampson, D. (1993), *Theology and Feminism*. Oxford: Basil Blackwell.

Henry, M. (1892), *A Commentary on the Holy Bible*, vol. I. London: Marshall Brothers.

Herzfeld, M. (1997), *Cultural Intimacy: Social Poetics in the Nation State*. New York: Routledge.

Irigaray, L. (2002), 'The Crucified One: Epistle to the Last Christians' in Morny Joy, Kathleen O'Grady and Judith Poxon (eds), *French Feminists on Religion*. London: Routledge, pp. 50–8.

——— (1993), *Je, Tu, Nous: Toward a Culture of Difference*. London: Routledge.

Isasi Diaz, A. M. (1989), 'Mujerista: A Name of Our Own' in Marc Ellis and Otto Maduro (eds), *The Future of Theology of Liberation: Essays in Honor of Gustavo Gutiérrez*, Maryknoll, NY: Orbis Books.

——— (1993), *En la Lucha/In the Struggle: A Hispanic Women Liberation Theology*. Minneapolis: Augsburg Fortress Publishers.

Iser, W. (1971), 'Indeterminacy and the Reader's Response' in J. Hillis Miller (ed.), *Selected Papers from the English Institute*. Columbia: Columbia University Press, pp. 2–45.

Isherwood, L. (2000), 'Erotic Celibacy' in Lisa Isherwood (ed.), *The Good News of the Body: Sexual Theology and Feminism*. Sheffield: Sheffield Academic Press.

Isherwood, L. and Stuart, E. (1998), *Introducing Body Theology*. Sheffield: Sheffield Academic Press, 1998.

Jauss, H.-R. (1982), *Aesthetic Experience and Literary Hermeneutics*. Minneapolis: University of Minnesota Press.

The Jerusalem Bible (1971), London: Geoffrey Chapman.

Josephus, F. (1886), *The Works of Flavius Josephus*, trans. William Whiston. London: T. Nelson & Son.

Kairós Centroaméricano: Un Desafío a las Iglesias y al Mundo (1988), Managua.

Karttunen, F. (1983), *Analytical Dictionary of Náhuatl*. Austin: University of Texas.

Kee, A. A. (1990), *Marx and the Failure of Liberation Theology*. London: SCM Press.

Kearney, R. (ed.) (1984), *Dialogues with Contemporary Thinkers*. Manchester: Manchester University Press.

Lapiedra, A. (1986), 'Religiosidad Popular y Mujer Andina', *Cuadernos de Teología* vii, no. 3, pp. 169–76.

León-Portilla, M. (1980), *Visión de los Vencidos: Relaciones Indígenas de la Conquista*. México: UNAN.

López Vigil, M. (1993), *Piezas para un Retrato*. San Salvador: UCA.

Malthus, T. (1991), *Essays on the Principle of Population*, II. New York: Dutton [1798].

Martínez Diez, F. and García F, B. (1989), *La Teología de la Liberación es Latinoamericana*. Caracas: Paulinas.

Marx, K. (1980), 'Teoría del Plusvalor'. México: FCE, vol. III.

Marx, K. and Engels, F. (1976), 'The German Ideology', *Karl Marx and Engels Collected Works V*. London: Lawrence & Wishart.

Mesters, C. (1989), *Defenceless Flower: A New Reading of the Bible*. London: CIIR/Orbis Books.

——— (1993), 'The Use of the Bible in Christian Communities of the Common People' in N. Gottwald and R. Horsley (eds), *The Bible and Liberation: Political and Social Hermeneutics*. Maryknoll, NY: Orbis Books.

Mitchell, J. (1974), *Psychoanalisis and Feminism*. Harmondsworth: Penguin.

Moffat, A. (1988), *Psicoterapia del Oprimido: Ideología y Técnica de la Psiquiatría Popular*. Buenos Aires: Humanitas.

Moi, T. (1990), *Sexual/Textual Politics: Feminist Literary Theory*. London: Routledge.

Montes de Oca, E. (1995), *Guía Negra de Buenos Aires: Marginación en la Gran Ciudad*. Buenos Aires: Planeta.

Navarro, González M. (1970), *Raza y Tierra: La Guerra de Castas y el Henequen*. México: Colegio de México.

Nelson, J. (1988), *The Intimate Connection*. London: SPCK.

Noya, E. (1987), *Corrientes entre la Leyenda y la Tradición*. Special issue of 'Todo es Historia', Buenos Aires, vol. 7.

Oakley, A. (1982), *Subject Women*. London: Fontana.

Perlongher, N. (1997), 'Matan a una Marica' in Néstor Perlongher, *Prosa Plebeya*. Buenos Aires: Colihue.

Plummer, K. (1995), *Telling Sexual Stories: Power, Change and Social Words*. London: Routledge.

Ramazanoglu, C. (ed.) (1993), *Up Against Foucault: Explorations of Some Tensions between Foucault and Feminism*. London: Routledge.

Rebón M. (2004), 'Ser Marginal en la Argentina: Charla con Alfredo Moffatt, Arquitecto y Psicólogo Social', *La Tecl@ Eñe: Revista Digital*. Available on line at http://www.icarodigital.com.ar/numero10/eldamero/coop.html

Rich, A. (1980), 'Compulsory Heterosexuality and Lesbian Existence', *Signs*, vol. 5. no. 4.

Ricoeur, P. (1969), *Le Conflit des Interpretations*. Paris: Ed. du Seuil.

——— (1976), *Interpretation Theory: Discourse and the Surplus of Meaning*. Texas: CU Press.

Rowland, C. and Corner, M. (1990), *Liberating Exegesis: The Challenge of Liberation Theology to Biblical Studies*. London: SPCK.

Sahagún, B. de (1938), *Historia General de las Cosas Nuevas de España*. México: Pedro Robredo.

Schüssler Fiorenza, E. (1993), *Discipleship of Equals: A Critical Feminist Ekklesialogy of Liberation*. London: SCM Press.

Segundo, J. L. (1982), *El Hombre de Hoy ante Jesús de Nazareth: Fé e Ideología. II/I*. Madrid: Cristiandad.

Shuttle, P. and Redgrove, P. (1986), *The Wise Wound: Menstruation and Everywoman*. London: Paladin.

Simeon, R., *Dictionaire de la Langue Nahuatl ou Mexicaine*. Graz, Austria: Akademische Druck.

Smith, D. (1990), *The Conceptual Practice of Power*. Boston: Northwestern University Press.

Sobrino, J. and Ellacuría, I. (eds) (1993), *Mysterium Liberationis: Fundamental Concepts of Liberation Theology*. Maryknoll, NY: Orbis Books.

——— (eds) (1996), *Systematic Theology: Perspectives from Liberation Theology*. Maryknoll, NY: Orbis Books.

Soustelle, J. (1961), *The Daily Life of the Aztecs*. London: Weidenfeld & Nicolson.

Spivak, G. (1993), 'Can the Subaltern Speak?' in P. Williams and L. Chrisman (eds), *Colonial Discourse and Post-Colonial Theory: A Reader*. Hemel Hempstead: Harvester Wheatsheaf.

Steven, E. P. (1993), 'Marianismo: The Other Face of Machismo in Latin America' in A. Minas (ed.), *Gender Basics: Feminist Perspectives on Women and Men*. California: Wadsworth Publishing.

Stuart, E. (1995), *Just Good Friends*. London: Mowbray.

——— (2002), *Gay and Lesbian Theologies: Repetitions with Critical Difference*. London: Ashgate.

Sugirtharajah, R. S. (2001), *The Bible and the Third World: Precolonial, Colonial and Post-Colonial Encounters*. Cambridge: Cambridge University Press.

——— (2003), *Postcolonial Reconfigurations: An Alternative Way of Reading the Bible and Doing Theology*. London: SCM Press.

Valdés, M. (1987), *Phenomenological Hermeneutics and the Study of Literature*. Toronto: University of Toronto Press.

Walsh, M. E. (1979), 'Desventuras en el País-Jardín-de-Infantes' in L. Caraballo, N. Charlier and L. Garulli (eds) (1998), *La Dictadura (1977–1983): Testimonios y Documentos*. Buenos Aires: Eudeba.

Warner, M. (1999), *The Trouble with Normal: Sex, Politics and the Ethics of Queer Life*. New York: Free Press.

Sources and Acknowledgements

The author and publisher acknowledge permission to use copyright material, written by the author and reproduced from the following publications:

'Walking with Women Serpents', *Ministerial Formation*, no. 62, July 1993, pp. 31–41. © World Council of Churches, Geneva; used by permission.

'When God is a Rich White Woman Who Does Not Walk: The Hermeneutical Circle of Mariology in Latin America', *Theology and Sexuality*, vol. 1, 1994, pp. 55–72.

'Do Not Stop the Flow of My Blood: A Critical Christology of Hope among Latin American Women', *Studies in World Christianity* (Orbis Books/ Edinburgh University Press, 1995), vol. 1, part 2, pp. 143–59.

'¿*Bién Sonados?* The Future of Mystical Connections in Liberation Theology', *Political Theology*, Issue 3, November 2000, pp. 44–63. With permission of Equinox Publishing Ltd © 2000. All rights reserved.

'On Wearing Skirts without Underwear: Poor Women Contesting Christ', *Feminist Theology*, no. 20, January 1999, pp. 39–51.

'A Woman's Right to Not Being Straight: *El Derecho a no ser Derecha*: On Theology, Church and Pornography' in The Concilium Foundation (eds), 'The Rights of Women', *Concilium*, 2002/5 (London: SCM Press), pp. 88–96.

'Does the Church Need Theology or Vice Versa? A Materialist Analysis Concerning the Current Theological Industry and its Church Market', *Ministerial Formation*, 82, July 1998, pp. 4–13. © World Council of Churches, Geneva; used by permission.

'Doing the Theology of Memory: Counting Crosses and Resurrections' in M. Best and P. Hussey, *Life out of Death: The Feminine Spirit in El Salvador* (London: CIIR, 1996), pp. 194–206.

'Gustavo Gutiérrez Goes to Disneyland: Theme Park Theologies and the Diaspora of the Discourse of the Popular Theologian in Liberation Theology', in Fernando Segovia (ed.), *Interpreting Beyond the Borders* (Sheffield: Sheffield Academic Press, 2000).

Index of Names and Subjects